D1334416

IMMACULATE CONCEPTIONS: THE POWER
OF THE RELIGIOUS IMAGINATION IN EARLY
MODERN SPAIN

ROSILIE HERNÁNDEZ

Immaculate Conceptions: The Power of the Religious Imagination in Early Modern Spain

UNIVERSITY OF TORONTO PRESS
Toronto Buffalo London

© University of Toronto Press 2019
Toronto Buffalo London
utorontopress.com
Printed in Canada

ISBN 978-1-4875-0477-9

Ⓢ Printed on acid-free, 100% post-consumer recycled paper with
vegetable-based inks.

Library and Archives Canada Cataloguing in Publication

Title: Immaculate conceptions : the power of the religious imagination in
early modern Spain / Rosilie Hernandez.
Names: Hernández, Rosilie, author.
Series: Toronto Iberic ; 42.
Description: Series statement: Toronto Iberic ; 42 | Includes bibliographical
references and index.
Identifiers: Canadiana 20190103426 | ISBN 9781487504779 (hardcover)
Subjects: LCSH: Mary, Blessed Virgin, Saint – In literature. | LCSH: Mary,
Blessed Virgin, Saint – Art. | LCSH: Mary, Blessed Virgin, Saint – Devotion
to – Spain. | LCSH: Devotional literature, Spanish – History and
criticism. | LCSH: Spanish literature – Classical period, 1500–1700 – History
and criticism. | LCSH: Immaculate Conception – In literature. | LCSH:
Immaculate Conception in art. | LCSH: Painting, Spanish – 17th century.
Classification: LCC PQ6063 .H47 2019 | DDC 860.9/351—dc23

University of Toronto Press acknowledges the financial assistance to its
publishing program of the Canada Council for the Arts and the Ontario Arts
Council, an agency of the Government of Ontario.

 Canada Council
for the Arts

Conseil des Arts
du Canada

 ONTARIO ARTS COUNCIL
CONSEIL DES ARTS DE L'ONTARIO

an Ontario government agency
un organisme du gouvernement de l'Ontario

Funded by the   Financé par le
Government   gouvernement
of Canada   du Canada

Canadä

 MIX
Paper from
responsible sources
FSC® C016245

To Antonia, Manuela, and Joaquín

who came before this book was conceived

To Michał

who made its conception possible

Contents

Illustrations

Acknowledgments

I am indebted to the College of Liberal Arts and Sciences, the School of Literatures, Cultural Studies, and Linguistics, and the Department of Hispanic and Italian Studies at the University of Illinois at Chicago, especially Dean Astrida Orle Tantillo and my fellow faculty members, for their unwavering institutional and personal support. I thank the University of Toronto Press Editorial Board and Toronto Iberic for embracing this project, and Suzanne Rancourt and her team for their careful editorial assistance. I also owe a great debt of gratitude to Noelia García Pérez, José Miguel Granados, Natascha Reihl, Ignacio Hermoso Romero, the Archbishop's Office of Seville, and the anonymous collectors who so graciously offered their assistance in securing illustrations.

This book project was in large part developed during my tenure as a Faculty Fellow at the Institute for the Humanities at the University of Illinois at Chicago. Early on, Ronda Kasal and Stacy Schlau generously wrote letters of support. Stephan Leopold and the University of Mainz, Germany invited me to offer two seminars that proved instrumental to fine-tuning some of its central tenets. Mercedes Alcalá Galán and Steven Hutchinson kindly allowed me to present a part of the final manuscript at the University of Wisconsin, Madison to their wonderful graduate students. The editorial assistance offered by my UIC doctoral students – Lisa James and Jill Quarles – was of great value.

Anne J. Cruz – wise mentor, thoughtful critic, and closest of friends – lent her watchful eye to the book proposal and continuously reminded me of the balance between rigour and passion that is required in order to successfully complete a book manuscript. She is a champion of and an exemplary model for women scholars across the profession, and I count amongst my luckiest the day I entered her classroom in spring 1992. I am also forever indebted to my loving sister, Arlene Hernández, who so often took the time to call and ask in the softest of ways, "¿y el libro?"

This book is dedicated to my children, Antonia, Manuela, and Joaquín. They spent several years being told to stay out of my hair when I was writing, and still every time the subject of this project came up their faces beamed with pride in and anticipation for the fruit of my labour. They did not write one word of this book, but without their patience and open hearts not one word could have been written. Finally, the idea for the book was first sowed at the small bookshop of the Iglesia de Santo Tomé in Toledo when, on a hot summer day, Michał Paweł Markowski identified and insisted on buying for me a four-hundred-page catalogue on images of the Virgin of the Immaculate Conception. He carried that book all day and many others in many cities after. Most significantly, he generously lent his immense wealth of knowledge and excitement for the topic of images and the imagination as I developed my own. The intellectual and emotional richness of our relationship has profoundly shaped this project and my life for the past seven years.

IMMACULATE CONCEPTIONS: THE POWER
OF THE RELIGIOUS IMAGINATION IN EARLY
MODERN SPAIN

The Anatomy of the Religious Imagination: Immaculacy and the Spanish Counter-Reformation

In 1615 Trinitarian Friar Miguel Ruiz takes to the pulpit at the Church of San Gil in Seville and imparts an impassioned defence of the doctrine of the Immaculate Conception. Published one year later, the "Sermon on the Immaculate Conception" ["Sermón de la Inmaculada Concepción"] is a testament to the religious fervour that the cult of the Virgin of the Immaculate Conception enjoyed in early modern Spain. Against the backdrop of theological uncertainty that clouded the exact conditions of Mary's immaculacy, Ruiz's sermon rehearses the fundamental scriptural and theological tenets that Immaculists upheld as proof of Mary's eternal purity. And yet, the "Sermón" goes well beyond a predictable recitation of orthodox beliefs. On the one hand, Ruiz intends to exert political pressure on the Spanish Habsburg court, hoping to intensify its support of the Immaculist cause. In doing so, he draws on the fickle ebb and flow of papal opposition and support to argue that the Holy See – despite its refusal to elevate the doctrine to dogma – positions Spanish Immaculists as defenders of the *true* Catholic faith. On the other hand, and just as significantly, Ruiz derives further authority from San Gil's lay congregation. In the spirit of post-Trent pastoral reforms, his parishioners' unqualified faith and zeal – surely moved and sustained by God's will and grace – offer the ultimate and incontestable substantiation of Mary's eternal holistic purity and the correctness of Seville and Spain's resolute devotion to and defence of the *tota pulchra*: "But Christian devotion, as we see, has been so inclined to honour the Virgin, that the Priest has a duty to avoid all scandals, and honour her with his words, and say that she was conceived without original sin, because these are the foundations of this Divine City."[1] Ruiz's assertion brings to the fore many of the queries I examine in this study. Within the religious and political context of the Spanish early modern period, what does it mean to have popular belief, alongside orthodox theological exegesis, determine the validity of doctrinal truth? How is this "us" distinguished and fashioned against those others – including those Catholic others – who fall outside of the umbrella of "Christian devotion"? And, what are the explicit and implicit competing meanings and ideologies – theological, social, and political – that underlie the phrase "foundations of this Divine City"? In a European Counter-Reformation context in which the defence of immaculacy was polemical and often proved contentious, the answers to these and other questions demonstrate how Spain – the Habsburg court, cities and local communities, theologians and religious thinkers, writers, artists, and devout lay individuals – positioned itself as the staunchest defender of Mary's exceptionality before, at the time of, and after her conception. The Spanish religious imaginary, fostered by a doctrine singularly characterized by the radical inscrutability of God's design, generated a rich and vast proliferation of cultural products that attempted to interpret and represent the conditions, meanings, and effects of a divine mystery that posited the existence of one human being – even more so, one woman – who was *never* touched by the stain of original sin. Indeed, the quality of this exceptionality, of purity itself – how it could be defined, identified, appropriated, internalized, particularized, transmitted, materially embodied, popularized, nationalized, and politicized – is at the crux of the Immaculist religious imaginary and is the principal concern of this book.

It is within this religious and cultural climate that I examine devotional writings, religious and literary texts, and paintings that feature the Virgin of the Immaculate Conception in early modern Spain. My analysis is motivated by the complexity and multivalent capacity of the doctrine and its icon at a time when the debates around Mary's conception imbued all levels of religious and social life. In doing so, I consider the many interests – political, religious, artistic, and gender-driven – that intersect and compete in the exegesis and textual and visual representations of the Immaculate Conception. The theological and institutional reactions to Luther's reforms, coupled with Spain's embattled political, military, and economic position in Europe, permeated the nation's collective consciousness. Within this historical context – and although the Catholic doctrine would not become dogma until 1854 – the Immaculate Conception of Mary, more than any other religious symbol or doctrine, proved to be a fertile ideological field wherein the identity of the Spanish state, cities and villages, convents and monasteries, and individuals was negotiated, variously defined, and contested.

My broader aim is to delineate a speculative category, the religious imagination. I expound upon the religious imagination as a spiritual, intellectual, and artistic pursuit in which the individual is committed to sacred truth yet articulates this truth through contingent, partial, and contextually determined theological propositions. At the threshold of the Enlightenment, with its privileging of reason over orthodoxy, and during the early development of scientific methods based on material observation and proof, the religious imagination of early modern Spain delves into the ineffable and miraculous through visionary, imagined, imaginal, and intimately subjective approximations. Instead of predictably reproducing given and transparent correlations, religious and secular thinkers, writers, and artists creatively appropriate the representational capacity afforded by the enigma of Mary's immaculacy. In *The Order of Things*, Michel Foucault posits that this period evinced an epistemological shift from an order of resemblance, fixed referents, and correlations to the emergence of the unbound sign and pure representationality characteristic of modernity; a transition which Foucault famously exemplified through Miguel de Cervantes's *Don Quixote*, a text contemporary with many of the cultural products I analyse:

> What is a sign in the Classical age? For what was altered in the first half of the seventeenth century, and for a long time to come – perhaps right up to our own day – was the entire organization of signs, the conditions under which they exercise their strange function; it is this, among so many other things one knows or sees, that causes them to emerge suddenly as signs; it is their very being. On the threshold of the Classical age, the sign ceases to be a form of the world; and it ceases to be bound to what it marks by the solid and secret bonds of resemblance or affinity. (*The Order of Things* 64)

Moving beyond Foucault's sequential epistemic schema, I trace how the Spanish early modern religious imagination admits an intermediary third order, one in which bonds of resemblance sustained by a fixed divine referent paradoxically depend on and flourish in a contiguous and open dialectic of transcendence and immanence, resisting a strict boundary between them. Considered in this manner, the religious imagination proves to be a powerful space for a renewed forging of the particular within the universal and of the human as an extension of the sacred. It is in this context that the Virgin's immaculacy – from doctrinal and biographical perspectives – performs as an unbound sign, characterized by its proliferating representational capacity. My contention, which I hope to prove in this book, is that at this transitional epistemic juncture the presumed closed system of signifying correspondences between the divine and the human incorporates and unpredictably deploys itself through the controversial and slippery indeterminability of the mystery of Mary's Immaculate Conception.

The motivating factors that buoyed the Spanish early modern investment in the belief in and promotion of the doctrine of the Immaculate
Conception appear to have been many and are often debated. Historians and cultural critics differ in how they gauge the degree of influence
the Crown and the Church Militant held over the communities and
individual practitioners that were subjects of and subjected to the entrenched hierarchies that these entities formally represented. Suzanne
Stratton, for example, opts for a top-down assessment of the historical
record, one in which religious and secular writers and artists respond to
the demands of an imposed or ideologically inculcated doctrinal belief:
"It has often been said that the proliferation of Immaculist art in Spain
in the sixteenth and especially the seventeenth century is a reflection
of popular devotion to the belief. The evidence contradicts that idea.
In fact, the belief in the IC filtered from Franciscan theologians to the
monarchs of Spain to the nobility and finally to the people" (*The Immaculate Conception in Spanish Art* 36–7). The opposite stance, intimated by
Stratton herself, stresses how popular belief instigated, from the bottom
up, institutional, political, and artistic commitments to the doctrine. My
own analytical position rejects this dichotomy and, instead, privileges
the dialectical bonds – immanent and transcendent, of sight and of
vision, rational and ineffable – that make possible the production of
theological thought and devotional zeal from multiple sites, and that
support the creative potentiality of national, communal, and individual
religious imaginaries.

The intensity of popular belief in the power of the Immaculate Conception played a crucial role in supporting *and* compelling the Habsburg
monarchy's penchant to make the doctrine central to Spanish Catholicism, and to demand that the papacy elevate the doctrine to dogma.
Representations of the Immaculate Conception in textual and visual
cultures enable us to examine how individuals secured their Catholic
identities through a standardized and institutionally determined set of
beliefs, doctrines, rituals, and generic conventions, while simultaneously
constructing local interpretations of these same beliefs, doctrines, and
rituals. The negotiation of particular Catholic identities was not exempt
from the compulsory authoritative power of the Church and Catholic
orthodoxy. Nevertheless, despite the imposition of institutional control
and the real possibility of censorship and punishment at the hands of
overzealous confessors and inquisitors, the Catholic religious imagination and the production of religious thought could not be thoroughly
determined by authoritative oversight. The Church and the practising
faithful were actively engaged in the common but not identical task
of translating (i.e., making intelligible) divine mystery and design. As

the texts and art I examine amply demonstrate, the permeability across learned theology and popular belief markedly expands the exegetical field. I argue that the religious imagination of the period generates a productive space for individuals and communities – through the ingenious citation and amplification of given theological concepts and sanctioned beliefs – to carve out singular identitary positions. This project, therefore, participates in recent efforts to revisit the coordinates of pre- and post-Tridentine Spanish culture, emphasizing the many ways in which individuals identified with and creatively interpreted and represented the doctrine and icon of the Immaculate Conception of Mary.

By reviewing the cultural products of sermon and treatise writers, painters, playwrights, visionary nuns, and amateur poets, this book challenges readings of Immaculist texts as self-evident, homogeneous, and repetitive, unequivocally submitting to the orthodox and propagandistic demands of the Church Militant. It honours, instead, the rich tapestry of religious identities that founded their singularity in the vast field – intellectual, ideological, and spiritual – afforded by the doctrine of immaculacy.

I. Orthodoxy and the Self in Counter-Reformation Spain

The temporal, ideological, and geographical assumptions that in the past guided the study of the Catholic Counter-Reformation have been challenged and rethought. Most prescient for this book, the traditional reading of the period that divided the Protestant and Catholic movements into two monolithic camps – one that led to modernity and one that staunchly held on to a medieval, and thus oppressive, past – is no longer understood as valid.[2] The characterization of the period and its theological and cultural products as a consolidated and closely controlled reaction to the Protestant threat indeed falls short when the period is understood to comprise a multiple and differentiated process that resulted in a variety of local and contingent iterations. As summarized by Mary Laven,

> [W]e might wish to identify distinct phases of reform and regeneration: "the Tridentine period" (c. 1550–1600), "the age of confessionalism" (c. 1600–1650), and "the flowering of Baroque Catholicism" (1650–1750). But this time frame is clearly less appropriate to the experience of Catholics living in Italy or Iberia, Peru or Japan. Apart from considerations of chronology and geography, *historians are ever more alert to the wide range of agents who shaped the Counter-Reformation.* Many of these (nuns, soldiers, painters of devotional art, or participants in pilgrimage) appeared

by turns to promote and to threaten the ideals of Tridentine Catholicism. What is clear is that our vision of the Counter-Reformation is no longer limited to top-down initiatives of the kind undertaken by bishops, inquisitors and princes ... *we now acknowledge far broader transformations, often driven from below.* We take account of gender and are beginning to engage with the equally important category of age. The twists and turns of the historiography continue to present us with yet more faces of "the Counter-Reformation." ("Legacies of the Counter-Reformation and the Origins of Modern Catholicism" 452; emphasis mine)

We must, therefore, consider the particular spaces, networks, and individual circumstances and ambitions that framed religious practices and products (treatises, literary texts, art, letters, etc.) during this period. Lines of inquiry are in turn made available that lead us – historians and cultural critics alike – to examine anew how the mandates and institutional expectations of the Tridentine Church were locally interpreted and creatively negotiated. Scholars increasingly discard the characterization of the early modern Protestant and Catholic movements as a clash between change and tradition, between a culture of individualism and a culture of standardization and compulsory uniformity. As Laven maintains, we need instead to recognize the development of local and even individual Catholic "identities," in flux and contingent: "The reforms and renewals experienced by the Catholic peoples of the world were propelled by conflict and opposition; their faith was dynamic, responsive and ever-changing. The value of the term 'Counter-Reformation' is in encouraging us to put 'encounters' at the centre of religious change" (Introduction 11).

Spain proves to be an intriguing case in the historical revision of the Counter-Reformation. Given its imperial and Inquisitorial history – coupled with the Black Legend that saw its first intimations in the sixteenth century and that persists to this day – early modern Spain is still often branded as authoritarian and conservative, staunchly monolithic, and prosecutorial; and yet, the historical record presents a much different picture. Admittedly, in a resolute effort to suppress plurality and before Luther ever uttered any of his protestations, Spain had already concertedly reacted against heresy with the expulsion of non-converted Jews and Muslims, the institutionalization of a permanent Inquisition, and the suppression of Erasmists and *alumbrados* amongst the aristocracy. In the days that followed Luther's first declarations, it was Charles V, not the papacy, who led the charge in defence of consolidating Catholic supremacy. Nevertheless, Spain is also where the abuses of the clerical class were first addressed through education and the encouragement of pastoral care; where the Jesuits emphasized the ability of the lay individual to practise spiritual exercises outside of an institutional context and encouraged the belief that God could be found in all things; where the reform of the mendicant orders was first instituted; where the Catholic *via mística* found its strongest base; and where devotional art and literature flourished in the service of instructing and promoting faith amongst individuals and their extended communities. To interpret the Spanish context solely as one where the institution strictly determined or was able categorically to dictate or repress localized beliefs and individual practices vastly underestimates the complex and dynamic conditions – political, social, geographical, familial, personal – that structured the relationship between the Church and the faithful in Counter-Reformation Spain.

A more productive paradigm is to understand how regulation and control coexisted with variability and adaptability in the production of the early modern Catholic self. Anne J. Cruz and Mary E. Perry, for example, investigate in *Culture and Control in Counter-Reformation Spain* the ways in which the Catholic Church "acted as an official organ of cultural production" (xi) but also how, in return, writers and thinkers (and here they are following Raymond Williams) "construe significance for themselves and the world around them" in response to the mechanisms of culture and control imposed upon them (x). Within these parameters, Cruz and Perry set forth the following working premise: "In the case of Counter-Reformation Spain, alternative means of coexistence were shaped both because of and despite the control imposed by the dominant social and religious groups" (x). A similar route is taken by Anthony Cascardi in *Ideologies of History in Golden Age Spain*, where, in dialogue with Cruz and Perry, he proposes that cultural control, and the ideological apparatus that sustains it, need to be understood in terms of what he concludes was a "crisis of subjectivity" during this period (114):

> It is only by locating the links between cultural control and the matter of self-control that we can use recent shifts in Hispanism's understanding of "ideology" as a way to go beyond the tasks of locating the material consequences of ideas or of describing the various mechanisms of psychological control to *a less reductive understanding of the various modes of representation through which individuals adopted a cultural identity as subject-selves.*
> (112; emphasis mine)

Admittedly, we must concede to the Church Militant's ideological promotion of mechanisms of control and oversight; however, we must not forgo the examination of the response – the production of particular meanings and modes of representation – fashioned in the interdependency between the institutional forces that regulate and the individuals who mediate (variably understood and particularly adapted) their selfhood (or subject-selves) within the resulting order.

To a similar effect, Allyson Poska has examined institutional and popular religion, basing her historical analysis on the idea that the "interaction" between these two levels "should be conceived of as a part of a fluid structure" (9). More precisely, the historian observes how in early modern Spain, even as authority and dogma were accepted and strictly followed as a matter of undisputed fact, at the local level the faithful maintained and practised individualized communal, regional, and familial traditions and beliefs. Regardless of the degree of oversight (sometimes high, other times low) that a bishop, parish priest, or confessor exerted, the practice of Catholicism after Trent was far from uniform. Taken a step further, as argued by Kathryn Edwards, the interaction between "official" and "popular" religious formations must be understood as interdependent, given how "popular beliefs and practices could revise, nuance, or even negate official doctrine" (342). In fact, the post-Tridentine Church deemed that, if the faithful commonly held a religious belief, the Church should consider whether God placed that belief in their hearts. In the Spanish context and as it pertains to the central theme of this book, the ardent devotion to the Virgin Mary played a crucial role in supporting and compelling the Habsburg kings and the Spanish Church to relentlessly push the papacy to elevate the doctrine of the Immaculate Conception to dogma.

In the examination of this context, Foucault's *A History of Sexuality Vol. 1: An Introduction* – where the concept of technologies of power and the relationship between individual and institutional power are formulated – provides a useful point of departure. Following its conceptual framework, power is omnipresent and ubiquitous throughout the social field and in all social relations, private and public.[3] And yet, far from being static or exclusively determined, technologies of power and their discourses are fluid, and they function – are confirmed, affirmed, manipulated, challenged, transformed, dismissed, and reinstituted – from multiple sites. To be precise, for Foucault one cannot speak of technologies of power if one does not consider the relationship between individual subjects, local communities, and institutions as dynamic: "[T]he rationality of power is characterized by tactics that are often quite explicit at the restricted [local] level where they are inscribed ... tactics which, becoming connected to one another, attracting and propagating one another, but finding their base of support and their condition elsewhere, *end by forming comprehensive systems"* (*History* 95; emphasis mine). Local tactics and global strategies combine and concatenate, and discourses of power are unevenly deployed, resulting in less restrictive "comprehensive systems" than one may assume: "Discourses are not once and for all subservient to power or raised up against it ... discourse can be both an instrument and an effect of power, but also a hindrance, a stumbling-block, a point of resistance and a starting point for an opposing strategy" (*History* 100). I do not argue for the religious imagination of individuals – their particularized rendering of the doctrine and image of the Immaculate Conception in early modern Spain – as a source of consistent or coherent resistance ("an opposing strategy") to a controlling Catholic institution and its ideological apparatuses. Albeit supported by Foucault's formulations, I explore something altogether different: an understating of the individual religious imagination – in its many and varied levels of manifestation and forms of expression – as taking part in and, therefore, imposing its particularized sensitivities, desires, and anxieties upon a "comprehensive" religious, social, and political system. If the Church Militant, following the Council of Trent, officially sought to delimit religious discourse and close ranks under the oversight of bishops, confessors, and inquisitors, individual practitioners took it upon themselves to prove their faith and loyalty to the Catholic Church by producing ever more imaginative religious discourses. Even when official orthodox ideology sought a regularized homogeneity, Counter-Reformation religious fervour (paradoxically also favoured and solicited by the Church) elicited a proliferation of religiosity with corresponding plural imaginations, local and global. Following Foucault's thoughts on power and its dispersal, I would thus like to

> [D]isengage my analysis from the privileges generally accorded the economy of scarcity and the principles of rarefaction, to search instead for instances of discursive production (which also administer silences, to be sure), of the production of power (which sometimes have the function of prohibiting), of the propagation of knowledge (which often cause mistaken beliefs or systematic misconceptions to circulate); I would like to write the history of these instances and their transformations. (*History* 12)

As I will demonstrate, Foucault's proposition on technologies of power – supported by early modern historiography – provides a nuanced conceptual framework for the varied positions and identities that together form a Catholic system of thought in defence of the doctrine of the Immaculate Conception.

Coupled with a reflection on "instances and their transformations," a consideration of the hermeneutical tradition as analysed by Paul Ricoeur in *Figuring the Sacred* also proves useful to my reading of Spanish early modern religious imagination. Ricoeur has commented on the long-established distinction between "sacred" texts (i.e., the canonized biblical texts) and "authoritative" texts produced as a result of the "critical activity" of a community in a given moment and space (69):

> And so the nature of the text, at least in Christianity, is not completely hostile to the critical approach ... in Christianity all the discrepancies were preserved, and a certain equivocity of the texts was assumed at the beginning. No one said how many days the passion lasted; no one said how many days intervened between the crucifixion and the resurrection, and so on. Maybe the opaque notion of the sacred is shattered by this critical activity; it is really the concept of "sacred" that changes. (69)

For Ricoeur, hence, the relationship between sacred and authoritative goes much farther than merely a detached exegesis unilaterally imposed; instead, he stresses the individuated identitary effect that happens in the interpretation of foundational "sacred" texts, resulting in a proliferation of "authoritative" texts:

> [I]t is a hermeneutical act to recognize oneself as founded by a text and to read this text as founding. There is a kind of reciprocity between the reading and the existing self-recognition of the identity of the community. There is a kind of reciprocity between the community and the text. There comes to mind the distinction that Augustine makes in *De christiana doctrina* between *signum* and *res*: we are aware that the *signum* is not the *res*, and there is a history of possible approaches to the *signum*. I wonder whether this actually implies a certain distance between the text and its reality, what it is about. It is really important to say whether critical activity is assumed by the community that learns to read its text in a different way as a result. *What happens to the reader and the community when critical activity is applied to the text? We might say that something arbitrary and uselessly compulsory is removed.* (69; emphasis mine)

Of course, one could argue that the Church Militant's most effective mechanism of control was its prerogative in the production of authoritative texts; or "the sacred/authoritative through the sacred and subjected to the sacred," mimicking Louis Althusser's formulation of the nature of ideology and its interpellation of subjects.[4] The weak spot of this assertion is that Counter-Reformation Spain – in accord with the

propagandistic needs of the Catholic Church and aided by the printing press and higher levels of literacy – saw a proliferation of religious
treatises, printed sermons, hagiographies, spiritual (auto)biographies,
commentaries, paintings, and sculptures that offered a multitude of complementary and competing interpretations of the Scriptures. As Ricoeur
has well noted, it is precisely because of this relationship between the
signum and the *res* that religious communities can stave off the sedimen-
tation of doctrine and belief; through "recognition" and interpretation,
the hermeneutical practice promotes renewal and offers the individual
and her community an opportunity to enter a reciprocal (I would add
dialectical) relationship with the sacred through the sacred. To be more
precise, the function of interpretation in a particular historical, social,
and geographical context allows for the faithful to mediate their relationship to the sacred, a process through which the community "learns
to read its text in a different way," moving away from the arena of the
"compulsory" and into the field of "critical activity."

Ricoeur's thoughts on the role of the imagination in biblical exegesis
are also very useful in drafting the category of the religious imagination. Rejecting the notion that the Bible is "a closed book, one whose
meaning is fixed forever ever and therefore the enemy of any radically
original creation of meaning" (144), Ricoeur takes up the cause for the
imagination as a dynamic partner to interpretation within the framework provided by orthodox Catholic ideology. As such, the imagination must be conceived of in two concurrent modes:

> First, imagination can be described as a *rule-governed form of invention* or,
> in other terms, as a norm-governed productivity ... Next, the imagination
> can be considered as the power of giving *form to human experience* or ... as
> the power of redescribing reality. Fiction is my name for the imagination
> considered under this double point of view of rule-governed invention
> and a power of redescription ... I would like to consider the act of reading
> as a dynamic activity that is not confined to repeating significations fixed
> forever, but which takes place as a *prolonging of the itineraries of meaning
> opened up by the work of interpretation*. (144; emphasis mine)

It is precisely in these "itineraries of meaning" that my exploration of
the varied religious imagination of Counter-Reformation Spain, as revealed through the Virgin of the Immaculate Conception, is anchored.
Subscribing to the possibility for a space of negotiation and the potential for fluidity in the system of belief and identification, I consider how
the Spanish early modern faithful translate and generate for themselves
and for others (rather than just overtly react to or ceremoniously repeat)

interested and particularized religious thought. Fully invested in the elaboration and dissemination of an expansive Catholic imaginary that is framed, but not vehemently overdetermined, by institutional control, the believer responds to the sacred text and the divine mysteries found therein as an act of self-recognition.

II. The Religious Imagination: Between Interpretation and Excess

As stated in the previous section, the conceptual focus of this book is the dialectical relationship between the Church as a guarantor of doctrinal and theological truths, and the communities and individuals who adopt and adapt those doctrines and truths to suit their own contexts and needs. I contend that we can best examine this reciprocity through the category of the religious imagination, a concept that I now need to historicize and define more concretely.

Theologians Paul Avis and Anthony J. Godzieba have written at length about the unequivocal role of the imagination in the nature and practice of Christianity. Avis, for example, states that, "unless we attempt to do full justice to the part played by the imagination, we cannot understand the Christian faith" (3); Godzieba, for his part, insists on the centrality of what he calls the "sacramental imagination" to Christian belief: "It is the way of envisioning reality through the eyes of faith that recognizes that the finite can mediate the infinite, that all aspects of created being can mediate grace" (21). The notion behind these assertions is that the most salient mechanism through which human beings move towards divine revelation is the imaginative capacity. We cannot know God directly but, through the imagination, we can receive and reproduce forms, concepts, and symbols that mediate divine truth (or, to be more precise, what the faithful construct to be divine truth). Indeed, this position recalls the long philosophical and theological tradition that grappled with the role of the imagination in facilitating a passage between the material world, reason, and the sacred realm of Being.

The medieval synthesis of Platonic and Aristotelian ontology with biblical theology produced an onto-theological system that incorporated into early Christian thinking philosophical concepts such as true form, reason, and imagination to address the relationship of humans with God. Concerning the specific role of the imagination in this framework, Richard Kearney explains:

> In both traditions of this conceptual alliance ... the imagination was essentially interpreted as a mimetic activity – that is, as a second-hand reflection of some "original" source of meaning which resides beyond man. In the

biblical tradition, this Origin was identified with Yahweh, the Father of all creation. While in the Hellenic tradition, it was usually equated with the highest of the Forms: something which mortals desire to emulate, contemplate or know in some way. (115)

Following this logic, Augustine of Hippo (354–430 AD) stressed seeking understanding primarily through reason, insisting that the imagination remain a secondary faculty. As noted by John Cocking, Augustine goes back "to Aristotle and his tripartite hierarchy of sensation-imagination-reason, and to Plato with his emphasis on the conceptual and his implication that thinking in images is a lesser or 'degraded' kind of thinking as compared with thinking in concepts" (71). Whereas theology can seek to discern divine truth or the essence of the world through the intellect – through reason – the imagination can only imitate, or reproduce; it cannot grasp the spiritual light "as it is in itself" (Kearney 117).

The medieval period saw a departure from this hierarchizing with Hugh of St Victor (1096–1141) and Bonaventure (1221–74), whose treatises reconsider the Augustinian paradigm in favour of the power of the imagination. For his part, Hugh of St Victor privileges the connection of images in the mind to the spiritual, rather than the material, realm. In *On the Union of the Body and Spirit*, he insists, "Nothing in the body is higher or nearer to the spiritual nature than what the force of the imagination, coming after sense, and beyond the reach of sense, conceives. What is more sublime than this is reason" (qtd in Cocking 146). This is a pivotal turn in the history of the imagination, and most especially of the Catholic religious imagination, since it frees this faculty from its function as a mere passage between the material and the intelligible (between things and the idea of things). Instead, as explained by Ritva Palmén, Hugh of St Victor's claim foregrounds the continuity of the imagination with the spirit on its way to divine reason: "Thus imagination may designate the faculty as well as the activity or content of the soul" (43). The imagination is thus secured as a productive (and not a conductive) capacity. From a complementary position, Bonaventure (whom I discuss in more detail in chapter 3) structures the relationship between truth and image as one of similitude. The human imagination is, in his system, analogous to the ineffable act of divine creation: "The human creature is a simulacrum of the divine Creator; and his highest vocation is to faithfully 'mirror' the Supreme Artist of the universe" (Kearney 124). For Bonaventure, therefore, the imaginative faculty draws on humans' likeness to the sacred by way of the creative function of the imagination; and it is through the imaginative creative function that we best confirm our bond with God.

Thomas Aquinas (1225–74), whose *Summa Theologica* remained highly influential during the period of the Council of Trent, offers the concept of the image as a phantasm – as a sensible impression – that arises by way of comparison and similitude. Closely following an Aristotelian paradigm, Aquinas sets the foundation for the analogical function of the phantasm in part I, question 85, of the *Summa Theologica*, where he discusses at length the function of the image as an analogous mechanism to abstraction and divine intellect: "But to know what is in individual matter, not as existing in such matter, is to abstract the form from individual matter which is represented by the phantasms. Therefore, we must say that our intellect understands material things by abstracting from the phantasms; and through material things thus considered we acquire some knowledge of immaterial things, just as, on the contrary, angels know material things through the immaterial" (part I, q. 85, art. 1). The imagination in Aquinas thus retains (as in Bonaventure) a productive function through which "immaterial things" of which we can have no knowledge – including the divine mystery – are made analogically accessible. Moreover, although for Aquinas many aspects of God's nature can be demonstrated through reason aided by the imagination, there are thresholds (the Trinity and the Incarnation, for example) that can only be perceived by way of "imaginary visions," divine illumination, and faith. Within this line of thought, Aquinas offers the following definition for "prophet" in his *Commentary on the Letters of Saint Paul to the Corinthians* on 1 Corinthians 14,

> For sometimes one is called a prophet, because he possesses all four [modes of prophecy], namely, that he sees imaginary visions, and has an understanding of them and he boldly announces to others and he works miracles ... Again, one is called a prophet, if he has the intellectual light to explain even *imaginary visions* made to himself or someone else, or for explaining the sayings of the prophets or the Scriptures of the apostles. In this way a prophet is anyone who discerns the writings of the Doctors, because they have been interpreted in the same spirit as they were edited; and so Solomon and David can be called prophets, inasmuch as they had the intellectual light to understand clearly and subtly ... Someone is also called a prophet from working miracles, as it says in Sir (48:14) that "the dead body of Elijah prophesied, i.e., worked a miracle." Therefore, what the Apostle says through this chapter of the prophets must be understood in the second mode, namely, *that one is said to prophesy who through a Divine intellectual light explains visions made to him and others.* According to this, what is said here about prophets will be plain. (1 Cor. 14:1–4. 813; emphasis mine)

As here described, the connection established between the imagination (in the form of the imaginary vision) and prophecy is essential to the category of the religious imagination, deepening the relationship between the image, reason, and divine intellectual light. In this schema, the imagination – images manifested as visions – enables the prophet to speak to higher truths that cannot be reached through the intellect alone.

Nevertheless, it is also in this context that Aquinas (like Bonaventure before him) warns against the potential dangers of the imagination that, if left unchecked, can quickly degenerate and become subservient to base instincts, or even worse to Satanic manipulation, fooling us into taking falsity for revelation. Despite elevating the imagination closer to the spiritual realm, Aquinas does not break with Augustine on the importance of judgment and knowledge; ultimately, reason must be the faculty that discriminates the essence of sacred truth, both in the assessment of what is imagined/imaged and in the event of prophecy. Thus configured, the imagination is the necessary extension that conveys the sensible and the spiritual to the intelligible; nevertheless, because of its proximity and attachments to the sensory and the sensual, it remains a vehicle that can be easily derailed. As Augustine had early on warned and as Cocking explains, "what we see depends on what we are looking for, and ... if we are looking for something with enough force of desire, or 'vehemence', we shall mistake our self-created image for the real thing, and give rise to hallucinations or to bodily reactions identical with those that would take place if the image were real and not fictional" (74). Necessary and analogous to God's creative power yet simultaneously corruptible and suspect, the capacity of the imagination to be either divine simulacra or a sinful degeneration into the fancy of the senses and the body was a core dilemma within the context of the Counter-Reformation. This quandary drove much of the anxiety in regard to mystical experiences: was the visionary positively experiencing the Divine through his/her imagination, or was the vision misguided by indulgence and diabolic intervention?[5] Sacred art (painting, especially) was likewise often critiqued and censored for its imagining of the Divine in a way that seemed too close to the material world, the phantasm leading back to the sensual instead of to the sacred. The predicament of how to determine whether the religious imagination of a believer and/or (following Aquinas) "prophet" arises from divine light or from some other source frames Counter-Reformation religious experience and artistic/textual production.

The supplementary nature of the religious imagination is fraught with peril, put to the test by the fact that divine mystery must always ultimately remain unavailable to human understanding; only through analogy and interpretation can we approximate that which is beyond our grasp. It is especially because of these ontological coordinates that the imagination must be vigilant of unchecked immoderation, remain subjected to reason and truth, and not turn wayward. As Kearney explains, summarizing Bonaventure and Aquinas, "As a mimetic faculty of representation and storage, imagination has its place. But it must be kept in its place. Any departure from its mandatory subordination to reason and reality, can only lead to error – and, at worst, satanic pride" (130). Consequently, the Counter-Reformation Church sought to oversee the imaginative faculty in two ways. On the one hand, within the parameters of orthodoxy but in the spirit of reform, the Church encouraged an expansive theological and biblical interpretative imagination (exegetical and heuristic) necessary to the spiritual, pedagogical, and propagandistic requirements of the movement. On the other hand, the imaginative faculty, as it is positioned in the realm of the human, had to respond to a scrutiny that considered its alliances with the body suspect. The validity of the interpretation of the sacred that is produced via the creative force of the religious imagination or an imaginary vision per se called for verification; its content and effects had to be deemed appropriate and mediate a passage to divine reason and truth, or else be considered as originating in sinful motivation or from an evil source. How and by whom these parameters and limits were identified and enforced is a matter, in practice, of local circumstance. Censure notably varied depending on the confessor, the local inquisitor, the familial or political connections of the individual, the physical location of production, and the intended audience. Under these conditions, religious practices, experiences, and products require in equal measures vigilance *and* creative ingenuity so as to navigate successfully a complex Counter-Reformation hermeneutical, cultural, and ideological field.

Within the framework of this double exigency, the mystical movement, mendicant reforms, and the Jesuit spiritual exercises forged a path for a profuse Catholic religious imaginary. Individuals were able to stake a claim as *conduits* for divine alterity through their imagination; to position themselves as *translators* between our world and the sacred; and, in their textual and artistic practices, to enact privileged Catholic identities. Certifying the presence of divine inspiration was a task that had everything to do with perception and the specific networks and social positioning of the author or artist; ironically, this undertaking often led to additional imaginative output, in the form of letters, framing texts, and glosses.[6] In the interstices between personal faith, political influence, social networks, and religious orthodoxy, individuals were more often than not impelled to generate additional writings, objects, and practices, resulting in an ever-expansive creative praxis.

As described in the medieval theological corpus, the religious imagination is a reproductive, not productive, capacity (what it would later become under Kant and the German Romantics): "It cannot create truth *out of itself*, but must always observe the strict limits *of reproduction*" (Kearney 118). In this sense it is a conservative faculty, dependent either on the senses or on higher concepts, never autonomous from an external source of truth, i.e., God. Yet, within a Counter-Reformation context (one which carries forth the heritage of Renaissance humanism and its confidence in human faculties), this derivative condition served as an advantage. Because the origin of truth resides in God and is fundamentally inscrutable, the Catholic self is compelled (perhaps paradoxically) to imagine, to elaborate on phantasms/images that analogize the sacred, to pursue the logic of divine reason in the biblical account, and to contemplate the sacred, envisaging its abstract and experiential possibilities: in other words, to perceive and render intelligible for oneself the Divine as made manifest in the physical and spiritual worlds. Justified in a Scholastic medieval theological apparatus, the potentiality of the analogical imaginative interpretation and translation of the sacred is in practice, and despite the pressures of orthodoxy, a rather open and fluid hermeneutical activity, full of idiosyncrasies, self-serving manipulations, and copious extravagances and exaggerations. From a purely theological perspective, the sacred mystery is designated as ineffable, uninterpretable, and untranslatable. Nevertheless, in lived experience, systems of faith rely precisely on the necessity of tracing a connection between what cannot be known, what is known, and what can be imagined; this, it could be said, is the work of the religious imagination (and, not surprisingly, of classical philosophical systems as well). At a minimum, sacred texts provide foundational narratives, parables, and prophecy; and the faithful – in oral and written texts, in art, and in their preferred practices and rituals – use their imaginative capacity to interpret and translate, bringing to bear in their particular contexts the mystery of divine design.

Along this same line of thinking, Stephen H. Webb, has argued for the inherent need for a capacious hyperbolic imagination in religious thought and practice; an "(il)logic of excess" that moves believers into the realm of "truth":

I want to confront the Enlightenment critique of exaggeration more directly. What is needed is a new perspective from which to view the relationship of religious event and exaggeration. A rehabilitation of hyperbole would direct enquiry not to ask about the reality that this figure distorts but rather the reality that [for the believer] could be expressed in no other way except through the excited and startling language of excess and extravagance. Hyperbole does not emphasize and magnify; it conjures and reveals. (23)

If we are to follow Webb's proposition, it is only through the hyperbolic religious imagination – excessive and extravagant – that the Divine can be revealed as reason. Philosopher William Desmond has taken a similar position, framing hyperbole as a way to "a rich poetic of religious practice" and towards transcendence:

Generally, by contrast with the symbolic, the hyperbolic indirection turns us to the *excess of disproportion*, but this time in terms of transcendence "above" rather than "immanence in the midst." The hyperbole gives us a figure of the overdeterminate ... "beyond" of immanence ... that "throws us above" immanence ... in the disproportion *between* immanence and transcendence ... This is why we need hyperboles to say what we mean, what indeed *we alone* cannot mean. (127)

Webb's and Desmond's formulations could not have been articulated in the cultural and theological context of the Counter-Reformation; still, religious texts and other cultural products of the period contain multitudes of examples that can only be understood as excessive and extravagant, hyperboles aiming at transcendence, pointing at meanings that cannot be fixed. Rhetoricians classically understand hyperbole as a straining of the truth;[7] and yet, as it regards the religious imagination, hyperbole provides a framework that attempts to capture a higher and otherwise illusive sacred truth. Most of the texts and paintings I examine could easily fall into the category of excessive in ways that I hope will become apparent throughout this study.

Not without reason, the topic of excess may seem to inevitably tie the category of the religious imagination to the baroque. In my estimation, this classification imposes interpretative limits that I want to avoid. The term "baroque" was originally coined in the nineteenth century and evolved mainly as an art historical designation whose function was to distinguish seventeenth-century art, described alternatively in derogative and laudatory fashion vis-à-vis its classical, restrained, and orderly Renaissance precedents. Within these parameters, the baroque was initially associated with visual arts and architecture sponsored by the Church, the state, or the high

aristocracy during the Counter-Reformation, and was typically identified as shaped and financed by those in power in order to showcase their supremacy and influence in a moment of religious and
political turmoil. As it refers to literature, the category evolved to
describe language that relied on double metaphors, extreme hyperbole, complex hyperbatons, and other tropes to communicate (when
successful) newfangled and often obscure conceptual connotations.
Alternatively, when elevated to the level of philosophical thought by
intellectual historians, the baroque is reserved for a poetics and met-
aphysics of immanence on the path towards secular modernity. As
Christopher D. Johnson explains in *Hyperboles: The Rhetoric of Excess
in Baroque Literature and Thought*:

> Baroque hyperbole helps goad as well as represent the dissolution of the
> analogical worldview. Surprisingly heuristic, hyperboles may be read as
> seismic markers that help chart the early modern "rupture" between what
> Foucault calls an *episteme* of resemblance and one of measure, identity,
> and difference ... a late seventeenth-century cosmos in which language
> becomes increasingly "transparent" and ontologically suspect, is filled
> with "ruptures" that clearly call for hyperbole. (17)

Given these coordinates, scholars of religious art and culture
have mostly moved away from anchoring their studies through
this designation. Recent monographs, such as *The Sensuous in the
Counter-Reformation Church*, edited by Marcia Hall and Tracy Cooper,
or Hall's *The Sacred Image in the Age of Art*, refrain from employing
the category as part of the methodological framework; the term "baroque" does not even appear in these books' indexes. I suspect the
issue is that the general parameters of what baroque has come to
signify – an appeal to the senses often at the cost of exegetical intent,
a unilateral imposition of orthodoxy, the visual display of the cen-
tralization of absolutist monarchical power, and conceptual obscu-
rity – lead us astray when we examine much of the religious-cultural
production (both high and low) of the period, especially in Spain. On
the one hand, when the category is thought of in terms of "immanence, aporia, and transcendence," as it relates to the spiritual im-
peratives and resulting culture of the Counter-Reformation we are
treading on fertile terrain (Greene and Cushman 122). On the other,
when strictly limited to an aesthetic of grandeur, accumulation, and
linguistic exuberance, as well as the cultivation of wit and herme-
neutic conceit, the category would seem to exclude most of the texts
(both literary and visual) that I examine. Admittedly, many of my

examples demonstrate an intensified visuality and theatricality, and a desire to stir the emotions – all broadly understood as "excessive" and often associated with the baroque. Furthermore, in its intent, Counter-Reformation religious art is squarely inscribed in the propagandistic needs of the Church Militant, following Trent's mandate to instruct and inspire contemplation, a description that has also been a constant in the general criteria used for the category. Nonetheless, in the final account, most of the cultural products analysed in this book are not exceptionally witty, do not use language in intentionally obscure ways, often are produced or consumed outside of centralized power structures, and resist interpretations that could lead to a rhetoric or a poetics of immanence. As I will demonstrate, they can only be well understood through the category of an excessive religious imagination, hyperbolic but not strictly baroque in its traditional prescriptions.

In its varied private and public manifestations, the religious imagination around the cult of Mary is at times profound and sophisticated, at others direct and raw, and invariably reveals the intricate and very distinct ways that the faithful recognized themselves in and responded to the mystery of immaculacy. Given the context of the Counter-Reformation, there is an added consideration: Immaculists deployed their imagination in the face of a competing Protestant paradigm that positioned itself as rational, not lured by excess, and opposed to an expansive Catholic religious sensuality.[8] Protestants, although accepting of Mary's essential role in the drama of redemption, outright rejected the doctrinal insistence on her absolute immaculacy and, therefore, understood the cult of the Virgin, with the apocryphal texts, theological treatises, images, and liturgies that framed and ritually supported it, as disproportionate and idolatrous. As noted by Hans Belting, the image of Mary was in turn fundamental to how Catholics responded to the Reformation:

[T]he Counter-Reformation's cult of images was an act of atonement toward them, each new image being intended symbolically to fill the place from which another had been expelled. This polemical use of images culminated in the figure of Mary, because Mary made it possible to present in visible terms the doctrinal differences between Catholics and Protestants. Older icons of the Virgin, now newly revered, served in their fashion to validate a tradition on the strength of their age. Publicly erected Marian columns, like paintings in other times, also were monuments to the church as an institution and to its triumph. The state, as the defender of the church, likewise associated itself with images and their cult. (2)

Along these lines, one can read the hyperbolic religious imagination in countless Spanish early modern religious texts and images, and particularly in those that feature the Immaculate Conception of Mary, as political insofar as they certify – both in terms of personal belief and in a broader communal public identity – an appropriate degree of loyalty to the Church Militant in opposition to Protestant theological reformations. The Catholic faithful respond to the Protestant penchant for exegetical and ceremonial restraint with an unswerving turn towards an exuberant religious imagination; and Mary's immaculacy – at least in the early modern Spanish Habsburg context – is the mystery through which to best ideologically and politically declare, feature, and legitimize that excess. The hyperbolic and extravagant, in this manner, is reframed in the Immaculist Catholic imaginary as fundamental and singularly revelatory of God's true – specifically Catholic and Spanish – enterprise.

As indicated above, divine reason can only be approximated (both as in getting closer to and being similar to) through a logic of abundance; the sacred exceeds us, and the faithful can only come to know it and of it through an imaginative surplus. One point of entry is to recall the relationship between imagination and reason made by the early Church fathers. The imagination is legitimately excessive in that it produces – in its analogous capacity and capaciousness – a surplus account of the sacred in the mind of the faithful. The ideas, images, and concepts produced by the religious imagination are not identical to the sacred; they emanate from humans, not from God, and can never aspire to capture the divine design thoroughly. And yet, the interpretative practice is perforce a framing of the sacred that generates an analogical and, thus, revelatory excess. It is only in this theological and cultural context, I argue, that the devotion to and the immense cultural production of texts and artefacts about the Virgin of the Immaculate Conception in early modern Spain can be explained.

III. The Doctrine of the Immaculate Conception of Mary: A Matter of Theological Debate

In a historical moment of perceived and actual attack on the Catholic faith and the dwindling of the Habsburg Empire, Spain seemed compelled to attempt to monopolize the sacred, both in the realm of reason and as unknowable mystery. The Church Militant, local communities, and individual practitioners tried to (re)create, promote, and proliferate religious images and doctrines that certified the superiority of the Catholic faith, alongside the Spanish Habsburg Empire, as the Chosen One; accordingly, the symbols, texts, and visionary experiences that accompanied this effort had to be vetted and proven authentic and divinely ordained. Only this framework and its cultural effects can explain the institutional, political, artistic, and literary commitments and resulting tensions over the doctrine and representation of the Virgin of the Immaculate Conception. In a context of reform and with a sacred mystery that bore diverging interpretations, the defence of the Immaculate Conception lent itself to often unexpected imaginative translations.

The religious imagination of the Spanish Counter-Reformation was fed by the slippery logic and often convoluted elucidations on immaculacy. The anxiety over the state of Mary's sinful nature was not unwarranted, given the imperative that Jesus' holy nature in no way be thought of as corrupted by his human mother's inheritance of Adamic nature and its propensity to sin. Originating in the early Church's liturgical practice, the doctrine of the Immaculate Conception fundamentally proposes that the Virgin Mary was exceptional in that the stain of original sin *never* touched her. Immaculist accounts of how this condition is possible in a human being vary. Against Augustine's proposition that "original sin was transmitted through sexual intercourse," those that followed Anselm (1033–1109) believed in an essential connection between the exercise of free will and sin, stressing the relationship between self-awareness and choice: "Although the potential for original sin is present in everyone from conception, it does not take effect until a child has reached the age at which it should have the possibility of exercising free will" (Boss, "The Development of the Doctrine" 208–9). This line of reasoning allowed for the sexual union of Anne and Joachim, insisting on a topography of sin found in the soul, not in the body. Mary's exceptionality is possible insofar as God, despite her acquiring free will, miraculously preserved her soul pure and untouched by the stain of original sin. Anselm's interpretation of the body/soul dichotomy and onset of original sin is fundamental for those who would insist on Mary's immaculacy as distinct from her parents' sexual union. Among many examples, Bernard of Clairvaux (1090–1153) – unsatisfied with the implication of the wholesale sanctification of any human being, even Mary – insisted on the purification of her soul after conception but before her birth. And yet, even if the Anselmian solution distinguishes the natural state of the body from the soul concerning conception, free will, and sin, Scholastic theologians sought a resolution to the persistent quandary posited by the threatening power of the flesh and its seepage onto Mary's immaculacy. These include suggestions that Mary was implanted in Anne's womb fully formed without sexual contact with Joachim, coupled with the proposition that Mary's placenta never touched Anne's body and that at birth she was miraculously protected from coming into contact with Anne's birth canal. Because Anne's body is not exempt from original sin, Mary's immaculacy must be shielded at all times, keeping her body free from any contact with her mother's sexualized and corrupted flesh.

Aquinas – and Dominican theologians by extension – formally struggled with the contradicting positions advanced in the early Church between the Feast of the Conception of Mary and the Feast of the Annunciation. In his *Summa Theologica*, Aquinas attempts to reach a degree of synthesis between these two oppositional doctrinal positions, the first locating Mary's immaculacy upon conception *in utero* and the second advocating for the Virgin's purification upon the incarnation of Jesus in her body. Expounding a view that is less decisive than that of the Dominican conservatives who followed him into the seventeenth century, Aquinas specifically addresses the matter of Mary's immaculacy in question 27 of the third part of the *Summa*, which not inconsequentially he dedicates to the "Blessed Virgin Mary Immaculate Seat of Wisdom." From the lengthy arguments, objections, and answers provided, we can surmise the following: 1) that Mary had to be redeemed, otherwise Christ's role would be diminished; 2) that she must have been sanctified first in the womb, then upon the incarnation of Christ, and third upon her assumption; and 3) that she was thus concurrently preserved from all sin, venial and actual. Despite a valiant attempt to formalize the necessity and parameters of Mary's purity, for Aquinas the actual moment of Mary's first sanctification and the divine logic for its specific occurrence remain a matter of deductive interpretation, not of certainty: "And although it is not possible to assign a reason for God's judgments, for instance, why He bestows such a grace on one and not on another, yet there seems to be a certain fittingness in [Mary] being sanctified in the womb, by [her] foreshadowing the sanctification which was to be effected through Christ" (part III, q. 27, art. 6).[9] In other words, Aquinas avoids settling the how and the when of the miracle of Mary's Immaculate Conception and, in doing so, leaves open a vast hermeneutical space for Immaculist thought – its causes, conditions, assumptions, and effects – in abundant theological debates, religious treatises, sermons, images, and literary texts all over medieval and early modern Europe.

The Franciscan John Duns Scotus (1266–1308) – who inherited a variety of accounts from Anselm, Eadmer (1060–1126), and William of Ware (? – 1305) – argued, for example, that,

[P]reservation from sin is better than deliverance. Consequently, to claim that Mary was preserved from contracting original sin is to say not that she did not need to be redeemed, but on the contrary, that she was the object of Christ's most complete redemptive action. Thus [for Scotus] the doctrine of the Immaculate Conception teaches that Christ's salvific power reaches to the fullest possible extent. (Boss, "The Development of the Doctrine" 212)

As this explanation makes clear, Scotus is – like Aquinas before him – attempting to preserve the necessity of Christ's incarnation by maximizing its scope and design; Christ's redemptive power is so perfect that it prevents Mary from having ever been touched by sin. William of Ockham (c. 1285–1347), the father of medieval nominalism and conceptualism, took a similar position on Mary's singularity by emphasizing God's voluntarism and prioritizing the absoluteness of divine will over divine intellect. From his perspective, God wills the scheme of original sin and salvation and, likewise, has the power to forgive sin and bestow grace with or without repentance, or, in Mary's case, to exempt her from original sin insofar as his will is absolute. Ockham's estimation of God's omnipotence – exempt from a predetermined logic – became a keystone of the Franciscan defence of the doctrine. Just as significantly, this nominalist strain in Franciscan thought also underscored, as explained by Michael Allen Gillespie, a reliance on revelation and visions: "God could not be understood by human reason but only by biblical revelation or mystical experience" (14), which meant that the contemplation of immaculacy was often intimately connected to the visionary and the imaginary. Given these hermeneutical conditions, questions regarding the *place* of immaculacy, whether God had to sanctify and preserve from sin both the body and the soul, or only the soul, continued to riddle medieval and early modern theologians and religious thinkers as they attempted to settle the manner in which Mary was conceived (i.e., generated through sexual intercourse or formed and miraculously placed in Anne's womb); the coordinates of her spirit and being (eternal and incarnated or resulting solely from Anne and Joachim's sexual union); and her standing vis-à-vis all other created beings (including angels) and the holy Trinity.

A particularly fascinating Spanish example in this last regard is Francisco Suárez (1548–1617) – one of the most renowned Franciscan theologians and philosophical thinkers in early modern Europe – who in his *De mysteriis vitae Christi* (a commentary on Aquinas's *Summa Theologica*) clarifies Mary's status as the most loved of all created beings, more so than all the angels and saints combined. As explained by Suárez, the Virgin's exceptionality is doubly carried out by God's grace and eternal wisdom: she is predestined to immaculacy before the fall of Adam and, when conceived under the law of Adam, preemptively cleansed via Christ's redemptive power:

> God predestined the Virgin before the expected occurrence of original sin, to a divine maternity as well as to the perpetual sanctity and innocence that her state necessitated, and he, nonetheless, incorporated her under the law imposed upon Adam; and again, once Adam's sin was forgone, so that his first intent for the Virgin remain firm, Christ preserved her from any and all stain; because among these things there is nothing repugnant; to the contrary these are very coherent and agreeable to reason.[10]

For Suárez, the correlation in Mary between immaculacy, grace, and free will structures the logic for the Virgin's exceptionality. A key concept of what has come to be known as *suarecianismo*, as summarized by Mindy Nancarrow, is that "In Suárez's calculations, Mary at the first instant of sanctification (immediately after her Immaculate Conception) received more grace than any saint or angel and her grace intensified by her continuous acts performed of her own free will in cooperation with God's grace so that by the end of her life her grace was more intense than the consummated grace of all of the saints and angels combined" ("Francisco Suárez's Bienaventurada Virgen" 20). Sarah Jane Boss further argues for the Scotian roots for Suárez's position:

> Moreover, following the teaching of John Duns Scotus (1266–1308) ... the incarnation of the Word of God in Christ was predestined from before the foundation of the world, and not only a response to human sinfulness; and since the incarnation consisted in part, at least, in Mary giving Christ his humanity ... Mary's divine motherhood must have been predestined in the same act by which God predestined the incarnation ... Since her whole life would have been ordered by this supreme dignity, according to Suárez we can be sure that God will have bestowed upon Mary an exceptional degree of grace from the very first moment of her life. ("Francisco Suárez" 258)[11]

Suarecianismo thus binds Mary's eternal spiritual superiority to an exalted terrestrial humanity. Preordained to be free of sin, she is conceived always already full of grace; nevertheless, it is through freely chosen acts in her capacity as a human being that her immaculacy is confirmed, maintained, and increased in grace. As Suárez's writings make clear, the logic of purity – tied to the mystery of the Incarnation and the unknowability and nominalist unpredictability of divine design – was for its defenders unshakeable and yet open to ever more detailed and elaborate rationalizations.

Mary's immaculate humanity, as made manifest in her maternal self, attends to only part of the doctrine. Genesis 3:15, the visions of John of Patmos in Revelation 12:1, and Proverbs 8:22–4 (as well as select verses in the Psalms and Ecclesiasticus) resulted in the fact that Mary was also theologically interpreted and popularly understood to be the eternal Apocalyptic woman. Following Scotus's lead, Mariologists in the early modern period (especially the Franciscans) often insisted that the Virgin was predestined to be the Mother of God before the beginning of time, *ab initio*, and thus should be considered eternal, incomparable, and the recipient of the highest degree of grace:

> Scotists argued that if God willed from eternity that the Word should take human flesh, then the woman from whom that flesh was to be taken must likewise have been predestined from eternity to be the Mother of God. Mary therefore shares in the predestination of Christ. Since Mary was predestined to her sacred office prior to Adam's fall, it was argued that her humanity was ordered in the first instance to her divine motherhood; so if the existence of original sin meant that there would be some tension between Mary's descent from Adam and her office as Mother of God, then – provided it was possible – the former must be subordinated to the latter. (Boss, "The Development of the Doctrine" 221)

The account of Genesis 3:15 (mistranslated from the Hebrew by Jerome in the Vulgate Bible) sets the stage for Mary as the woman who crushes the head of the serpent.[12] Revelation 12 tells John of Patmos's vision of a pregnant woman whose superiority to the angels in the realm of Heaven enrages a seven-headed red dragon. She is dressed in the sun and crowned with twelve stars, births a son who is immediately whisked away by God, and is hidden by God in the wilderness for 1,260 days so as to keep her untouched by evil. Revelation also tells of an encounter between the forces of good and evil which ends with a war led by the archangel Michael. John of Patmos's vision is today read by the faithful as a prefiguration of the end of time when Satan will be finally defeated. In the medieval and early modern periods, however, a preterist interpretation of Revelation (as retold, for example, in John Milton's *Paradise Lost*) placed the encounter with the seven-headed dragon and the resulting war at the beginning of time, before the fall of man, when Lucifer and the rebellious angels were cast from Heaven. In this account, Proverbs 8:22–4 confirms Mary's existence before time, before the fall of man, and offers further proof of her immaculacy: "The LORD possessed me in the beginning of his way, / before his works of old. / I was set up from everlasting, / from the beginning, or ever the earth was." For Immaculists, the identification of Mary as the Apocalyptic woman not only assured her exemption from sin but, just as significantly, positioned her as eternal, purer than the angels and coexisting in the Heavens under the protection of the Trinity. Not insignificantly, this interpretation extricates Mary from her Jewish context, eternalizing her being and freeing her from any typological relationship with her Old Testament earthly mothers and precursors. In sum, Mary's immaculate existence, inclusive of a prelapsarian heavenly presence and spiritual birthing of Christ, is framed so as to erase Adam's inheritance and trump any association with the stain of original sin.

Despite its growing acceptance and proliferation through the sixteenth and seventeenth centuries, the doctrine remained polemical amongst the ever more influential and contentious religious orders. As noted by Robert Goodwin, the subject of Mary's exemption from sin had become "contentiously politicized" as a result of the opinions issued by Aquinas and the subsequent splintering of the Franciscans on this matter (360). The Dominicans, with Aquinas's hesitation and Anselm's propositions as their primary sources, challenged the belief that Mary was conceived free of the stain of sin, since this claim seemingly denied the need for Mary's redemption and thus lessened Christ's role as *universal* Saviour. In its place, the Dominicans argued for an immaculacy fashioned in the womb after conception but before birth; a redemption that stems from Christ's sacrifice at the cross *retroactively*. Following Scotus, the Franciscans retorted that Christ's salvific grace, an extension of God's omnipotent and nominalist power, extended to Mary preemptively and eternally. Additionally, the claim of Mary's eternal and privileged fellowship with the holy Trinity in Heaven, and the assertion of her role in the prelapsarian battle with Lucifer, only deepened the dispute between Franciscans and Dominicans. These theological positions were ultimately reconciled by the time that the doctrine was elevated to dogma in 1854; during the early modern period, they remained a source of considerable tension.

Alongside these theological disputes, popular Catholic sentiment insisted that, as the Mother of God, Mary's whole humanity – her body and soul – must be pure, regardless of how it may be elucidated by scholars. As Boss notes,

> This argument holds that since the flesh of the incarnate Word was taken from the flesh of the Virgin, it is inconceivable that the Virgin's flesh would ever have been united to a soul contaminated by sin ... Since everything about Christ must be as holy (and therefore as clean) as possible, the flesh from which he is made must never have been bound to anything impure. ("The Development of the Doctrine" 220)

Circular in its structure, the argument in the popular imagination is that Mary's purity is entwined with Christ's purity – one leads to the other and back as a necessary given. Following this logic, the *tota pulchra* prayer – which originated in the fourth century and is taken from language found in the Book of Judith and in the Song of Songs 4:7 – served as the clearest and most accessible template for the faithful to recognize and internalize the notion of Mary's unquestionable exceptionality, her transcendent humanity, and her role in our redemption.

> You are all fair, O Mary,
> And the original stain (of sin) is not in you.
> You are the glory of Jerusalem.
> You, the joy of Israel.
> You are the honour of our people.
> You are the advocate of sinners.
> O Mary,
> Virgin most wise,
> Mother most merciful.
> Pray for us,
> Intercede for us with Jesus Christ our Lord.
> In your conception, Holy Virgin, you were immaculate.
> Pray for us to the Father, whose Son you brought forth.
> O Lady! Aid my prayer,
> And let my cry come unto thee. (Lasance 554–5)[13]

As the prayer amply reflects, Mary's freedom from sin results in several key notions: a) her exalted humanity; b) the pride that humans can draw from having one of their own be "all fair," "most wise," and "most merciful"; and c) the extraordinary sanctified position afforded to her by her immaculacy as "advocate of sinners." Immaculacy is, accordingly, conceptually and affectively bound both to the capacity for goodness found in all humans and exemplified by Mary, and to the redemption from sin for her/him who prays the *tota pulchra*. As shown by Lesley Twomey in *The Serpent and the Rose*, the phrase *tota pulchra* became shorthand for the doctrine of immaculacy and indicative of Mary's crucial intercessory role, resulting in its linguistic and visual proliferation from medieval *cancionero* poetry to the countless images of the Immaculate Conception all the way through the late seventeenth century.[14] To be sure, it was the simplest and most easily accessible theological formula to be consumed and repeated by the broadest spectrum of believers during the period, and the banner that confirmed their faith and commitment to the religious and political cause.

IV. Spanish Habsburg Devotion and Popular Belief: The Politics of Immaculacy

The doctrine of the Immaculate Conception found an early and robust devotional base in Portugal and Spain.[15] Beatriz da Silva y Menezes, a Portuguese nun with close ties to the Castilian court, instituted the Order of the Immaculate Conception and founded its first monastery in 1484 in Toledo with the sponsorship of the Catholic monarchs. The Catholic monarchs proved to be fervent believers and advocates for the doctrine during their reign. The Virgin, alongside Saint James, was figured as the patroness of the Reconquest, and Isabel I was symbolically identified with the Virgin as the Woman of the Apocalypse who defeats the seven-headed dragon, a metaphor in this period for the Moorish heathens that occupied southern Spain. As documented by Linda B. Hall, "The birth of Prince Juan reinforced the identification of Isabel with Mary. It was reported that when she gave birth she exclaimed, 'Oh, Sweet Mary.' This report may have been an invention designed to link Isabel with the Woman of the Apocalypse of the Book of Revelation (in turn linked iconographically with the Immaculate Conception) who, with a cry, gives birth to a son" (43). This symbolic connection was further solidified by King Fernando, who carried on his sword "a message invoking her (the Virgin of the Immaculate Conception's) aid and protection, and even before he became king he founded a chivalric order dedicated to the purity of the Virgin and to the final conquest of the Moors with the Virgin's help" (43). The Catholic kings understood their own situation as one in which they – like the Apocalyptic Woman – would fulfil their role as victor-protagonists over the devil in the widely recounted prophecy of the imminent appearance of the Antichrist in Seville (43).[16] As proof of the Catholics' faith and commitment, Isabel I sponsored three chapels dedicated to the Immaculate Conception (one in Guadalupe, one in Toledo, and one in Seville) with monies secured for the yearly celebration of the feast of Mary's conception. The Catholic queen's devotion was not only public and political but also very personal, as demonstrated by the Polyptych Altarpiece, a miniature "intended to be framed as a retablo ... greatly scaled down to serve for Isabel's personal devotions" (Levenson 163). The Polyptych includes Michel Sittow's *Assumption of the Virgin* (National Gallery of Art, Washington), in which the assumpted Mary is returned to the heavens as the Immaculate Conception, garbed in the blue robe, standing on a crescent moon, dressed in the sun, and surrounded by a halo of angels (Levenson 162).

Following the family's commitment to the defence of the doctrine, "Juana the Mad established a convent in Mallorca under the patronage of *La Inmaculada*, while Charles V had an image of the subject displayed on his armor and was closely associated with confraternities devoted to the doctrine" (Goodwin 360). Just as it had come to be defined in the *Pietas Hispanica*, the *Pietas Austriaca* also saw a definitive Marian bent with the Immaculate Conception doctrine at its core.[17] In fact, as traced by Anna Coreth, the specificity of the cult of Mary in her guise as the Immaculate Conception was not only first and foremost a Spanish religious-political phenomenon but was also "certainly inherited from Spain" by the Austrian side of the empire, with Ferdinand I, Ferdinand II, and Ferdinand III standing as staunch defenders of the elevation of the doctrine to dogma (48). Within the Habsburg imaginary, Mary's immaculacy functions as a symbol of the purity of the Catholic faith and the superiority of the imperial house that had taken up its cause. The competition and animosity between religious orders often complicated what ideally should have been a united diplomatic Austrian front. Prominent members of the Dominican and Franciscan religious orders occupied key advisory and consular roles through which they felt entitled to promote their causes and exert enormous pressure at court and on the papacy. By the late sixteenth century, the Spanish king's personal confessors were typically Dominicans, whereas the Franciscans occupied the same position for all queens regnant and queens consort – a division of labour, should we say, that replicated itself in various forms within the court and in the delegations sent to the papal state.[18] And yet, despite the debate amongst the religious orders on the definition of the doctrine, the Spanish Habsburg royal family and their extended Austrian relatives persisted in continuing the tradition established by the Catholic kings and promoted, with varying degrees of fervour, the doctrine's elevation to dogma. Religion being imbricated with politics during this period, the defence of the *tota pulchra* was identified as pivotal to the dynasty's religious identity and the Spanish Empire's unwavering protection of the Catholic faith in the face of heresy.

The Austrian and Spanish Habsburg *Pietas Mariana*, as filtered through the image of the Immaculate Conception, also offered an important martial symbol, for they, as the prefigured Mary of Genesis 3:15, would crush the heads of their infidel enemies:

> Mary was elevated to the role of patroness of the Christian, that is, especially the Catholic armies. In this sense, she was invoked as "the help of Christians." It is well known that the Catholic victory at Lepanto [1571] ... [was] attributed to her, that many thought that the rosary united a spiritual army, as it were ... Mary was of foremost importance during the Counter-Reformation and at the time of the Turkish threat. Without a

doubt, the symbol that most effectively captured the idea of Mary victori-
ous was the Immaculate Conception. (Coreth 45–6)

The constant state of war with the Turks and its connection to the decree of expulsion of the *Moriscos* from Spain between 1609 and 1614
intersected, as has been convincingly argued by Peter Broggio, with
the debates on the conditions that make necessary and possible Mary's
exceptional immaculacy and her existence *ab initio*:

> I therefore wish to raise the following question: might there have been
> some connection between the decision to expel the *Moriscos* and the ex-
> istence of these tense relations between Madrid and Rome over Spain's
> request – sometimes interpreted by the Secretary of State as being
> over-ambitious – for doctrinal definitions of the issue of grace and the
> Immaculate Conception? I believe that the answer is in the affirmative.
> Petitions requesting that Rome take a clear stand in its definition of the
> "solid Catholic truth," as the phrase ran in the communiqués of the time,
> formed part of a political and ideological climate in which Philip III's
> monarchy was striving to make the purity of faith and religious orthodoxy
> one of the cornerstones of its image both at home and abroad. (171)

Devotion to the Virgin of the Immaculate Conception, especially in her
guise as the Woman of the Apocalypse, thus perfectly fitted the Spanish
Habsburg religious and political imaginary, its claim of purity – religious
and racial – and its ambition for supremacy within a contentious diplomatic and militarized European arena.

At a personal although not less political level, the family's devotion
found its most fervent members in the Spanish Habsburg women,
who as queens, mothers, wives, and aunts influenced or outright
strong-armed Philip II, Philip III, and especially Philip IV into advocating for the promotion to dogma, including pushing for a succession of
Reales Juntas sent to the Papal Courts.[19] A case in point is Margaret of
Austria – Queen Consort of Spain and wife of Philip III – whose confessor, Francisco de Santiago, reported two visions of the Immaculate
Conception in 1606 that fuelled her zealous defence of and campaign
for the definition of the dogma (Goodwin 360). Her personal belief and
political will to support the cause are showcased in Juan Pantoja de la
Cruz's 1605 portrait, in which she is holding open a book of hours and
pointing to an illumination of the Woman of the Apocalypse, standing
on the crescent moon with a child in her hands (figure 1.1).

The bottom right corner of the painting includes a letter on the floor that
is traditionally interpreted as a representation of the communications

Figure 1.1. Juan Pantoja de la Cruz, *Margaret of Austria* (1605). Royal
Collection Trust.

Margaret sent to Rome pleading for papal recognition.[20] Interestingly,
the portrait was gifted to James I of England by Philip III in 1605, a year
after the Treaty of London was signed – an event for which Margaret
was present and where the Spanish Catholics relinquished and recognized the Protestant monarchy in England. From a political perspective,
therefore, Margaret's Immaculist devotion, as represented by Pantoja
de la Cruz, flaunts Spain's unwavering Catholic devotion despite its
reluctant acceptance of England's official departure from the faith. Following in the queen's footsteps, between 1621 and 1622 Margaret of

the Cross, a discalced nun at the Royal Convent in Madrid and aunt of Philip IV, exchanged several letters with Gregory XV, who, in turn, copiously praised and attempted to reassure her despite his ultimate unwillingness to grant her petition:

> Because your letter ... has shown us how much study you have dedicated in praising the Mother of God, for you write as if you would arrive at the summit of all glory on the day that the disputes of theologians and the common people finally come together in a single judgment about the Immaculate Conception ... Because of this, your Majesty will know how truly we desire to please you with affectionate propensity, as we love you with fatherly charity, especially knowing that from the royal palace you brought examples of Christian virtues to that holy monastery, so that you may incite those religious virgins through the imitation of your nobility ...[21]

As made patent in Gregory XV's letter, the Royal Discalced Convent in Madrid was a focal point for Immaculist devotion for the Spanish Habsburgs during the reigns of Philip III and Philip IV, and the letter confirms the commitment to the cause in the closest family circles and relationships. Notably, it is in the matter of the *Juntas* – in which Margaret of Austria and Margaret of the Cross exerted a notable degree of influence – that the intersection of the highest political stakes, religious fervour, and the Habsburg women's individual drive makes itself most present.

The Habsburg personal and official pleas to the papacy have been thoroughly studied, most especially by Stratton, who impeccably documents the connections between the political-religious arena and the development of the iconography and popularity of the doctrine of the Immaculate Conception, principally in the seventeenth century. Instigated by his aunt, Margaret of the Cross, and pressured by the Immaculist movement in Seville, Philip III established the first *Real Junta* on 2 June 1616: "Its mission was to impose silence on the calumniators of the doctrine, or to define the doctrine as dogma" (Stratton, *The Immaculate Conception in Spanish Art* 74). Plácido Tosantos, Bishop of Cadiz and Philip III's emissary to the pope, stayed in Rome for three years, making official the Habsburg endorsement. Ultimately, Tosantos's *Junta* did not achieve its goal, with the French manipulating the controversy over the doctrine to impose their increasing political influence on the papacy. Not surprisingly, the *Real Junta*'s inability to convince the pope of a final elevation to dogma only fed the flames at home and fuelled rebelliousness amongst devout Immaculists who challenged papal oversight of this matter.[22] The *Regis Pacifici* of 1616, tendered by Paul V before

Tosantos had reached Rome, "in which he appealed to the disputing Immaculists and the Maculists to allow for time to judge the matter," did little or nothing to assuage the demands of believers in Spain, and instead only caused more turmoil (Duerloo 466). The papal nuncio in Madrid, Antonio Gaetano, for example, "wrote to Philip III, blaming both the Immaculist clergy and the Dominicans for the disputes that were an embarrassment to the church. He placed special blame on the archbishop of Seville for permitting a serious theological issue to be literally dragged through the streets and for ... contravening a decretal of Pius (Paul) V" (Stratton, *The Immaculate Conception in Spanish Art* 75). Devout members of the Habsburg court (especially at the Royal Discalced Convent), important members of the Church hierarchy in Spain (particularly in Seville), and the populace demanded more. Paul V relented with a new decretal in 1617, the *Sanctissimus Dominus Noster*, in which the concept of sanctification (that Mary was sanctified in the womb only post-coitus) was prohibited. The reaction – despite the prohibition of celebrations on this matter by the pope – was widely commemorated in public and private gatherings that insisted on the *Sanctissimus* as a victory for the Immaculist movement (Stratton, *The Immaculate Conception in Spanish Art* 80). In Madrid, even though Philip III refrained from commemorating the decree with a public procession, the Habsburg family celebrated in the company of other interested parties within the confines of the Royal Discalced Convent (Stratton, *The Immaculate Conception in Spanish Art* 80). However, given the lack of closure and the uncertainty of the papal commitment, Philip III was pressured to send additional *Juntas* (1618; 1619) that would again make a case for dogmatic definition.[23] Internal court and papal politics between Franciscans and Dominicans proved equally to be a motivation and a distraction for the king, driving Philip III to convene the Dominican order in Madrid and pressure them to sign a letter promising to "celebrate the Feast of the Immaculate Conception and preach in defense of the doctrine," which was then sent to Rome (Stratton, *The Immaculate Conception in Spanish Art* 82). Predictably, a large contingency of Spanish Dominicans who maintained their disapproval sent an accompanying document to Rome, prompting the pope to take sides and respond in their defence.[24]

Ardent support of the doctrine, and the religious and political lobbying that accompanied it, was not limited to the Habsburg court and family; it encompassed other centres of power and geographies, official and popular. Ironically, the stage for fervent and uncompromising advocacy had been set during the fifteenth and sixteenth centuries, motivated by the wavering of the papal state and the tentative decrees of the councillors at Trent. A stronghold of the Franciscan order and firmly positioned as Spain's richest port city holding exclusive trade rights with the American colonies, Seville, for example, became a focal point of Immaculist activity. The Andalusian city's political and economic power translated in the first half of the seventeenth century into sumptuous public feasts and commemorations, accompanied by enormous pressure exerted on the court and the papacy to promote Mary's Immaculate Conception as a dogma of faith. Goodwin describes how when news arrived that Paul V had acceded to favourably assert the doctrine – "nobody dare to affirm the opposite opinion" – Sevillians (unlike the Habsburg court in Madrid) publicly declared victory (362). Ignoring the tentative, partial, and transitory nature of the *Sanctissimus*, the Sevillian Church "celebrated with an outpouring of piety and a very long solemn mass was said in thanksgiving at the Cathedral, while the church bells were rung, and the ships on the river fired their guns in salute" (362). Not missing the opportunity to display their investment in the matter, the nobility put on secular celebrations that were "riotously extravagant, with fireworks, masques and jousting," and featured a bullfight (362). Responding to the city's international economic power and its political and religious clout, a more substantial victory was granted in 1622 when Pope Gregory XV formally praised Seville for its devotion and declared its exclusive right to celebrate the Feast of the Immaculate Conception on 8 December; no other community in Europe would enjoy this privilege.

The celebration of the Feast of the Immaculate Conception of Mary, in fact, constitutes a particular cultural, social, and political site where the religious imagination of the Church Militant, its specific communities, and individuals was elaborated, negotiated, and contested. Unofficially celebrated since at least the eleventh century in England, it prompted disagreement, given that, in the liturgical calendar, the birth of sinners cannot be observed (only their redeemed death); as such, the celebration of the feast throughout Europe suggested as a matter of indisputable fact Mary's eternal immaculacy. In other words, the feast underscored the conception of the always already *tota pulchra* (before, during, and after conception), for whom redemption was not necessary. For this reason, Sixtus IV in 1477 issued a bull recommending instead the celebration of the "birth of the Immaculate Virgin" (attempting to side-step the status of Mary's conception) and tried to keep the peace by condemning the accusations of heresy made by the opposing parties. Reacting to the denial of Mary's privileged sanctity by the Protestants and the growing contentiousness amongst the Catholic orders, close to a century later the councillors at Trent – pushed by the Spaniard Cardinal Pacheco,

Bishop of Jaén – recalled Sixtus IV in the *Decree Concerning Original Sin* (Fifth Session, 15 June): "This holy council declares, however, that it is not its intention to include in this decree, which deals with original sin, the blessed and immaculate Virgin Mary, the mother of God, but that the constitutions of Pope Sixtus IV, of happy memory, are to be observed under the penalties contained in those constitutions, which it renews" (Schroeder 23).[25] On the face of it the councillors at Trent, who were largely sympathetic to the cause, seemingly affirmed Mary's purity and exceptionality. What should be understood, nonetheless, is that the they avoided determining how or when immaculacy exactly ensues: whether it is a matter eternal or a redemptive miracle that occurs after an initial conception tainted by sin. By leaving the question open yet again, the councillors attempted to achieve several distinct goals; they avoided privileging one side over the other, either Franciscans or Dominicans, and affirmed papal authority. Inadvertently, the residual vagueness on the event of Mary's absolute purity gave licence to decades of debate that encouraged the production of innumerable devotional texts (theological, exegetical, and artistic) on the description and desired resolution of the matter.

Papal decrees after Trent continued to waver and only managed to raise the stakes even higher for both defenders and detractors. Pius V kept the Feast on the Tridentine Calendar but suppressed the word "Immaculate" altogether, instituting instead on the celebration of the Mass for the Nativity of Mary. Gregory XV, persuaded, as mentioned above, by Spanish pressure, backtracked and prohibited any public or private assertion that Mary was conceived in sin. Urban VIII in 1624 allowed (even if reluctantly) the Franciscans to establish a military order dedicated to the Virgin of the Immaculate Conception, which in Spain opened the door for local communities to revert to the celebration of the Feast of the Immaculate Conception. Cognizant of complaints by the Dominicans, Urban VIII issued from his deathbed in 1644 an Inquisitorial decree, "prohibiting use of the word 'immaculate' to describe Mary's conception, but permitting references to the conception of 'Mary Immaculate'" (Trevor Johnson 376). The general reaction in Spain over the wrangling of what is considered a sacred mystery, coupled with Urban VIII's prohibition, was met with great despair and open rebelliousness in localities such as Seville, and beyond, where the populace vehemently continued to publicly swear devotion to the Virgin in formal institutions, such as the university and confraternities, going so far as to post the prohibited words everywhere. Even the cathedral defiantly exhibited a canvas of the Virgin by Murillo under the legend "conceived without sin" (Trevor Johnson

376). After almost twenty years, the pendulum once again swung in favour of the Immaculists with the *Bull Sollicitudo* of 1661, in which Alexander VII reinstituted the Immaculate Conception decrees and shifted the debate from theological exegesis to the importance of popular belief, as reflected in the quotation from the Bishop of Lérida that opens this chapter. In the last stretch of the seventeenth century, with the Spanish Habsburg monarchy nearing its end, Innocent XII offered a compromise and declared the Feast of the Immaculate Conception universally obligatory throughout the Church, even if still refusing to elevate the doctrine to dogma.[26]

Throughout this institutional and civic history, we should not overlook the powerful influence wielded by the local communities and individuals who structured their belief and support for the doctrine in particular and highly imaginative ways. Even if not successful in having the papacy declare dogma, the Spanish kings and people forced the Church hierarchy to react and again restate its position vis-à-vis Mary's immaculacy. What is evident in the historical record is the papacy's inability to convincingly and finally fix the time or site of Mary's stainless conception. The result is a persistently open field of interpretation, with Mary performing as an unbound sign whose most pivotal signifier – her immaculate nature – insists on its status as a mystery.

For this very reason, insofar as it concerns the doctrine of the Immaculate Conception, the relationship between the sacred, Church hierarchies, and the faithful is structured through multiple and shifting vectors. At a minimum, we need to consider the triangular structure between Immaculists, Maculists, and the bounteous faithful who imagined and framed their individual religious selfhoods through the debate. Predictably, however, the angles proliferate: Franciscans against Dominicans; Immaculist theologians in disagreement with other Immaculist theologians; members of the Habsburg court and the populace over whom they ruled but who also exerted immense pressure and expected definitive results; Immaculist confessors, censors, inquisitors, and the faithful (both communities and individuals), whose justifications and practices differed; religious artists and writers who variously rendered the doctrine; distinct arguments produced by religious men and women in differing contexts; and so on. The point is that the structure of the religious and cultural phenomenon I describe is not binomial; instead, we must recognize the abundance of interests and interpretative positions that come into play and shape the many and varied discourses and debates around the Immaculate Conception in early modern Spain.

All told, taking into account the theological, historical, and political conditions I have here described, and as stated at the beginning of this chapter, it is my contention that the Virgin of the Immaculate Conception assumes in Counter-Reformation Spain the function of a multivalent sign on which the imaginary coordinates of national and personal identity and selfhood are drawn, manipulated, and contested. On the one hand, the Virgin's analogical function assumes the representation of Spain as God's chosen imperial seat – militant, physically and spiritually pure, exceptional among all peoples, full of grace, and eternal. Spain thus overshadows competing Catholic states and overthrows the Jewish, Muslim, and Protestant threat, which in the Catholic imaginary could only be figured as impure. On the other, local citations of the doctrine and its image reveal competing ideologies, unresolved contradictions, and conscious and unconscious needs, desires, and anxieties at the core of early modern Spanish individual and collective Catholic identities.

V. Immaculate Conceptions: The Virgin as a Multivalent Sign

Why, specifically, is the Virgin of the Immaculate Conception such a ripe symbol for the Spanish early modern religious imagination? This is the core question that leads the analysis of texts throughout the remainder of this book. The following provisional thoughts can be put forth. It seems clear that the controversy around the theological question of immaculacy and redemption is fundamental. Figuring the logic for God's design as it pertains to the conditions that prefigure the incarnation of his Son – both as a matter of reason and as a matter of mystery – offers theologians and lay believers alike a wide field in which to express their varied perceptions of God's omnipotence, grace, and the legacy of sin. Within this domain, the figure of Mary demands a consideration of the enigmatic relationship between the sacred and the human, wrought in the ineffability of divine design. Conceptually, the doctrine probes into the conditions and limits of redemption of the body/soul dichotomy that Mary encompasses. Moreover, the extrication of Mary from the legacy of original sin allows for a vision of humanity as not altogether lost, not entirely cast out of Eden – one of "us" untouched. As I will show, the texts and paintings examined in this book delve deeply into the hermeneutical challenges and creative opportunities granted by the representation of Mary's privileged humanity.

As noted above, within the field of politics the defence of Mary's eternal immaculacy is folded into the defence of Catholicism itself, a matter that in early modern Spain was closely identified with the integrity of the state and of a "common and shared social identity" within a privileged geography of faith (Baranda, "Beyond Political Boundaries" 64).[27] Luther, when attempting to establish a revision of the scriptural canon, had rebuffed the book of Revelation (and, therefore, John of Patmos's visions) as theologically suspect, a position known as the *Antilegomena*. The Spanish Catholics would, in opposition, embrace John of Patmos's mystical narrative and adopt the Apocalyptic Woman as one of their most consequential symbols and a touchstone of their faith.[28] Like the Apocalyptic Mary, Spain was chosen by God to carry redemption forwards. Spain, like the Virgin of the Immaculate Conception, is of pure blood, untainted by sin or heresy, which in the Iberian political and social imaginary coincided with purity of blood statutes and the expulsion of Jews and Muslims from its collective body. Just as importantly, the fervent defence of the doctrine featured Spain's categorical rejection of any Protestant heresy in its midst. Spain, like the Immaculate Mary, was made to be "exceptionally" uncontaminated, a privileged representative of the Church on earth, an eternal Catholic political and spiritual geography, entitled to special treatment by the papacy, as well as to a dominant position as a world power. Granted, the historical record, replete with nuances and contradictions, denies the possibility of an imaginary wholesale construction of a shared Spanish Catholic identity. The Protestant reforms could not simply be ignored; purity of blood was often illusive (even Saint Teresa of Ávila had Jewish grandparents); other European centres of power (France and England, most notably) did not simply acquiesce to Spain as *redentora*; and the Spanish Habsburg Empire found itself embroiled in multiple depleting war fronts that made patent Spain's decline as an economic and military powerhouse.[29]

And yet, it is precisely within this context of instability and contradiction that I argue the doctrine of the Immaculate Conception provided – from the king to the lay believer in cities all over the peninsula – an imaginary of exceptionality and purity, a joint undertaking, and a common symbolic referent in an otherwise conflictive and increasingly disillusioned world. This religious, political, and social imaginary conflated in a particularly fascinating manner in the *votum sanguinis*, a "blood vow" first formally proclaimed at the University of Granada in 1617 that proliferated thereafter, but whose ideological conditions had long been in the making. In its pronouncement, the faithful swore to defend the doctrine of the Virgin of the Immaculate Conception to the point of shedding blood, if necessary. For the vow to make sense, the shed blood was presumed pure and untouched by Jewish or Muslim ancestry, as well as free from the heresies of Protestantism. It is within this imaginary field that we see, as Trevor Johnson summarizes and as this book will demonstrate, an explosion of cultural production around the concept and image of immaculacy:

> An Immaculist campaign was waged throughout Catholic Europe, although most intensively in Spain, and led to the notorious "blood vow". It produced an unprecedented volume of Marian literature of all kinds, polemical and panegyric, plays, theses, sermons and poetry, in a campaign which rested on rhetorical force rather than theological originality and which also placed great stress on visual representation, establishing a new and lasting iconography. (373)

From a gender perspective, there is much to add. Mary's conception is, no doubt, a theological and narrative framework that values, above all else, purity (sexual and otherwise), reflected in the undisturbed innocence of the Virgin of the Immaculate Conception's childlike appearance. No less important, typically portrayed in a prayerful stance looking down at the earth, she is an exemplar of silent contemplation, especially for the women who venerated her. Concurrently, as the Apocalyptic Woman, she is a symbol of strength, both spiritual and physical, the only being capable of crushing the head of the serpent. She is positioned in the liminal heavens, before the beginning of time, spiritually and physically imbricated in the story of human redemption. Powerful and chosen, *tota pulchra* and in existence *ab initio*, the Virgin of the Immaculate Conception motivates an imaginary that far exceeds the typical limits of frail femininity and subjugated maternity that we typically think of when examining the figure of Mary. This is a point not lost to the authors and artists whose texts and paintings I analyse in this book. As I hope to make clear, the multiple and competing ways of deploying the doctrine and image of the Virgin of the Immaculate Conception intercept, inform each other, get tangled, and allow for even less expected – thus ever more imaginative – representations. In the abundant theological discourses and cultural products that simultaneously promoted and confirmed popular belief, reflections on the mystery of immaculacy and its implications flourished, responding to the identitary needs, specific interests, and creative impulses of Spanish communities and individuals from the earliest examples in the late fifteenth century to the height of the cult in the seventeenth.

Chapter Two

An Army of Peers: The Virgin of the Immaculate Conception for the Popular Imagination

It is a thing worthy of candid wits, and of noble hearts, and of pious wills, not to await the determination of the Council, or decree of the Supreme Pontiff, but to follow the opinion of which we speak, knowing all Prelates of the Church, that in her honour the world is full of temples and altars, in great excess ... given what we know, no one up to now would be moved to carve, I dare not say an entire monastery or a Church, but not even one image, in protest, that Our Lady was conceived in original sin.

Vicente Justiniano, *Tratado de la Inmaculada Concepción de la
Virgen Santísima Nuestra Señora*[1]

"Where are you going, señor don Quixote? What the devil do you have in your heart that incites you to go against our Catholic faith? Watch out – may I be damned! – that's a procession of penitents, and that woman that they're carrying on the litter is a statue of the very holy Virgin without blemish. Careful, señor, what you're up to, because this time one could say you don't know what you're doing."

Don Quixote 487[2]

In the 1640s, Pedro de Valpuesta (1614–68), a Madrilenian Franciscan priest and minor artist, received a commission to paint a portrait of Philip IV displaying his devotion to the Virgin of the Immaculate Conception. Meant for the Hospital of the Conception of Our Holy Lady (Hospital de la Concepción de Nuestra Señora, also popularly known as the Hospital de la Latina) in Madrid, *Philip IV Swearing to Defend the Doctrine of the Immaculate Conception* (Municipal Museum of History, Madrid) recreates the 1621 ceremony in which the king, upon the death of his father, swears in the presence of the *Cortes de Castilla* to defend the mystery of immaculacy (figure 2.1).

Figure 2.1. Pedro de Valpuesta, *Philip IV Swearing to Defend the Doctrine of the Immaculate Conception* (1640s). Municipal Museum of History, Madrid.

On the one hand, Valpuesta pays homage to royal power and its influence upon the spiritual priorities over whom it rules, featuring the Crown's appropriation and promotion of the Immaculist symbolic capital. On the other hand, the painting – the happening it depicts together with the particular context of its commission and placement – has more to tell. Firstly, from a socio-political perspective, Philip IV's pledge of loyalty to the doctrine was not wholly a vehicle for the imposition of Habsburg power over the kingdom of Castile. To the contrary, it was equally an opportunity for the people of Castile, represented through the members of its *Cortes*, to require that Philip IV publicly align himself with their social, cultural, and religious expectations. Philip IV's pledge secured Castile's influence – vis-à-vis the competing interests of Seville and Aragon – within a religious-political field in which the defence of the Immaculate Conception was synonymous with the promotion of the Spanish Habsburg national project and the true Catholic faith. Secondly, Valpuesta renders Philip IV with one hand placed on the Bible and one on his heart, his gaze lost in a contemplative visionary state; a stance that echoes for the viewer the textual and mystical experience represented in the painting within the painting, in which Bonaventure (the Franciscan Immaculist theologian) is shown having a vision of the Apocalyptic Woman. As such, Valpuesta's portrait features Philip IV's appropriation of the Franciscan saint's singular and intimate visionary experience of the Virgin of the Immaculate Conception. In a room full of Church dignitaries and aristocratic members of the Castilian *Cortes*, Philip IV's devotion leads not outwardly to the public political field but to an inward religious imagination that translates Saint Bonaventure's experience to his own. Thirdly, historical memory within the convent and hospital walls would have allowed a contextualization of Philip IV's devotion as encouraged by his first wife, Elizabeth of France; by the Habsburg family nuns, who relentlessly exerted their influence at court from within the walls of the Royal Discalced Convent; and by María de Ágreda, author of the Immaculist treatise *Mystical City of God* [*Mística ciudad de Dios*] (which Philip IV kept at his desk) and who served as his personal confidante and religious guide for more than twenty-two years.[3] The spiritual and political influence of women upon the Immaculist cause would have been further noted, given the source of the commission itself; the hospital and the adjacent convent were founded in 1499 by Beatriz Galindo, *La Latina*, a historical figure who was not only a fascinating intellectual force in the humanist Castilian court of Isabel I but also (as was the queen) a fervent early defender of the promotion of the doctrine to dogma. Valpuesta's painting thus keenly displays the intersection between imperial authority and local power, political symbolism and personal devotion, the patriarchal social field that Philip IV represents and the women who exerted their influence upon his religious convictions and devotional practices, and the religious imagination of the nuns and patients who ultimately viewed the painting at the Hospital de la Latina and convent of the Conception of Our Holy Lady.

I draw the idea for the title of this chapter from Pedro de Alva y Astorga's (c. 1602–67) *Army of the Immaculate Conception* [*Militia Immaculatae Conceptionis*] (1663). Beyond Alva y Astorga's personal context and specific project, what interests me is the notion of an imaginary "army" of random believers – evoking Paul's and Erasmus's *militia christiana* – of varied stations and ranks, educational levels, genders, and professions, unified in their common project as defenders of an ineffable mystery.[4] In what remains of this chapter, I examine the *Militia* alongside exemplary sermons, treatises, religious theatre, and popular poetry. Together, these texts constitute an army of textual peers and exhibit the range of mediums through which the doctrine of the Immaculate Conception was reproduced and consumed in a "battlefield" that puts into contact national and local politics, abstract theological propositions, a multiplicity of religious discourses and art forms, and popular devotional practices. If the Habsburgs privileged the Virgin of the Immaculate Conception as a common national symbol, these texts exemplify the capacious religious imagination of innumerable localities and individuals that took the defence of immaculacy and the image of the Apocalyptic Woman as a template upon which to fashion their own Catholic selfhoods, each demonstrating the depth of their belief and their imaginative contributions to the common Spanish cause.

I. Righteous Soldiers Use Their Pens as Swords: The Immaculate Virgin's *Militia Universalis*

Alva y Astorga was born in Spain (probably near the town of Carbajales), moved to Cuzco, Peru when he was eight years old, and there eventually took the Franciscan habit as a Friar Minor of the Strict Observance around 1621. By 1641 he was a Doctor of Divinity and around the same time returned to Spain, where he served as a *procurador* and a *custodio*; by 1645 he was named the *procurador general* of the Franciscan Order in Rome, a post that he left to return to Spain soon after. Around 1661 he relocated (or most probably was forced to move) to Louvain in the Catholic Netherlands, where he founded a printing house dedicated to the Immaculate Conception. In Belgium, marginalized from the centre of Habsburg political power but also paradoxically empowered to pursue without restraint his Immaculist project, Alva y Astorga prolifically wrote and published his books, as well as those of other Franciscan Immaculists.[5] A careful look at his literary production reveals a man truly obsessed with conceptionism, an outspoken opponent of Thomas Aquinas – a position that caused the two editions of his *Nodus indissolubilis* (1661; 1663) to be placed in the Index of Prohibited Books – and an indefatigable graphomaniac and self-plagiarizer. The following volumes are habitually listed as his most significant works: *Bibliotheca*

Virginalis, 2 vols. (1648); *Armamentarium Seraphicum et Regestum universale pro tuendo título Immaculatae Conceptionis* (1649); *Sol Veritatis* (1650); *Militia Immaculatae Conceptionis* (1663); *Monumenta antiqua Immaculatae Conceptionis* (1664); and *Monumenta antiqua seraphica pro Immaculata Conceptione* (1665). The complete catalogue of Franciscan works lists another nine volumes, for a total of sixteen major works, written in Latin, each exceeding six hundred pages. He also published three additional volumes in Castilian, the *Rosa Seráfica* (1663), the *Pleitos de los libros y sentencias del juez* (1664, written under the pseudonym Rodrigo Rodríguez), and the *Respuesta limpia* (1667), as well as several *memoriales* dedicated to Philip IV in defence of the doctrine.

As noted by Trevor Johnson, the *Militia Immaculatae Conceptionis* is a compendium of Immaculist sources assembled to counteract the malice of those who would deprive the Virgin of grace (377). This description is certainly correct; yet, it does not do justice to the excessiveness of the project, its prodigiousness, the way it imposes itself on the reader, and the manner in which it constructs Alva y Astorga's identity as the self-appointed captain of this global and trans-historical Immaculate army. The printed manuscript contains 1,534 columns contained in 767 large folios, plus preliminary materials including a *memorial* dedicated to Philip IV, an onomastic index, an index of titles, and an index of biblical references. Alva y Astorga claims to include about 6,000 soldiers from across Europe and the Americas, covering several centuries. Entries vary in length from a few lines to full columns and typically include the name of the "soldier" and his/her familial and religious affiliations (orders, specific convents, etc.), followed by an account of the texts (oral and written) that attest to the individual's militancy. Each entry is dutifully accompanied, if applicable, by a detailed bibliographical citation. The *Militia* moves through a vast imaginary battalion, singling out names, texts, and specific references, provoking admiration in readers who must have marvelled at the sheer number of records and Alva y Astorga's godlike omniscience. Entry after entry, he displays detailed knowledge of thousands of individuals who have – according to his estimation – properly defended the doctrine; those named include well-known theologians such as Scotus (*Militia* 754), but also hundreds of virtually unknown individuals whose identities would have otherwise been lost to history. In doing so, he ascribes to himself a great deal of authority, judging and interpreting the actions and writings of men and women from across time and the most remote corners of the Catholic world, from different social stations and with widely varying degrees of recognizability and power. Collectively, their efforts are portrayed as overwhelming proof of the incontestable truth of the doctrine and as weapons against those who sully the Virgin with the legacy of the fall. Not insignificantly, these soldiers are joined by the Catholic Church and the Virgin of the Immaculate Conception herself, who (as documented in separate entries) take their place among the rank and file.

The desired effect is to have the believer think of him/herself as a soldier in this invincible vast army, and of course to make the "enemy" feel defeated. Admittedly, the personal politics of the project are rather transparent. Alva y Astorga's need for support – social and economic – must have been especially keen around the time of publication of the *Militia*; he had only arrived the previous year in Louvain, now removed from the core positions of influence he had occupied when he had access to the court in Madrid. The dedication of the volume to Philip IV reveals his staunchness as well as his anxiety, citing his controversial *Nudo Indisoluble* (the text whose anti-Aquinas rhetoric probably motivated his unwilling departure from Castile), while expressing the desire to be recognized for the service done in defence of a doctrine tied to the king's religious and political projects: "To this end, I offer to your excellency this army of almost six thousand soldiers that, although a flying squadron, is composed of only feathers; under your military discipline, they will serve as wings that carry steel points to the target and the aim that they pursue."[6] The creative word play reads as both playful and ominous; the quills act as wings and as swords, offer a fanciful flight and simultaneously threaten. It seems obvious, given what we know about the sheer volume of texts produced by Alva y Astorga, that he fashioned his pen as the sharpest of swords. In the *Militia* he positions himself as the convener of an army of believers under the protection of the Virgin of the Immaculate Conception, thereby strategically paying homage to thousands of potentially sympathetic patrons (or their surviving extended families), as well as to powerful networks of fellow Immaculists. All of them, given Alva y Astorga's ambiguous situation as an exile in Louvain, could potentially offer protection and come to his aid. The many entries connected to the Habsburg family are a case in point; they include, among many others, Margaret of the Cross, whose letters to Gregory XV (which I discuss in chapter 1) appear as part of the entry: "She wrote letters to the Pope ... in the year 1621 in defence of the definition of the mystery of the Immaculate Conception, which begin: And of the obligations of your office ..."[7] Given Margaret of the Cross's position and influence on Philip IV, Alva y Astorga could have well estimated that her inclusion could only help resolve his circumstances as an exile and advance his cause.

Interpretation, or better yet, a masterful manipulation of his "soldiers'" words, texts, and actions – contextualized in favour of the Immaculist cause – is pivotal to an analysis of the *Militia*. Not to be missed is, for example, Alva y Astorga's insertion of Martin Luther's sermons and writings in which the German friar, despite his Reform theology, enthusiastically confirms the validity of the doctrine (1016–17). Perhaps most surprising, given the Dominican theological basis for contesting the Virgin's Immaculate Conception and Alva y Astorga's controversial positions, the *Militia* includes a three-column entry on Thomas Aquinas in which each of the theologian's major works are scoured for support of the belief (1437–40). To be clear, Alva y Astorga pits Aquinas against Maculist Thomists (i.e., Dominicans), a gutsy strategic move that aims to redress his own past position in the *Nudo Indisoluble*. Additionally, the *Militia*'s scope allows for readings that go beyond an assessment of political self-interest or hermeneutical grandstanding. For example, numerous entries that single out the influence of religious and secular women thinkers and writers are notable indeed. From the Habsburg family women to Teresa de Ávila, Valentina Pinelo, countless minor nuns, and each of the amateur women poets included in Sancho Zapata's *Poetic Tournament on the Defence of the Purity of the Immaculate Conception of the Virgin* [*Justa poética en defensa de la pureza de la Inmaculada Concepción de la Virgen santísima*] (which I examine later in this chapter), all make substantial appearances as "soldiers." There are inexplicable (at least to me) absences, most especially Ágreda with her *Mística ciudad de Dios*. Nevertheless, it is truly outstanding how, in his penchant to include as many entries as possible, Alva y Astorga inadvertently produces a significant record of female religious writing and influence in early modern Spain.

The *Militia* constructs an impressive authorial identity for Alva y Astorga, supported by his apparently cosmic knowledge that incorporates every corner of the world. From a psychological perspective, the obsessive-compulsive components of the text reveal the construction of a self whose mania is channelled through an exhaustive and meticulous encyclopaedic process that gathered, documented, and reported on every (or almost every) traceable defence of immaculacy. To be sure, the *Militia* creates a community fashioned through a sense of mission, agency, and intrinsic value; this "we" is defined by a collective cause and a common privilege found in the Virgin's protection, as something given to her and as something received from her. It also offers the reader the figure of "Alva y Astorga" as an all-knowing presence; as the commander of a *militia universalis*; as a superior man on the right side of a war against those who cannot recognize God's truth; and as a man who, despite his displacement to Louvain, will not be dissuaded from using his pen as a sword. The *Militia* is a cultural product driven by Counter-Reformation zeal. I would suggest that an equally satisfactory approach is to read it, despite the formal constraints of the encyclopaedic genre, as a tour de force of the religious imagination and as a textual space where a highly inventive and defiant Catholic identity is affirmed.

As the *Militia* clearly attests, the Spanish cultural and religious landscape is replete with texts (hundreds of them) whose aim is to widely promote the doctrine of the Immaculate Conception and train its "soldiers" in the fight against those who cannot recognize or are unwilling to embrace the mystery of immaculacy and the co-redemptive power of the Virgin. Printed treatises, sermons, dialogues, songbooks, *relaciones*, religious theatre, and poetry competitions abound, each displaying the specific imaginary relationship of its author or authors with a set of given theological premises and doctrinal beliefs. As I established in chapter 1, these texts evince the varied novel ways in which the popular imagination appropriated and independently reproduced the conditions of Mary's conception, her status as *tota pulchra*, her eternal existence *ab initio*, the meanings and effects of her exceptionality, and her singular function as an intercessor between the human and the sacred. It would be impossible to do justice in the scope of this chapter to the countless examples of texts produced for popular consumption that address the question of Mary's Immaculate Conception. The selection I make reflects my personal preference. As such, I believe it offers a strong foundation for understanding how the question of Mary's purity lent itself to a rich popular religious imaginary that bridges the immanent and the transcendent.

II. Treatises, Sermons, Dialogues, and Lily Bulbs: Ineffability and Revelation in the Popular Discourses of Immaculacy

The vast catalogue of printed treatises, sermons, dialogues, and *relaciones* in the vernacular on the mystery of immaculacy forms part of a prolific popular imaginary that simultaneously reinforces and is bolstered by Habsburg politics and devotion. Authored almost exclusively by male members of the Franciscan order (I discuss women religious writers in chapter 5), these documents reflect in equal measure a methodical approach to the subject and an exuberant zeal that drives the hundreds of pages, citations, examples, justifications, and comparisons that populate these texts. Written in the context of the defence of the doctrine, they alternatively announce themselves as documentation of proof, theological instruction, sources of spiritual solace, and instigators of zeal for the masses of Spanish believers whose Catholic selfhood was imbricated with a fervent devotion to the material and symbolic causes and effects of Mary's purity. As professed by Francisco de Torres on the cover page of his 1620 *Solace for the Devotees of the Immaculate Conception of the Holy Virgin* [*Consuelo de los devotos de la Inmaculada Concepción de la Virgen Santísima*], "Contained in this treatise is the historical record about this paramount mystery, and it is for persons of every station."[8] On the one hand, Torres's declaration showcases the ultimate inscrutability of God's design and will, which, predictably, results in a proliferation of texts that delve into approximate explanations of the conditions of immaculacy and its material fulfilment, the identification of need (why Mary *had to be* immaculately conceived), clarifications of the theological corpus, and provisional allegorical, tropological, and anagogical interpretations of the Scriptures. On the other, the account of this "paramount mystery" offers *all* the faithful, "persons of every station," discursive access to sacred knowledge that, even if necessarily partial, leads to the (re)production of more knowledge and an affirmation of the singular self as a contributor to a larger cause. These texts elicit a strong sense of inclusion, a common discourse guided by shared premises and ideological frameworks, and a pooled sense of purpose; no less significant, they also carve out a space where each individual author can add his own inventive (and often copious) account on the question of Mary's excessive humanity. Finally, they generate a common enemy – Maculists, those who have not experienced true divine revelation, have limited understanding or would limit God's omnipotence and will, and all those who are themselves "no limpios de sangre" – against which to claim the supremacy of an immaculate Spanish Catholicism. As declared by Gonzalo Sánchez Luzero in the dedication of his *Two Theological Speeches in Defence of the Immaculate Conception of the Virgin* [*Dos discursos teológicos en defensa de la Inmaculada Concepción de la Virgen*] (1614) to Luisa Manrique de Lara, Countess of Valencia: "give her [the Virgin of the Immaculate Conception] your hand so that you are well received by all and move safely among a million enemies, that without reason and truth, dressed in malice and vain wisdom have wanted to slander her although they have not been able to, all have stopped in uproar and barking like dogs and at the end leave with nothing and will leave with less."[9] The enemy, dressed in malice and animalistic, provides the perfect foil – as the seven-headed dragon of John of Patmos's vision had – for believers to affirm their faith and expound upon their version of the ecclesiastical teachings and divine design that frame the event of Mary's Immaculate Conception.

A theological dissertation dedicated to a laywoman, Sánchez Luzero's *Discursos* corroborates the considerable access that common men *and* women had to exegesis on immaculacy. In a context where it was correctly assumed that readers, both secular and religious, were highly committed to the defence and propagandizing of the doctrine, the instructional function of these texts is, in fact, what drives their content and organization. Vicente Justiniano's *Treatise on the Immaculate Conception* [*Tratado de la Inmaculada Concepción de la Virgen Santísima Nuestra Señora*] (1615), dedicated to Margaret of the Cross at the Royal Discalced Convent, similarly insists on this broad educational goal, asserting the author's intent to present theological matters, both practical and speculative, in a straightforward manner to his readers: "[I] propose with simplicity some considerations worthy of being pondered by those who are devoted to the service of Our Lady, who will (I believe) be pleased by finding them together in this treatise."[10] Justiniano's "considerations" include a summary of papal judgment on the matter; an outline of the core concepts and clarifications that Church fathers have offered in order to explain the Immaculate Conception; errors that have been promulgated and need to be corrected; and examples of the unwavering devotion that the belief in Mary's purity has occasioned as proof of God's will and perfect design.

Perhaps the most direct and efficient genre in terms of instructional value is the "dialogue" because it explicitly outlines for believers the legitimate questions and appropriate answers that should anchor their belief. Pedro Suárez de Castilla's *Diálogo entre Maestro y Discípulo* (1615), for example, sketches a Socratic-style exchange in which the teacher lucidly delineates for the student the correct way to structure his own deliberations on the matter of Mary's status. On the essential question of the act of conception, the *Diálogo* reads:

> D: So if the Virgin Mary wasn't conceived in sin, then she was conceived by the Holy Spirit?
> M: She was not conceived by the Holy Spirit, but rather, by an act of man, like all of us, as she was the daughter of Saint Joachim and Saint Anne, and, despite all of this, we affirm that she was not conceived in sin.
> D: Then would it follow that she was conceived in grace?
> M: I say that at the same moment and point that the soul of the Virgin joined the body (with special favour from God), she was full of grace, being privileged in this unique gift among all other descendants of Adam by natural generation, and by God's having preserved her with this particular providence, she could not have original sin, nor was there any reason for her to have it.[11]

Advocating for one of the accounts of immaculacy – that Mary was sanctified at the moment that her soul entered her body post-coitus – the *Diálogo* upholds certainty in the face of ineffability. In doing so, it circumvents what cannot be rationally known by our limited understanding (how *exactly* God materially and spiritually generated this "particular providence") through a linguistic and discursive register that can be easily understood, adopted, and repeated.

Although writings on the Immaculate Conception in the vernacular widely circulated in Spain from the end of the fifteenth century on (I examine, for example, Isabel Villena's *Vita Christi* and Juana de la Cruz's *El conorte* in chapter 5), the first formal treatise on the subject for a wide audience is Diego Pérez de Valdivia's *Treatise of the singular and pure conception of the Mother of God* [*Tratado de la singular y purísima concepción de la Madre de Dios*] (1582), establishing a template for the popular imaginary coordinates of the Marian exception. The title is already a clear indication of the logic of singularity, which as we see in text after text encompasses both God's absolute will and the Virgin's exalted humanity. Chapter 2, "On the difficult matter of original sin, and how God in this point is especially incomprehensible" ["De cuán dificultosa material sea la del pecado original, y como particularmente en este punto es Dios incomprensible"], presents the reader with the paradox of an incomprehensible act – the Immaculate Conception of Mary excepted from the burden and logic of original sin – that nevertheless, and precisely because of its incomparable status, must be believed *and* somehow tentatively explained: "What I cling to is that God is incomprehensible and that I must not account for what he does, neither can his works be completely understood, nor can we explain all of them ... for if God were comprehensible by finite understanding, he would not be God."[12] It is in the crux of this contradiction where Immaculist fervour flourishes. Mary's immunity from sin indexes God's unbound omnipotence and will. If divine design best displays its capacity through nominalist inscrutability, it likewise facilitates for the author an ample textual field wherein to imagine and assert the conditions and meaning of God's grace upon Mary:

> From the point that she began to be in the womb of the blessed Saint Anne, she was holy: she was not sanctified, if sanctified means changed from a sinner to a saint, because she never sinned, she was always holy. However, if sanctified meant that she was made a saint to which the holy Scripture sometimes speaks, she could well be called sanctified: like the Angelic Spirits that together had being and grace; like Adam and Eve who were raised in grace; like Jesus Christ, our Lord, whose soul, from the moment of his Conception, had infinite grace.[13]

Mary's sanctity is a *signum* (as defined by Ricoeur), comprehensible only as it relates to the ineffable sanctity of angels, the originary lost (and thus foreign) state of Adam and Eve, and Christ incarnate. To be more precise, her status is discursively recognizable and yet open to an ongoing critical activity that allows each reader to contemplate the Virgin's status and mould discrete avenues of identification with Mary's transcendental humanity.

Rodrigo Manrique's 1615 *Sermon on the pure conception of the Virgin Mary Our Lady* [*Sermón de la Limpia Concepción de la Virgen María nuestra Señora*] is a ten-part schematic presentation of the concept of immaculacy and its realization in the spirit, body, and soul of the Virgin before, during, and after her conception. In keeping with the parameters of a genre whose main thrust is the exhortation to faith and action, Manrique calls on the listeners (and now readers) of Seville to stand firm in their belief and defence of the doctrine, describing in the first and last sections the city's rituals and the clout of its leaders and citizens as they swear loyalty to the Immaculist cause while pressuring the papacy to declare the dogma.[14] Similar to what we see in Pérez de Valdivia, the body of the *Sermón* focuses on explaining the unexplainable, the event of a human being preserved from the sinful nature that vexes the rest of humanity. At the height of its theological discourse on the (il)logic of Marian exceptionality, Manrique's sermon takes on the ways in which we as humans attempt to make sense of the nonsense of divine design:

> ... be warned that when you hear that God our Father determined one thing and that afterward he determines another, you must not understand it as a concept that changes, because he is immutable, neither does he have various acts of understanding and will, nor is one first and the other last, and [you must not understand] that this undoes what was first ordered, nor that he contradicts himself and has different ideas, like you and like me, because in his majesty, everything is a pure act and a totalizing indivisible essence: although we, because of our little understanding, being unable to comprehend it, divide it into various acts, and so we comprehend some acts before others; in order to explain it to ourselves and intimate our concepts ...[15]

It is in the fissure between God's totality and our own postlapsarian state where the condition of Mary as a human, exempted from the legacy of Adam as well as from the strictures of time and materiality *ab initio*, must be rationally and spiritually acknowledged, even as it necessarily remains obscure. It is precisely this abstruseness that compels and validates the work of the religious imagination.

Justiniano and Torres repeat this pattern by offering as essential to their defence of the doctrine a series of Marian miracles. In the *Tratado*, for example, Justiniano privileges early on in his *consideraciones* the

visionary experiences and other forms of revelation that certify the verity of the Virgin's absolute purity. Mary's visit to Beatriz da Silva, "after
a certain revelation that she had, the Queen of Angels appearing to her
with a white habit and scapular, and a blue cloak,"[16] sets the stage for
numerous other accounts of the visionary and the miraculous as proof:
"one cannot deny that, in affirmation of the Conception of the Virgin,
there have been many true miracles."[17] These include not only those experienced by highly regarded religious figures, such as Saint Brigit (12),
but also apparitions of the Virgin's image experienced by unknown
women, such as María Peñuela and another nameless woman from
Cañavete, "who was very notorious in all of Spain, which happened
because of an image of the Conception."[18] Similarly, Torres opens his
Consuelo de los devotos with a chapter titled "On how miracles are effective testimonies for the confirmation of truth" ["De como los milagros
son eficaces testimonios para confirmación de la verdad"]. The correlation between Mary's miraculous conception and the Virgin's miraculous apparitions is straightaway established: "the efficacy of these
miracles ... confirms the truth that Christ's holy mother, in the instant
of her mysterious Conception, was freed from original sin."[19] Furthermore, the framework of Marian miracles is coupled with the concept of
sacred truth as infallible (despite its unknowability) and God's design
as miraculous and excessive (because it exceeds our understanding):
"So that miracles exceed the limits of nature, and are not made by ordinary law; a good foundation is to have truth as infallible, that in confirmation of this truth, God has worked miracles."[20] Visions and miracles
filter the indefinable through the experiential; or, alternatively, break
the barriers between the transcendental and the immanent. Their effect,
both rational and revelatory, is to confirm in the hearts of the knowing
faithful the enigmatic truth of Mary's exceptionality (Consuelo de los devotos 4). The miraculous serves as a discursive and conceptual scaffold
for the entire 543-page treatise. Torres places the exegetical and theological work of Church fathers, such as Aquinas and Scotus, alongside
visions, healings, and other inexplicable events. Together these examples offer the truly devout the solace needed when they are confronted
by all those infidels who would place doubt on the eternal purity of the
Virgin. The signifier for the Marian sign is itself an ineffable miracle.
Consequently, Mary compels three distinct levels of meaning. Literally,
she is a woman and the physical mother of Christ; allegorically and
tropologically, she is the Mystical Rose, the Morning Star, the Tower
of David, the Gate of Heaven, the Bride of the Church, and the many
other titles and representative qualities that are attributed to her in the
Litany of Loreto; and anagogically, she is a mystery that dialectically

binds the eternal, pure, and sacred to the human. She is a channel between a prelapsarian and our postlapsarian condition, in a manner that can only be received through faith and revelation, rejecting any logic that would bind God's will and design to our limited understanding. It is for this very reason that Justiniano and Torres see no better way to explain and defend the truth of Mary's Immaculate Conception than through the logic of the miraculous and inexplicable.

This logic is perhaps taken to its most enigmatic and yet accessible mode in the *relaciones de sucesos* genre, or more specifically, in the *True Account of the Image of the Immaculate Conception of the Virgin Mary that was found in the root or bulb of a lily in the valley of Mount Carrascal in the Village of Alcoy, in the kingdom of Valencia* [*Relación Verdadera de la Imagen de la Inmaculada Concepción de la Virgen María, que se halló en la Raíz o Cebollita de una Azucena de los Valles del Monte del Carrascal de la Villa de Alcoy, en el Reino de Valencia*], written in 1665 by Pedro Núñez Bosch. In these medieval and early modern short pre-journalistic texts – generally meant to inform, promote, persuade, praise, and entertain – there are numerous *relaciones de fiestas* in honour of the Virgin in cities and institutions all over Spain, as well as accounts of the foundation of the military order of the Immaculate Conception, the work of the *Reales Juntas* sent to Rome, poetic competitions, and the like.[21] Altogether, these texts are meant to demonstrate the faithfulness of communities and individuals all over Spain, evidencing the nation's elevated Catholicism and continuing to pressure for the declaration of the dogma. Núñez Bosch's *Relación* shares in this broader religious and political ambition, but, much more urgently, it substantiates the veracity of an apparition of the Virgin of the Immaculate Conception in a series of lily bulbs and, through it, speaks to the unconstrained dialectic of immanence and transcendence that frames the popular belief in Mary's Immaculate Conception. Anecdotal in its tone and without any formal theological or hermeneutical intent, Núñez's *Relación* stands out as testimony to the popular imagination's engagement with the doctrine and image of the Immaculate Conception. As noted by Lorenzo Borras, theologian and scholar of the University of Valencia, in his "Aprobación" to Núñez Bosch's text, the apparition is symbolically linked to the Song of Songs 2:1–2, verses which were interpreted by Immaculists as proof of Mary's purity and the totality of divine design: "I am the rose of Sharon, and the lily of the valleys. As the lily among thorns, so is my love among the daughters." Shoring up the believers' faith in Mary's "celestial purity," the image's presence in the root of a plant demonstrates the solidarity of all creation in defence of the doctrine, "nature adding its own applause."[22] The telling of the miracle itself starts, nonetheless, not in the countryside but in the main cathedral in the village of Xàtiva, where in the middle of the night a Maculist had posted a declaration against the Immaculate Conception: "Mary conceived in original sin."[23] Scandalized, the provost of the parish, Paborde Guerau, sets out to offer a sermon in which he uses as a point of reference the Song of Songs 2:2, "sicut lilium inter spinas" (11), which, as noted by Núñez Bosch, the provost took not in a literal sense but "in a mystical and spiritual sense, as Theologians and Evangelical Pastors commonly understand it and as it is in the Divine Service of Nogarolis approved by Pope Sixtus IV."[24] This is an important distinction precisely because what follows is the opposite, both in form and in content; the miracle, as we shall see, depends exactly on the material, literal, and non-orthodox manifestation of the transcendent in the immanent. Much like Mary, a human being descended like all other humans from Adam, the *cebolla* is filled by the sacred and the ineffable, miraculously blessed and made to embody a divine will that could hardly be explained or expected. Having performed his duty, Guerau goes to a country setting, the Carrascal de Alcoy, and from there to the Fuente Roxa to rest and recite the rosary, which elicits a continued meditation upon the metaphor of the thornless lily. Perhaps steered by the natural setting, but even more so by the obscure course of divine design, he begins to think in literal terms about the flower and its physical characteristics, at which point he sees a lily flower surrounded by thorns, "that there truly were white lilies among thorns."[25] The encounter with the material – i.e., not allegorical – object leads him, nevertheless, to further symbolic associations with the root of the tree of Jesse and the scriptural referent, "Egredietur virga de radice Iesse, Flos de radice eius ascendet" (15). A local priest and friend of Guerau, the Curate of Confrides, joins in on the search, finding nearby his own specimen, except that he, unlike the provost, digs up and peels the bulb, unveiling the miraculous image of the Virgin: "he discovered under an Effigy, or Image of the Virgin Mary, as she is usually painted in her Conception, white and perfect."[26] Astonished in the face of this marvel, the provost and the curate insist on corroborating their discovery with two *labradores* who, because of their knowledge of the land and their lack of prejudice, "as to a person who would look at the lily bulb with sincerity,"[27] could verify the presence and supernatural character of the image. It is very significant that not only is the site of this rural miracle far removed from the cathedrals, monasteries, hospitals, and universities where the cult of Mary was theologically and artistically "managed," but also the authority is placed in the physical sight and spiritual vision (a topic I examine at length in chapter 4) of the most common and uneducated members of the Catholic Spanish nation. The chain of confirmation eventually duly returns to the provost, who finally also peels the bulb of his lily and discovers yet another "perfect effigy of the image of the most Pure Conception of the Virgin Mary, Mother of God, with her eyes, nose, mouth, and crown, and her hair falling down her back and shoulders."[28] As such, Núñez Bosch's *Relación* documents not only a miracle but also Provost Guerau's conversion from knowledge based on theological discourses and allegorical symbols to a deeper faith founded on the material manifestation of God's inscrutable design. The image of the Virgin is found in each and every lily bulb at the Monte de Alcoy, an event that is qualified by the narrative voice as a "supernatural effect of the supernatural Providence of God,"[29] and that directly speaks to the growing and sincere devotion of the faithful to the mystery of immaculacy, as well as to the hyperbolic nature of the popular religious imagination.

Despite the depth of faith that the miracle both reveals and responds to, Guerau returns to Valencia conflicted as to whether he should divulge the happening, unable to reconcile in his mind the incongruence of a sacred doctrine and image proliferated in the dirty and lowly root of a plant (18). Ultimately unwilling to dismiss the "great devotion due to and exaltation of this most devout Mystery,"[30] Guerau tells of the miracle to his superior and spiritual guide, who advises him to spread the news, whereupon he summons the faculty and students of the University of Valencia: "He recounted the entire marvellous event of the Lily of the Valleys, with all of its circumstances, and all of the audience was left so amazed that they were greatly ignited in their devotion to this holy Mystery."[31] Moved and convinced, the city leaders build a hermitage at the Fuente Roxa, consecrated in front of an audience of "innumerable people of different stations,"[32] emphasizing the ways in which the miracle of the *cebolla* emanates from a popular and material, rather than a scriptural or exegetical, imaginary. Moreover, the miracle keeps perpetuating its effects and influence upon the religious and social hierarchy of Valencia. Guerau finds one even more perfect miraculous bulb at the Monte de Alcoy and delivers it to Church officials and members of the high nobility; in their shared belief in the verity of the miracle as a sign of the inscrutable design and will of God, they place the *cebollita* in a silver box and send it to Philip IV. The king, overcome by the image, keeps it as a sign of the truth of the mystery and miraculous nature of Mary's Immaculate Conception: "your Majesty, whom God keeps with his usual piety, has commanded you keep the lily, and to hold it with special veneration and decorum, as an image of the holy Virgin, Mother of God. That God shall be exalted and praised, and so shall the clean and pure conception of our holy Mary, conceived without original sin in the first physical and real instant of her Being."[33] In a context where the royal family had unfettered access to the full extent of the scriptural and theological canon, as well as to countless artistic renderings of the Virgin by court painters, Núñez Bosch fixes Philip IV's faith to the inexplicable image on a lily bulb authorized by *labradores* from the remote Monte de Alcoy.

In many respects both Borras's introduction and Núñez's account of the details of the miracle suggest a closed circuit of correspondences and cosmic sympathies that leave little room for new or unexpected meanings; this would be Foucault's reading, following the characterization of an episteme where the contingency of the sign is still not thinkable. Just as Mary is singularly pure in a world of sin, the lily – white and without thorns – would be interpreted to mimic and faithfully represent, in its natural capacity, the concept of Marian purity. Nevertheless, if on the one hand the signifying system seems to be settled and apparent, on the other the *Relación* tells of a sacred mystery in which what is symbolically pertinent is materially transposed to a mundane corm and confirmed by the everyday experience of villagers in a valley in Valencia. Stated differently, if in the sermons and treatises examined above Immaculist belief is shored up by the theological discourse of ineffability and the mystical experiences of prominent religious figures, Núñez's *Relación* transposes the ineffable to the ordinary – the bulbs of lilies in a mountain populated by *labradores*. In my opinion, this text goes well beyond the common formulation that ensures the verity of immaculacy because God has placed the belief in so many people's hearts. God's will and Mary's exceptionality are signified in a temporary and degradable natural object and in a site that only a rural popular imagination could certify. The transcendent and unknowable mystery of the Virgin's exceptional purity is brought down literally to the earth, and thereby to the immanence of everyday life; its onto-theological meanings are appropriated by a popular religious imaginary whose Catholic identity is intimately bound to Mary's hyperbolic and excessive sacred *and* human condition. As told in the *Relación*, the Virgin of the Immaculate Conception is not exclusive to scriptural references, the hermeneutical exercises of Scotus and Anselm, the visions of ascetic mystics, or the paintings and sculptures commissioned for churches, hospitals, and the houses of the nobility. Her purity can be shown to and perceived by all of us, belongs as much to the heavens as to the soil of the earth, and is even pertinent to and revealed in the roots of our wild flowers. The ineffable and miraculous are inexplicably present in the most unlikely of places, whether it is the *cebolla* of a white lily or the body and soul of a woman immaculately conceived by her very human parents.

III. Performed Visions: The Virgin of the Immaculate Conception Materializes on the Stage

The apparition of the image of the Virgin of the Immaculate Conception on a lily bulb is an event that, as I proposed in the previous section, populates the immanent with the transcendent in a way that parallels Mary's being: the sacred and the earthly contiguous and inexplicably existing in one site. It also amply demonstrates how the popular religious imagination asserts itself and is deployed in order to confirm and promote the belief in Mary as *tota pulchra*. Unlike the singular visionary experiences of chosen ascetic individuals, the sight of the image on the lily bulb is framed as a communal experience, shared in time and space by the provost, his friends, the *labradores* of the Monte de Alcoy, the scholars at the university, and, finally, Philip IV. On the other hand, the miracle of the *cebolla* calls upon the imagination of each individual "seer" to transform the inanimate into the spiritually animate and germane; in other words, matter – the bulb root of a flower – feeds into the conceptual anagogic field of the mystery of immaculacy. In Núñez Bosch's *Relación* the work of the imagination is to make present the Virgin of the Immaculate Conception upon the sight of her image on the surface of a bulb. When thought of in a parallel manner, seventeenth-century *comedias* in which an apparition of the Virgin of the Immaculate Conception is staged provide an exceptionally rich analytical possibility; in them the apparition of the sacred image acquires the form of an extant being, seen and heard by the audience alongside the actors in what may be understood as a shared visionary experience. In turn, we must think about the issues – textual, political, and ideological – that arise when the image of the Virgin of the Immaculate Conceptions is transformed into flesh and blood by an actress and given a physical voice. In other words, the audience's reception – both didactic and contemplative – is tested by the contrast of the ineffable character of the mystery of immaculacy vis-à-vis the embodiment of this same mystery in an actress, vacillating between complex theological precepts and the imaginary immediacy of a theatrical "lived" visionary experience. As I will show, these *comedias* offer another fascinating example of how the dialectic of transcendence and immanence – the relationship of the sacred that exceeds us and the sacred that is manifest in us – permeated and fuelled the social and religious imaginary of Counter-Reformation Spain.[34]

To delimit the scope of the analysis, I have chosen three historical plays that represent the events that lead to the late fifteenth-century constitution of the first religious order of the Immaculate Conception. Lope de Vega's *El milagro por los celos*, Tirso de Molina's *Doña Beatriz de Silva*, and Blas Fernández de Mesa's *La fundadora de la santa concepción* are faithful to the model established by Lope de Vega's *Arte nuevo de hacer comedias*, in which theatre was prescribed to follow a new mimetic imperative of joining tragic and comedic elements. The visionary appearance of the Virgin of the Immaculate Conception takes place in what are otherwise amatory plot lines, where events and relationships amongst conflicted, and at times rather corrupt, human beings are related. Each of these plays has as a point of reference the legend of Beatriz da Silva, recounting her difficult trajectory from a beautiful and marriageable lady-in-waiting to the admired lay sister and founder of the order of the Immaculate Conception in 1484, with numerous twisted love plots, death threats, and political intrigue as background. As is typically the case with *tragicomedias*, the plays end on a positive "comedic" note with Beatriz redeemed and free to proceed with her religious mission. It should also be noted that these *comedias* were written to be performed on public stages – or *corrales* – and were not thematically fit for inclusion in religious feasts, such as the *corpus Christi*, or meant for cathedrals or cloisters. As such, these plays navigate an equivocal religious and artistic field, between entertainment and spiritual didacticism with the embodied apparition of the Virgin of the Immaculate Conception introducing the miraculous and visionary into the midst of very human actions and emotions.

All three plays reach a climax at the moment that the image of Mary is represented on the stage. As the historical narrative goes, Beatriz is encased in a trunk for three days, a punishment imposed upon her by a jealous Isabel of Portugal, queen consort of Castile and León and mother of Isabel I of Castile; it is during this time that the Virgin of the Immaculate Conception appears to Beatriz and instructs her to institute a religious order in her honour. When eventually found by her uncle, Beatriz is neither dead nor weakened by the trauma she is presumed to have endured; to the contrary, she is more beautiful than ever and now entirely committed to living a cloistered life away from the temptations of the court, advocating instead for the Immaculist cause. From a purely political perspective, seventeenth-century Spaniards would have recognized Beatriz's revelation and staunch activism as part of an ongoing project in which Immaculist devotion was weaponized to promote communal and national identification in the face of religious and military conflict in the Mediterranean and beyond. For that very

reason, these plays can easily be read as part of the wide-ranging propaganda effort that called for the completion of the papal process and
that positioned the Spanish Habsburgs as the most stalwart defenders of the doctrine, a commitment that is corroborated within the plot
when Isabel of Portugal turns her wrath into support of Beatriz's new
order. As it regards the parameters of representation, I am interested
in the specific ideas, beliefs, and codes that come into play when the
Virgin of the Immaculate Conception physically appears on a stage and
what was required from and called for by the audience.

Early modern religious culture – both official and popular – depends
on a porous set of beliefs and uses of doctrinal tenets. As such, the religious imagination of the period lends itself to what may seem, from
our modern perspective, unconventional and surprising deployments
of biblical exegesis and lay theology. Theatre is a critical genre in this regard, since it is explicitly produced for a shared public consumption and
it is – within a humanist early modern cultural milieu – conceptually
bound to mimesis and the constitutive mechanisms of resemblance, interpretation, recognition, and understanding that Aristotle had long established as the foundation of poetics.[35] Spanish Counter-Reformation
religious theatre stood – much like sacred visual art – at the intersection of Church doctrine, the artist's individual religious imagination,
popular belief, and the broad cultural imaginary that nourished and
validated it. As noted by Stephen Halliwell in his *Aesthetics of Mimesis*,
"the 'intentionality' of mimetic works is not located simply in the specific designs of the particular artist but also in the shared conventions,
traditions, and possibilities of a culture. The mimetic status of certain
art objects is a matter of their having a significant content that can and,
if their mimetic status is to be effectively realized, must be recognized
and understood by their audiences" (153). Furthermore, and more so
than any other literary genre or visual medium, religious theatre dealt
in matters of immanence (in the mimetic representation of everyday
human life) while incorporating an illusion of the presence of the transcendental – that which exists beyond the material universe, ineffable
and eternal – that exceeds everyday human experience. In other words,
these *comedias* exponentially play out what has already been secured
by a Counter-Reformation religious imagination that allows for (even
depends on) the transcendental showing itself – revealed even if not fully
understood – in the realm of the immanent; or from a different perspective, a religious imagination that needs and insists upon the eventuality
of visions and miracles as a constitutive component of the experience of
lived faith. As such, these miracle plays or *comedias de santos* offer a privileged space where the coterminous experience of the sacred alongside

the human – upon which the Spanish Counter-Reformation religious imagination hinges – is profitably displayed.

Despite their commonalities, these three plays demonstrate noteworthy differences in how each imagines Mary's timely apparition. Lope de Vega, for example, materializes the Virgin as a grown woman whose sacred words focus the audience's attention on what is to be swapped: Beatriz's deliverance in exchange for the founding of convents and her service to the Catholic cause. Appearing on stage upon Beatriz's desperate promise of devotion, "Your conception I would defend, with reverent worship," the Virgin transfers her heavenly existence onto the domain of Beatriz's miserable prison: "'This prison is covered in celestial radiance, the ceilings have opened, Heaven rains light; thousands of cherubs descend from the empyrean; the messengers properly declare the news of who comes to the earth.' Our Lady of the Conception appears on a stage machine. She comes to the earth."[36] Recalling the debt occasioned by Beatriz's immoral behaviour, the segment hinges on the Virgin of the Immaculate Conception's role as co-redemptress and intercessor: "Beatriz, you will leave this prison very briefly; if you are grateful, walk to Toledo, where you will build a celebrated temple in honour of my conception, a universal refuge for devout women. You will give them precepts for the coming age; you will dress my nuns with the same habit you see me wear. Do not forget about Isabel and Fernando, the Catholic monarchs, Beatriz, remember what you owe me."[37] Not only does the Virgin intervene on Beatriz's behalf, turning her away from her sinful nature to a life of redemption and grace, but she also adjudges Beatriz's future as Mary's representative in Spain, authenticated by her role as founder of the order. The Virgin's and Beatriz's roles as protectors of the future monarchs, Isabel and Fernando, confirm a Counter-Reformation imaginary that links the theological defence of Mary's purity, the Catholic king's wars against infidels (the Moors) and heretics (the Jews), and the sacred mission inherited by the Spanish Habsburgs.

In Tirso and Fernández de Mesa, the Virgin of the Immaculate Conception materializes as a literal *niña* dressed in a blue robe, crowned by twelve stars, and standing on a crescent moon, thus announcing her identity to the audience, despite her youthful physical appearance, as the Apocalyptic Woman. Her enactment as a girl-child is fully congruent with the Virgin of the Immaculate Conception's iconicity and reception. In the vast corpus of painting of the Immaculate Conception produced in seventeenth-century Spain, and which I discuss in chapter 4, the Virgin is most often represented as a nubile young woman, with artists such as Zurbarán and Murillo occasionally taking the extra step of using child models for their work. The Virgin's youth is symbolic of her purity, the innocence of a child visually translated as the eternal prelapsarian incorruptibility of Mary. And yet, we must assume that the reception by the theatre audience of this young girl on the stage was complicated by a number of factors. First, the Spanish theatre rarely includes children, and they most definitively never perform a central role in the action, a fact that plays against the naturalization of this living image and in favour of her radical exceptionality amongst her fellow human beings. Second, although the body may be that of a child, she stands in for the Immaculate Mother of God and the Apocalyptic Woman. Mirroring John of Patmos's vision, in both plays she appears hoisted onto the stage on a machine as if floating on a moon, surrounded by twelve stars, recalling her eternal existence and role as mother and co-redemptress. This is a set of doctrinal tenets of which the *niña* Inmaculada explicitly reminds Beatriz in Tirso's play, declaring, "I am the privileged one, a guileless creation made by God *ab initio*, chosen to be his mother."[38] The simultaneous familiarity and strange admiration occasioned by the *niña* on stage offers the audience a tangible manifestation of the sacred in the familiarly human. Fernández de Mesa provides a similar juxtaposition between the body of the Virgin-child and her mystery and eternal holy mission, reminding Beatriz of her "sacred Son" while commanding with full authority, "You will leave this prison to be Beatriz, defender and first founder of my holy Conception."[39] The contrast figured in the staging of her small delicate body wrapped in Apocalyptic garments with her voice as a commanding Mother and Warrior must surely have been striking. That in Tirso's play the *niña* also scolds Beatriz for her previous lustfulness and reveals a secondary vision – a vision imbricated within the vision – of Beatriz's brother, Juan, as a hermit in the miraculous company of Saint Jerome offers yet another layer of exceptionality made manifest in the identifiable body and voice of the young girl. The *niña* Inmaculada is symbolically constructed by both playwrights as a textual image come to life, made present through Beatriz's visionary experience for the audience's viewing, at the threshold of what is familiar and similar – the image of a child – and what is extraordinary – Mary's radical singularity as the only eternal *and* immaculate human. She is revealed to Beatriz in a mystical vision and delivered on the stage for the benefit of an audience that is called upon simultaneously to recognize and to marvel. Paralleling the *pintores divinos* category widely used in the period, Tirso and Fernández de Mesa (as well as Lope de Vega) position themselves as *dramaturgos divinos*, offering the audience their interpretation – visual and dramatic – of a mystical encounter that nourishes and feeds on the audience's expansive religious imagination and their capacity to incorporate Beatriz's vision into their own experience.

The imaginary parameter through which the audience would have perceived and filtered the visionary happening that they behold on the stage thus requires some further consideration. The representational status of the body of the Virgin of the Immaculate Conception invites a doubling of the experience for the audience. Unlike the ethereal and sensuous contemplative stasis offered, for example, by the visionary paintings of Velázquez, Zurbarán, and Murillo (and which I discuss in detail in chapter 4), Lope de Vega's, Tirso de Molina's, and Fernández de Mesa's plays ask the audience to surrender their individual religious imagination – both as a motivating cause and as a propitious effect – to an evolving plot narrative. The point is not that the audience would confuse the actress playing the part of the Virgin with a miraculous apparition of the Virgin or would think that they were truly witnessing a vision, drawing no distinction between the image/actress on stage and the thing for which it stands or which it represents. Nevertheless, the performative nature of theatre offers a complex intensification of the theatrical experience as an act of witnessing, allowing the audience to temporarily bracket and transpose their expectations, needs, and desires to the dramatic context; like Beatriz, the audience can hear the Immaculate's voice, respond in kind, see the girth of her body, allow themselves to be taken in by the narrative, and participate virtually in the experience of this vision. Historically, Beatriz's vision is fundamental to the Spanish religious imaginary and the cultural and political attachments that the Spanish nation staked on the cult of immaculacy. Structurally, the event it represents is the climax of the play and calls upon the audience's historical memory and religious belief. Affectively, the staged presence of the Virgin of the Immaculate Conception allows for a heightened degree of identification. Therefore, if from a purely theological perspective the mystery of immaculacy is true and yet opaque to our finite understanding, the theatrical representation of the Virgin of the Immaculate Conception – translated from religious concept and eternal spirit to the material body of an actress, woman or child, on a stage – frees an imaginative capacity potentially unmatched by any other devotional media. The playwrights offer a dramatic interpretation and enactment of a sacred mystery within a mystical experience. Each audience member, in response, is impelled to imagine his/her distinct relationship to the exceptional, holy and radical other that has been placed breathing, talking, and floating – physically present even if theologically exceptional – before their eyes. Responsive to the didactic and contemplative functions that the Counter-Reformation posited as constitutive to religious art, these plays squarely insert themselves in a dialectical continuum between the sacred and the human, offering the audience a performed resemblance of the revealed and the ineffable.

IV. "Más que la luna hermosa, que escogida triunfa homicida": Amateur Women Poets in Defence of Immaculacy

Sancho Zapata, an influential nobleman of Zaragoza and nephew of Cardinal Antonio Zapata – one of Philip III's closest councillors and viceroy of Naples – sponsored and published the *Poetic Tournament on the Defence of the Purity of the Immaculate Conception of the Virgin* [*Justa poética en defensa de la pureza de la Inmaculada Concepción de la Virgen santísima*] in 1619 at the height of Immaculist debates and Habsburg papal missions.[40] As regards the literary context, the poetic tournaments are a rather particular type of event and publication. Independent of literary academies or professional *gremios*, a self-designated organizer – individual or group – would post an open announcement calling for the general amateur public to submit poems on a proposed topic with stipulated guidelines concerning form and content. Once the poems were submitted, a public contest would take place with a jury of experts designated to speak to the merits of the poems submitted and choose a selection of winners. The organizer would subsequently compile and publish a *relación* in which a selection of the winners was included with the authors' names indicated.[41] As the focus and title of Zapata's publication make clear, the *Justa* evinces the popular fervour that supported Spain's national claim as the locus of the true Catholic faith intimately imbricated with the theology and iconography of the Immaculate Conception. If Lope de Vega's, Tirso de Molina's, and Fernández de Mesa's plays stage the specific legendary (historical and visionary) moment in time when the Virgin of the Immaculate Conception appoints Spain as the locus of her defence and devotion, Zapata's tournament proudly displays the way in which the Counter-Reformation's popular imaginary digested and enthusiastically reproduced the theological discourse, religious commitments, and local devotional practices tied to conceptionism. And yet, as Nieves Baranda and María Carmen Marín Pina have noted, there is an added component that makes the study of these tournaments critical to contemporary early modern Spanish studies: significant numbers of women participated and were subsequently published in the *relaciones*.[42] In Zapata's *relación*, thirty-one of the over one hundred published entries are by women. Thus considered, as Marín Pina states, "the numbers reveal women's interest in poetry at a moment of clear poetic effervescence in all of Spain, and especially in Aragon."[43]

Additionally, Baranda and Marín Pina both remark on the public and non-exclusionary nature of the tournaments and the evidence they provide of an active, even if not formally recognized, women's poetic practice: "women tend to belong to the group excluded from literary society, to which they can only have access precisely through a public invitation."[44] For her part, Marín Pina adds, "In these competitions, the differences from a genetically marked society are erased, and there is no distinction drawn between men and women."[45] The only requirement that seems to limit access is the implicit assumption of a degree of literacy and literary aptitude in those willing to submit their entries. More specifically, the rules and parameters established by the organizer and measured by the judges require a particular set of proficiencies: "Knowledge is required of current poetic models, as well as training in the noble art of composing verses."[46] Given this context, the palpable participation of unknown and non-professional women poets in the tournaments allows us to gauge the public presence of women writers throughout the sixteenth and seventeenth centuries, the social groups to which they belonged, their literary expertise, and the general social acceptance of women's writing (Baranda, "Reflexiones" 315–16). The poetry contests in which we can document the highest degree of female participation were called in Madrid and Zaragoza, with the latter seeing a larger number of noblewomen contestants from the urban elite.[47] For Marín Pina, therefore, these women's poetic practice may be understood as a way to make an impression in the local milieu, precisely as "a welcome ability, a social distinction at a time in which the literary is achieving certain social prestige."[48] For these educated women, "poetry occupies a specific place, it has a function of personal affirmation or reaffirmation, of belonging to a group, of political and religious propaganda, of social promotion, in which they also want to share."[49] Beyond its use as a vehicle for public recognition and personal prestige, female participation and inclusion in the contests and their published *relaciones* demonstrate the availability of an artistic practice that has often been thought of in literary histories as foreclosed to them.[50] Zapata's *Justa* stands out in this regard, since it takes place at the peak of activity for these contests – between 1600 and 1650 – and sees by far the largest number of women included in the *relaciones* within that fifty-year span in Aragon.[51]

Certainly, Zapata's *Justa* lends itself to the literary and social type of analysis here suggested. However, I am equally interested in these women poets' engagement with and demonstrated comprehension of the complicated and often abstract theological premises that anchor the mystery of the Immaculate Conception of Mary. As I noted in the

previous chapter, Stratton has argued for a top-down orthodox dissemination of the doctrine – most often through the sermons of Franciscan preachers and the visual images abundantly found in churches and
homes – with a rather limited proper theological expertise demonstrated
by the general public (*The Immaculate Conception in Spanish Art* 73). We
could, therefore, surmise that, given the limited formal educational contexts in which laywomen participated, the absence of hermeneutical
experience would have been even more pronounced for non-religious
amateur women poets. Although this reading of the cultural context is
not without merit, the sources of theological knowledge were in fact not
as scarce as Stratton suggests. Baranda documents in some detail, for example, how even though women were prohibited from reading the Bible
in the vernacular (which limited its study only to those women who had
access to and could read in Latin) there do remain selected sources of
religious and theological knowledge in vernacular translations that continued to be officially sanctioned and were accessible: Saint Augustine,
Saint Jerome, Luis de Granada, and Loyola, among others (*Cortejo* 29–
30). Additionally, this period also sees a proliferation of new or revised
hagiographies, including Pedro de Ribadeneyra's widely available 1616
Flos Sanctorum or *Libro de la vida de los Santos*, which was dedicated to
Margaret of the Cross (daughter of Empress Mary of Austria and a professed nun at the Royal Discalced Convent in Madrid), whose devotion
to the Virgin of the Immaculate Conception was crucial to the promotion of the papal definition of the doctrine within the court of Philip
III. Religious books, such as Martín Carrillo's 1627 *In Praise of Illustrious
Women of the Old Testament* [*Elogios de mujeres insignes del viejo testamento*]
(also dedicated to Margaret of the Cross), were also widely available to
women readers as a source for scriptural exegetical instruction.[52] Specifically concerning the doctrine, we can also point to the proliferation of
published treatises, *relaciones*, and sermons on the topic that circulated
widely during the period and which I examine in the first section of this
chapter. Just as significantly, women religious authors, such as Isabel
Villena, Juana de la Cruz, Valentina Pinelo, and María de Ágreda (all
of whom I discuss at length in chapter 5), provide a practicable corpus
of published theological discourses on immaculacy available to women
inside and outside of the convents. Finally, the introduction authored
by Zapata that frames the reading of the *Justa* – in which he extensively
quotes Gregory, Bonaventure, and key passages of the Old and New Testaments in translation – is yet another fine example of precisely how lay-
people, and women specifically, would become familiar with the more
complex theological tenets that are not customarily attainable in the
visual iconographical program of most paintings and sculptures of the

Virgin of the Immaculate Conception. Given what we know of the public nature of the tournaments, together with the access to religious and devotional texts that women during the Counter-Reformation generally could have, I intend to examine the demonstrated exegetical knowledge that the *poetas* in Zapata's tournament display, and how their erudition is translated to a religious-artistic imagination. More precisely, I read these poems not as a literary curiosity or anomaly, but rather as religious literature that exhibits women's comprehension of and engagement with religious debates and discourses. The women I examine are only published in Zapata's *Justa*, and no other examples of their poetic production have been documented.

Upon denouncing the uneducated ignorant who would deny Mary's eternal purity, Gerónima Marqués defines the Virgin's beauty as an effect from her decapitation of the sinful dragon:

> More beautiful than the moon, which chosen
> triumphs homicidal, in superior beauty
> with the head of the prostrate dragon
> not bloody: because of her beauty
> nothing could stain such a pure thing.[53]

Immediately evident is that Gerómina Marqués's conceptual framework exceeds the commonplaces that equate Mary's beauty with purity as a symbolic abstraction. Rather, Immaculate splendour concretely emanates from strength, violence, and the resulting victory of the Virgin over a dragon whose foul blood cannot touch her. The referent here is, of course, Genesis 3:15. And yet, Gerónima Marqués is not citing her source exactly but rather creating a reimagined account in which the Virgin, in her status as *tota pulchra*, outright defeats – beheads and not just steps on the head of – the dragon; this is a narrative that certainly recalls but does not exactly reproduce either the biblical text or the popularized versions of John of Patmos's Apocalyptic vision retold in sermons and other religious discourses. Her account is most certainly motivated by her desire to create an image of the Virgin's immaculacy as an unequalled force against the bestial supremacy of sin. Following this logic, Gerónima Marqués's imagery picks up on the theological rationale and belief in the Virgin of the Immaculate Conception as co-redemptress. Like her Son, the Virgin outright defeats the source of all sin, miraculously exempted from being touched by its nature or effects; the result is that, alongside her Son, the Virgin can thus intercede in favour of the redemption of humanity's sins. Far from the floating and ethereal childlike image that almost exclusively populated the visual iconographical program, Gerónima Marqués's

Immaculate Virgin warrior reveals the enigmatic conditions of purity as a simultaneous and perplexing contact and non-contact – a defeat of the dragon that inexplicably and yet tellingly produces a severed head while precluding the association of the Virgin warrior with the sinful blood of her victim. Possibly transposing well-known Old Testament accounts of David and Judith onto the allegorical symbolism of Genesis 3:15, Gerónima Marqués makes of the Virgin a slayer.

Just as remarkable is when Gerónima Marqués shifts her attention to the eternal nature of the Virgin created by an omnipotent and eternal God:

> If God could, if God since *ab eterno*,
> had the government, of the invisible
> and the visible, and in his quintessence
>
> ...
>
> who could doubt
> that from *ab eterno* he preserved Mary?[54]

The logic of God's omnipotence is pivotal to the theological defence of immaculacy. Treading on nominalist Franciscan theological ground, Gerónima Marqués emphasizes the changeableness of divine design and will; going against his condemnation of all human beings, God creates Mary as an immaculate spirit and body. Moreover, the reference to God's eternal government links the Virgin to a time before time; she has existed pure for all eternity in God's invisible realm. At this point, Gerónima Marqués ventures into the arena of abstract religious thought as found in the theological corpus – professional and lay – where the unknowable, yet perceivable, asserts its claims. In the verses "who could doubt that from *ab eterno* he preserved Mary?" the reference is Proverbs 8:22–3, "The Lord possessed me in the beginning of his ways, before he made any thing from the beginning. I existed from the beginning, and of old, before the earth was made," a scriptural touchstone for exegetical discourses that tackled the relationship between Mary's earthly stainless conception and the idea that she had been created before the beginning of time, following the timeline afforded by Revelation 12 and 21. The poet places Mary's eternal purity at the juncture between no-time and time, between the visible and the invisible, eternal spirit and human incarnation, in each instance displaying her religious imaginary and comprehension of God's "government," the mystery of his wisdom, divine will, and enigmatic omnipotence.

Juana Garcés follows a similar path, with particular emphasis on the Virgin's power over Satan, describing her as a strong captain, *mulier fortis* (Proverbs 31:10) or *mulier militans* (Revelation 12). This is an image that, as in Gerónima Marqués's poem, stresses the Immaculate Virgin's physical strength through the crushing of the dragon's head:

> Archetype, and not surrendered,
> called the Virgin Saint John
> who as a strong captain
> left his opponent defeated.
> If she has come to place her foot
> upon its bold forehead,
> erroneously they will say that she was defeated,
> the one that earned victory
> giving to the world such glory,
> as well as to the One whom she also gave life.[55]

Reproducing the import of John of Patmos's visionary account in Revelation, as well as the account in Genesis 3:15, Juana Garcés compares the Virgin to a mighty commanding captain who defeats Satan in the heavens. The logic follows, of course, that Mary could not have been defeated by sin on earth. More significantly, Juana Garcés focuses on the ineffable circularity of the Virgin's creation and conception: God creates her as a singular being both in the heavens and on earth, in spirit and in body, in order for her to bear God incarnate. As such, the verses "giving to the world such glory, as well as to the One whom she also gave life" suggest one of the most prescient concepts in the theological defence of the doctrine. Because the Virgin is created by God the Father to carry God the Son in human form, there must be an exceptional and necessary purity that positions her as contiguous to the sacred, explicates her eternal being, and results in her ability to bear the Divine.

Bárbara Amigo de Cariñena pays tribute to the Virgin's immaculacy by reminding her audience that in heaven, where Mary has always existed, there can be no sin:

> Saint John, in his vision
> thinking of her dressed in light
> and a ghost in heaven
> where sin cannot settle,
> clearly he represents her to us
> conceived without sin.[56]

As reproduced by Bárbara Amigo de Cariñena, Saint John's visionary experience visually and textually translates and confirms the category of immaculacy as evident and necessary. Especially noteworthy is how the poet deploys the image of the heavenly sun and the dawn fundamental to Conceptionist iconography, but here reframed as signs of an eternal symbiotic relationship between God and the Virgin, united in the redemptive light of salvation that they jointly offer the world:

> As when the dawn appears
> with its red glory
> manifesting the sun to the world
> without being offended by it,
> the Virgin with God united
> shone more than the dawn,
> with the light that she received,
> from the divine sun in heaven,
> to restore the ground,
> remaining a virgin, she gave birth.[57]

The sun, God, may be the original source of light, but it is the dawn, the Virgin, who brings that light and a new day to the dark world. Like the relationship between the sun and the dawn, God and the Virgin are inextricably coextensive. This premise demonstrates Bárbara Amigo de Cariñena's familiarity with the theological implications of Mary's exceptionality in the schema of the holy Trinity and the Virgin's position of co-redemptress. An agent in the event of redemption, the Immaculate Virgin bears Christ "to restore the ground," and without her there is no restoration possible.

In one of the poems that glosses Sancho Zapata's assigned topical phrase for the contest, "Without sin conceived, Mary of Adam was born" ["Sin pecado concebida María de Adán nació"], Margarita Zapata explicates Mary's belonging to a time before sin:

> but two eras that passed
> could be considered
> that if the second is understood,
> that it was after he [Adam] sinned,
> Mary was excerpted
> By divine omnipotence,
> Kept in the first era of innocence,
> Mary of Adam was born.[58]

Despite coming from the lineage of Adam in her bodily incarnation, Mary is kept, singularly as no other human, in that first prelapsarian time before Adam's fall. As in Cariñena above, the concept of eternal time once again displays the poet's familiarity with the theological premises extracted from John of Patmos's vision and the biblical symbolic corpus. Mary is the Apocalyptic Woman, pristine, superior to Adam, *ab initio*, and immune to the effects of sin, eternally "excerpted" from its consequences. Zapata's verses also demonstrate, as we saw above, how Franciscan nominalism – with its emphasis on the unbound and unpredictable nature of divine design – permeated the lay religious imaginary and its symbolic and artistic constructs in these women's poems.

In her own interpretation of the sun/dawn metaphor, Antonia de Mendoza postulates that, despite her secondary status to God, the Virgin occupies the same position as God in her role in the incarnation of Christ:

The Virgin in which he [the divine sun, Christ] shows himself
with her purity, gave us
the same thing as the eternal father
even though she is less than God.[59]

These verses evidently allude to the Virgin's role as the mother of God, but it is thought of as a matter of continuity: the sun/Christ comes to us through the dawn/Virgin, who is not God but coextensive with the Trinity, created by God and bearer of God. In the light that she and God bring to the world, they are one, "the same thing as the eternal father." If Christ is incarnated in order to redeem humanity, Mary, in her own incarnation and purity, participates in the mystery of salvation; she is an extension of Christ on earth just as she is a continuation of the Trinity in heaven. The proposition of sameness in difference, of an equality brought about by the core function of the Virgin as Immaculate Mother of God, stands out in Mendoza's poetic formulation and speaks to a religious imagination that awarded Mary with primary agency in the narrative of God's intervention in the redemption of humanity. She is not simply a chosen mother; she is, like God, a source and a bearer of purity.

Zapata's *Justa* includes a hieroglyphic section, which is especially fascinating given the play on visual images that have to be linguistically "translated" by the contestants. Contestants were offered images with corresponding Vulgate verses that held the key to their meaning. Within these parameters, these poems produced were meant to display the contestant's iconographic and verbal dexterity, as well as his/her biblical erudition. Among the contributions by women poets in this section, one salient example is Ana María de Gotor's:

The sky was painted very clear and serene, after the storm, with Saint John's arch and the sun rising, and on the ground a dove with an olive branch in its beak, and the writing says: *Columba venit ad vesperam portans ramum olivae virentibus solis in ore suo*. Genes. Cap. 6.

> Anne has been the restoration of man
> As this dove with weightless flight
> Brought us news from the serene heavens.[60]

The inclusion of Saint Anne in Ana María de Gotor's interpretation is significant in several ways. Certainly, a personal identification of the poet with her saint's name may have played a role. And yet, by 1619, the role of Mary's mother and father in the narrative of conception – iconographically represented as a kiss or embrace under a golden gate – had been pushed to the margins of exegetical inquiries on immaculacy by most theologians and religious thinkers. The reasons for this exclusion are not surprising, given the thorny questions of sexual contact, as well as the labyrinth of retroactive stainlessness that Saint Anne's maternity seemed to elicit. Did Saint Anne and Saint Joachim engage physically beyond a kiss? How can Anne's sinful body not contaminate Mary? Ana María de Gotor, nonetheless, is keen to imagine and assign absolute purity to Saint Anne through metaphor. Mary's mother is like a rainbow ("the sky was painted") that conveys the pure dove of redemption. The Virgin – and her Son implicitly through her – brings the good news from the heavens, indicating once again how the theological concept of *ab initio* circulated and was reproduced. But, as directly stated in the first verse, it is Saint Anne to whom Ana María de Gotor retroactively assigns the pivotal charge of carrying and delivering, incarnated in human form, the "news" from the heavens – the redemptive bodies of Saint Anne, Mary, and Christ symbolically made one. Holy grandmother, mother, and Son are thus inextricably united in the singular mystery and task of human salvation.

The women-authored poems of Zapata's *Justa* suggest a level of engagement with the theology of immaculacy that goes well beyond the limits of the visual iconography or commonplace tropes about Mary's purity. Instead, the poems reveal how concepts related to her eternal existence and coextensive relationship with the holy Trinity were received and reproduced in at least two critical ways. First, the poems demonstrate these women's intellectual and contemplative capacity – what they knew and how they interpreted the theological corpus. Second, they display the manner in which women's poetic practice can broaden and enlighten the theological discourse through the deployment of a capacious female religious imagination. In fact, the scope of women authors' treatment of the doctrine of the Immaculate Conception is the focus of chapter 5. What surely the women poets of Zapata's tournament display is their investment in the necessity and primacy of the Virgin of the Immaculate Conception, and of Saint Anne before her, whose fundamental and exalted positions in the narrative of redemption reflect upon them and elevate their own standing as women and as mothers. There is no salvation without Mary, and it is her absolute purity – with the power and agency it bestows – that brings light (*dar a luz*) to our world.

The larger point, as I have shown in this chapter, is that the mystery of and the theological premises that frame Conceptionist thought were readily available to be appropriated and reproduced by male and female authors with widely varying degrees of theological and artistic formation for a popular audience. Ready to document, describe, explain, and witness, an "army of believers" stood prepared to lay claim to the imaginary field of Mary's immaculacy in ways that simultaneously conform to, expand, and often unexpectedly transform the conditions and effects of the Virgin's enigmatic exceptionality.

ↄ

Pintor Divino: The Painter as Divinely Inspired Liberal Artist and the Conditions of Representation for a Sacred Mystery

Vicente Carducho, born in Italy in 1568, moved as a boy to Spain and spent the rest of his life working as a painter for Philip II, Philip III, and Philip IV at the Escorial and the Prado. In his art treatise of 1633, *Dialogues on Painting* [*Diálogos de la pintura*], Carducho focuses the seventh dialogue on religious painting with the heading "On the differences and modes of painting events and sacred stories with the dignity that they are owed" ["De las diferencias y modos de pintar los sucesos e historias sagradas con la decencia que se debe"] (244). After numerous questions from the student to the master regarding the appropriate parameters for the representation of religious subjects and the categories through which sacred images can be conceptualized (same, similar, and metaphorical), the student ups the speculative ante and asks: "Can one avoid Painting in the world?"[1] In his lengthy response, the master reminds the student that God is an artist: "It was God who just after creating the world made a painting or image of himself that could talk to our first parents, and then made an image of an Angel that could eject them from Paradise."[2] After citing numerous other divine beings transformed by God into intelligible image form, the Master proclaims:

> What is all this but images and paintings from the hand and brush of God, who speaks to us in this language, which seems to follow from this, and tells us that this Art is necessary and unavoidable, and that men are not exempt from imitating him, that they imitate this universal Painting of the Heavens and their luminaries ...? No Art is of such importance as this, for the news of all things, and mostly for the reverence and praise of God, and of his Saints, for the telling of divine and heroic miracles, made for the good and for edification, for all divine and human stories that beautify and adorn the Republics.[3]

The artist paints images that lead to and bridge the gap to the Divine by offering, through the visual medium, aspects of the holy that cannot be otherwise communicated. More precisely, the painter's interpretation, translation, and transmission of the sacred bring forth in an intelligible visual form what in oral or written language would remain invisible and inaccessible.

In what follows, I examine what it meant – both as a theological prescription and as a social phenomenon – for painting to be thought of as a conduit for the interpretation of the holy. The ideas I presented in the Introduction on the definition and parameters of the religious imagination frame the discussion below. The connection is clear because, as I indicated previously, the slippage between the imagination and the image is inescapable: the imagination is, in its mediation between materiality and reason, cognized as a mechanism of perception that allows the production of knowledge and mimics the structure of God's creation.[4] I focus on what treatise writers and painters understood were the conditions that allowed for the transmission of sacred knowledge – rational *and* mysterious – through the holy image. The early Church and medieval theological tradition, which led to the Council of Trent's prescriptions regarding the representational status and veneration of images, provides the necessary ground for this task. From a social and materialist perspective, I am interested in how Carducho (1576/8–1638), Francisco Pacheco (1564–1644), and Jusepe Martínez (1602–82) – three of the most important art theorists in early modern Spain – deploy these same theological tenets in the advancement of the status of the painter as a liberal artist, a rank that has tangible professional, economic, and social consequences.[5] These dual claims – painting as a sacred medium and painting as a liberal art – do not explain the fascination with and deployment of the Immaculate Conception, either as doctrine or as image. However, the juncture of the two provides fertile ground for the examination of the notable production of Immaculate Conception paintings by some of the most celebrated artists in Spain, including Velázquez, Zurbarán, and Murillo, amongst countless others. Moreover, and no less importantly, this detour to art treatises and an examination of their intersections with theological thought and discourse – most especially when they address the dialectical bind between immanence and transcendence, or perhaps even more so the opening to the transcendent through the immanent image or text – provides a conceptual framework not only for the paintings that I examine in chapter 4 but also for the examination of women-authored texts that I offer as a conclusion to this book in chapter 5.

I. The Representational Status of the Image; or the Logic of the Painting as Sacred Medium

The theological background for Carducho's declaration cited above has a complicated history that spans from Byzantine iconoclasm to the prescriptions set by the Council of Trent. Even though the purpose of this section is not to retell that history, its central concerns are fundamental to the arguments that Carducho, Pacheco, and Martínez provide in order to elevate their status as painters; and, just as importantly, to how during the Spanish Counter-Reformation the function and potentiality of the sacred image (visual and textual) were understood and deployed. The representational condition of the image and, therefore, the relationship of art to the sacred were the central concerns of the vehement icon/idol disputes of the seventh and eighth centuries. Were images to be interpreted as icons that represented/pointed towards/recalled the Divine for the viewer? Or did images pretend to substitute the Divine itself in the mind's eye of the viewer?[6] Certainly, the ability of the image as copy to ignite the viewer's memory and promote exemplarity through the visual depiction of a scriptural or hagiographic narrative underlies the didactic function of sacred art. If this were the only claim made on behalf of religious art, the history of the holy image would be less contentious. But it is clear that, from the early Church to the early modern period, the image was thought of and experienced beyond its capacity as a mnemonic device. As noted by Juan Luis González García, religious images performed instead as "painted sermons" in a visual space that blurred the firm boundaries between the reality depicted in the pictorial plane and the reality perceived as sacred by viewers within churches and private chapels (364).

The councillors in Nicaea, despite the accusations of idolatry that they withstood, also insisted on the relationship of the image to the holy as one based on resemblances and revelation. Religious painting and sculpture (material objects created by human hands) in themselves are not sacred and thus can only be venerated. Nonetheless, adoration is precisely what makes possible a higher level of worship of the holy being or divine substance that is communicated by, and yet transcends, the image. In other words, the image allows the believer to find his/her way – beyond the rational and narrativizable – to the sacred: "Indeed, the honor paid to an image traverses it, reaching the model, and he who venerates the image, venerates the person represented in that image."[7] The holy mystery is predicated, in fact, on the assumption that images (we as humans, the objects of the natural world, the cosmos itself) "resemble" (in a Foucauldian sense) the ineffable in ways that are not evident or even demonstrable, and yet are constitutive to existence. The conditions, implications, and effect of this similitude will prove fundamental to the discussion of the Spanish Counter-Reformation art treatises I present in the following section.

But first, it is important to trace further the history of the representational claims leading up to the Council of Trent and the aesthetic culture of the Spanish Counter-Reformation. The potential of the image to embody – remind us of but also stand in for the Divine to which it refers and which it simultaneously and necessarily replaces – finds its theological reasoning in the incarnation of Christ, the impenetrable mystery of God transformed into and thereby represented in human form, i.e., as an image. Christ, in his limited corporal materiality, denotes a perfect, infinite, and ultimately unknowable divinity. The body of Christ as an image (its limited sensuous materiality performing as a representation of the Divine) showcases the figurative mechanism of all sacred images. Holy images, in general, are thus proper and necessary, precisely because God as Christ, in his manifestation as a human form, is Image.

The relationship of the image to the Incarnation was drawn upon by John of Damascus in his "Apologia against Those Who Decry Holy Images" and would continue to serve as an important referent all through the Council of Trent.[8] As the title of his apology indicates, Damascus defends the production and consumption of holy images because they are conducive to worship and divine knowledge. Despite his initial claim regarding the unavoidable difference between the model and the copy – "The image is one thing, the person represented another" – Damascus also posits that the image contains "in itself the person who is imagined." This "in itself," as noted by Michał Paweł Markowski, complicates Damascus's position, since it seems to point towards a loss of transitivity to what is beyond (transcendence), "given that the image now shows what it represents 'in itself,'" a claim which could potentially lead to the threat of idolatry on the one hand and to a fissure of representation from any referent (as we think of in our present modern context) on the other (68). Despite this impasse, Damascus's proposition regarding the status of the image offers a clear trajectory for what the Council of Trent and Spanish Counter-Reformation art treatise writers would, ten centuries later, reiterate and refine:

> Every image is a revelation and representation of something hidden. For instance, man has not a clear knowledge of what is invisible, the spirit being veiled to the body, nor of future things, nor of things apart and distant, because he is circumscribed by place and time. The image was devised for

greater knowledge, and for the manifestation and popularizing of secret things, as a pure benefit and help to salvation, so that by showing things and making them known, we may arrive at the hidden ones, desire and emulate what is good, shun and hate what is evil. ("Apologia")

The desired outcome of the representation of the holy is to impart knowledge not bound to the descriptive or empirical, but which extends to a recognition of the mystery of divinity – so that "we may arrive at the hidden ones" – even though it resists interpretation. The power of the image for Damascus lies precisely in its "manifestation and popularizing" of the divine mystery.

Medieval theologians continued to reflect upon the coordinates of these principles in an attempt to resolve the dialectical tension between the transitive representational capacity of the image and the danger of having the image supersede "in itself" – or in the mind of the believer – the sacred referent; more precisely, the slippage of the icon into idol. Following the same framework that I touched upon in the Introduction regarding the function of the imagination, Bonaventure, in his *On the Reduction of Arts to Theology*, insists on the continuity between Creator and creation, since we live in a world "that bears at least the vestiges (foot-prints) of God, and at some levels even the image and the similitude of God" (11).[9] The possibility of a comparison between God and the artist is thus conceivable for Bonaventure, since all images created – by God and by humans – contain similitudes that emanate in order to bring us closer to the Supreme Mind, even if they only partially "reflect the mystery of the Divine" (25). In his remarks on the Incarnation, Bonaventure echoes the idea that God's most perfect image is Christ: "[U]nderstand that from the Supreme Mind, which can be known by the inner senses of our mind, from all eternity has emanated a Similitude, and Image, and an Offspring ... Through Him all our minds are led back to God when, through faith, we receive the Similitude of the Father into our hearts" (47). Like God, who creates the perfect image of his Son, the artist produces artefacts that, when illuminated by divine wisdom – Bonaventure proposes that we measure the illumination by "the skill of the artist, the quality of the effect produced, and the usefulness of the product that results" – can make manifest three truths: "the generation and incarnation of the Word, the pattern of human life, and the union of the soul with God" (49). In the sensual experience of finite beauty as found in art and the forms it reproduces, we experience the mystery of God's infinite Beauty. For Bonaventure, art does not exclusively function at the level of the senses, bereft of intellectual cognition. As the title of the treatise states, art is "reduced" (i.e., treated analytically) to a form of theology, and the artist is, in his analysis and under the right conditions, akin to a theologian.[10] The role of painter as theologian is connected to the double nature of the image as an instructional device and as a vehicle to the sacred. This is a point to which I will return.

Aquinas's *Summa Theologica* is often cited as the principal theological reference for issues regarding the representational status of the image in the early modern Catholic context: a simulacrum for what can only be truly seen through faith and grace (Marcia B. Hall, *Sacred Image* 1). The schematization of aesthetics (the perception of beauty, the correlation between things and the idea of things, between beauty and pleasure, etc.) in Aquinas's writings is exceptionally complex, as Umberto Eco has proven.[11] If we limit ourselves solely to the potentiality of the image, the general terms of the discussion revolve once more around the nature of representation vis-à-vis what it refers to beyond itself. In response to whether images of Christ should be adored to the degree of *latria* (adoration reserved only for the holy Trinity), Aquinas offers a description of the viewer's approach to the Image (i.e., Christ) as a double movement, one towards the thing as image and one towards the Thing as driving referent:

> As the Philosopher [Aristotle] says, there is a twofold movement of the mind towards an image: one indeed towards the image itself as a certain thing; another, towards the image in so far as it is the image of something else. And between these movements there is this difference; that the former, by which one is moved towards an image as a certain thing, is different from the movement towards the thing: whereas the latter movement, which is towards the image as an image, is one and the same as that which is towards the thing. Thus, therefore, we must say that no reverence is shown to Christ's image, as a thing – for instance, carved or painted wood: because reverence is not due save to a rational creature. It follows therefore that reverence should be shown to it, in so far only as it is an image. Consequently, the same reverence should be shown to Christ's image as to Christ Himself. Since, therefore, Christ is adored with the adoration of "latria," it follows that His image should be adored with the adoration of "latria." (*Summa Theologica*, part III, q. 25, art. 3)

Following his logic, holy images are seen only to be unseen in favour of their divine referent. For Aquinas the image is not a vessel "in itself" of the Divine (Damascus) or a contiguous emanation of Beauty (Bonaventure), but rather a sign whose sensuous materiality (via the cognitive process) signifies for the faithful, beyond its surface, the sacred. The movement towards the image is analogous to the movement towards God, and the material image becomes a site where transcendence shows itself and is revealed through the image/imaginary process. Aquinas applies the same signifying structure when speaking about sacraments or physical objects of this world that acquire a sanctified status: "[A] thing may be called a 'sacrament,' either from having a certain hidden sanctity, and in this sense a sacrament is a 'sacred secret'; or from having some relationship to this sanctity, which relationship may be that of a cause, or of a sign or of any other relation" (*Summa Theologica*, part III, q. 60, art. 1). To the question "Whether every sign of a holy thing is a sacrament?" Aquinas accordingly replies, "Signs are given to men, to whom it is proper to discover the unknown by means of the known. Consequently, a sacrament properly so called is that which is the sign of some sacred thing pertaining to man; so that properly speaking a sacrament, as considered by us now, is defined as being the sign of a holy thing so far as it makes men holy" (*Summa Theologica*, part III, q. 60, art. 2). The holy image calls attention to its transitivity, showcasing its sacramental power to reveal through what is familiar ("by means of the known") that which exceeds it. The image has no self beyond its function as a sign; and yet, it is through the holy image that man can be made holy.

The early modern Catholic Church continued to deliberate the double nature of the image (as variably found in Damascus, Bonaventure, and Aquinas) and, in the face of the Protestant Reformation, attempted to succinctly define its potential and function in clear, practical terms: didactic and contemplative. Not surprisingly, the value of an image, or more precisely its representational capacity, was determined in the context of the Counter-Reformation by its ability to visually impart the teachings of the Church (scriptural and hagiographic narratives and holy events) and simultaneously move the viewer towards a spiritual reckoning with the mysteries of the Divine. If the labour of painting was susceptible to changing techniques, recent discoveries in other fields, such as mathematics or astronomy, and evolving tastes and styles (topics treated amply in the Italian and Spanish art treatises), the nature and effect of holy images needed to be (hopefully finally) secured. This imperative became officially systemized in the Second Decree of the final session of the Council of Trent in 1563 titled "On the invocation, veneration, and relics of Saints, and on sacred Images," where the criteria for the veneration and censorship of sacred images were reaffirmed. After declaring that the honouring and veneration of images was necessary, the Second Decree states the following:

Moreover, that the images of Christ, of the Virgin Mother of God, and of the other saints, are to be had and retained particularly in temples, and that due honour and veneration are to be given them; not that any divinity, or virtue, is believed to be in them, on account of which they are to be worshipped; or that anything is to be asked of them; or, that trust is to be reposed in images, as was of old done by the Gentiles who placed their hope in idols; but because the honour which is shown them is referred to the prototypes which those images represent; in such wise that by the images which we kiss, and before which we uncover the head, and prostrate ourselves, we adore Christ; and we venerate the saints, whose similitude they bear: as, by the decrees of Councils, and especially of the second Synod of Nicaea, has been defined against the opponents of images. (Schroeder 219)

Following Aquinas and responding to the accusations of heresy and idolatry launched by the Protestants, the Second Decree insists upon the image as a conduit for the veneration of the sacred, as a "prototype," denying the image any direct surrogacy for the Divine: "not that any divinity, or virtue, is believed to be in them." The image's function is to instruct and to move the spirit, "so that they [people] may give God thanks for those things; may order their own lives and manners in imitation of the saints; and may be excited to adore and love God, and to cultivate piety" (Schroeder 219). For by "the histories of the mysteries of our Redemption, portrayed by paintings or other representations, the people is instructed, and confirmed in (the habit of) remembering, and continually revolving in mind the articles of faith" (Schroeder 219). The councillors at Trent explicitly deny the image status on its own terms and stress its dependency on the prototype. The task for the image is, nonetheless, not small. The double function to instruct and move the spirit, even if apparently straightforward, is enmeshed with difficult questions that include the selection of narrative elements to be represented and obviated; the ways in which the faithful need to simultaneously be moved by the image and yet remain cognizant of the empty materiality of the image as thing; the porous frontier between the copy and the prototype; and the desire for and simultaneous apprehension produced by the individual's access to the Divine.

We should note, additionally, that the Council speaks to the veneration of relics (parts of bodies or objects that share a sacred substance – both material and spiritual – with a sanctified or holy being) in the same article as sacred images. In doing so, the Council theorizes sacred images as structurally similar to relics. But how are they so, beyond their apparent correlation as loci for the veneration of the sacred? One potential link is to understand relics and images as synecdoche, with an emphasis on two different aspects of this figure of speech. Regarding relics, it is clear that the focus is on contiguity. In other words, the relic is a part of a sacred whole through which the faithful may receive the benefits bestowed by the whole: "through which (bodies) many benefits are bestowed by God on men" (Schroeder 219). As it pertains to images, the synecdochical relationship is instead closer to the etymological origin of the concept, the Greek *sunekdokhē*, which translates as "receiving together or jointly" or, more refined, as "simultaneous understanding" (Roberts 550). Thus interpreted, the image allows the person who venerates to concurrently understand the immanent scriptural teaching and the transcendent mystery through the eyes of the soul. As noted by Stuart Clark, "While external vision, like all sense perception, was limited, fallible, and uncertain, internal vision might 'see' fully and perfectly and thus compensate for these defects – grasping, for example, what was miraculous about the Eucharist: the real presence of Christ. The evidence of the eyes and the testimony of faith were thus not in conflict after all" (185).[12] From this viewpoint, the Eucharist, relics, and holy images participate in the Whole (refer to it, recall it, shed light on it, manifest it) through a mechanism of belief whose rational and spiritual operations are not as tidy and easy to demarcate as the councillors at Trent may have wished.

Upon first consideration, it may seem that, even if Trent had once more confirmed the importance of images as legitimate objects of veneration and catechism, its prescriptions also limited the ability of painters to act independently and creatively. The final admonition found in the Second Decree famously addresses the issue of decorum, the placement of images, and the direct role of the Church hierarchy in overseeing artistic practices: "[I]f any doubtful or grave abuse is to be eradicated, or if indeed any graver question concerning these matters should arise, the bishop, before he settles the controversy, shall await the decision of the metropolitan and of the bishops of the province in a provincial synod" (Schroeder 220). Reacting to the threat of the Protestant condemnation of images, but also to the new emphasis the reformed orders placed on the significance of individual devotion (within the tradition of the *devotio moderna*) and to the persistence of popular belief, the councillors felt it necessary to include a system of surveillance for the production of sacred images.[13] In theory, painters would strictly adhere to the dictates of clergymen, who alone prescribed the limits of how the sacred could be represented. In practice, nevertheless, by assigning the responsibility to ecclesiastics who had no clear directives coming from Rome and no jurisdiction officially adjudicated to any religious or legal body, enforcement was irregular at best. Paolo Prodi clarifies this point: "The way bishops applied the Tridentine decree could vary widely from place to place. The bishops themselves were individuals, and ... decisions to commission works of sacred art, might come from a variety of sources, including religious orders and confraternities. The degree to which there was cultivated discourse about the theory and practice of art in local circles was another significant variable" (13). Consequently, artists and patrons inevitably "negotiated," through responses and compromises, the limits of representionality stipulated by Trent (Marcia B. Hall, *The Sensuous*, Introduction 4). Marcia B. Hall concludes, hence, that "the challenge for artists and patrons was how to implement it [the Tridentine decree]. In the wake of the decree, it was the treatise writers who spelled out how sacred images should be reformed" (*The Sensuous*, Introduction 11). Moreover, the councillors at Trent did not issue an extensively developed analysis of the theological and philosophical principles summarized above; in fact, the Second Decree was composed and included at the last minute on the last session held by the Council. As a result, there was plenty of room for treatise writers and artists to navigate the bounds of what it meant, in a post-Trent milieu, to produce sacred images. In Counter-Reformation Spain, for example, Aquinas's sacramental attribution to the image proved fundamental to the theoretical conception and popular reception of religious art, including the innumerable images of the Virgin of the Immaculate Conception, as signs that lead to transcendence and revelation.

This is the religious, social, and textual space through which the treatises of Carducho, Pacheco, and Martínez must be considered. Beyond examining technical examples and necessary skill sets, these writers took it upon themselves to highlight the importance of painting and painters for religious conversion, instruction, and the deepening of faith; an artistic venture that activated the two types of vision (outer and inner) necessary for spiritual enlightenment. Their hope was to advance and secure the position of painters as liberal artists. As I will now show, they do so by invoking the connection between the painting, the painter, and the sacred, echoing the medieval theological corpus I have here described, embracing the image as a privileged site where the religious imagination intimately led to the transcendental Divine.

II. *Deus Pictor*: Theology and the Defence of Painting as a Liberal Art

Typically, theological deliberations around the status of the image are studied as distinct from socio-historical investigations on the assignation of painters as craftsmen or artists, the development of art academies, and the evolution of the system of patronage. In other words, the aesthetic issues central to the theological discourse I discussed above are often divorced from the artistic, professional, social, and economic conditions in which artists found themselves. For example, Marcia B. Hall's *The Sacred Image in the Age of Art* structures its analysis around the "conflict" between the religious mission of the post-Tridentine Church and the secular calling of the artist: "For the Church these images were spurs to devotion; for the artists, and for more sophisticated patrons, they were works of art" (*The Sacred Image in the Age of Art* 21). Even though Hall's objective is precisely to complicate the effects of this conflict by examining how "it was possible to make a truly creative response to the new conditions imposed by Trent – calling this possibility a 'miracle' – the assumption remains that theology and art were perpetually at odds" (*The Sacred Image in the Age of Art* 6). I approach this topic from the opposite perspective: given the concepts presented in the previous section, I consider the way in which treatise writers and painters defined their artistic practice through the discourse of theological aesthetics and how they saw their work as tied to the representational capacity of the image in its sacramental relation to the Divine.

One manner of pursuing this line of thinking is to examine the juncture between theology and an additional set of preoccupations for treatise writers and artists: the status of painting as a liberal art and by extension of painters as thinkers and translators of knowledge, rather than as mere artisans. Or, as Umberto Eco states concerning medieval Latin civilization, "to establish how the theories current at the time (Scholastic philosophy) were related to its actual sensibility and its actual artistic products ... and whether, and how, theory was a stimulus and orientation for artistic experience and practice" (*Art and Beauty* 1). The "field of forces" (loosely borrowing Pierre Bourdieu's term) that touches upon these two aspects (theory and artistic experience/practice) is expansive and, in late sixteenth- and seventeenth-century Spain, includes court politics, the *Cortes* and its taxation schemes, the patronage system, both secular and religious, the status of guilds vis-à-vis the rising presence of artists' academies, and the social and religious climate created, or at least supported, by a Counter-Reformation mentality.[14] Within this ideologically populated field, religious prescriptions on painting as a theological, didactic, and contemplative medium provide painters and treatise writers, especially in post-Tridentine Spain, an avenue through which to justify and promote their claims as liberal artists.[15] I would like to go further along these lines and examine in more detail the specific strategies deployed in the definition of religious painting as a way of knowing (theology) and as a truth-bearing medium (contemplation) for the Divine, within the context of Spanish treatises and their investment in the elevation of painting from craft to art. More to the point, I am interested in how the intersections between the material and the spiritual, as well as the relationship of the artist to the image and of the image to the viewer, are framed in the Spanish treatise tradition as evidence for the resemblances and continuities that unify the human and the Divine, and by correlation the artist and the *Deus Pictor*.

Still, my aim is not solely to suggest that treatise writers deployed theological aesthetic theories in favour of what ultimately were personal interests, i.e., to be considered liberal artists and thus exempted from the financial obligations imposed on craftsmen. There is a second vector to this account around how treatise writers and painters showcase what Victor I. Stoichita has called the "phatic function" of religious art, "where 'contact' is established between the spectator-believer and the theophany" (22), or "the communication between mystical imaginary and artistic imaginary" (48). Painters as believers in and spectators of the divine mystery reproduce through their religious imagination and human skill the image that allows others to experience the holy. It is in this sense that we can best understand their positioning as theologians. The painter translates the sacred into visual form, systematically (through his/her artistic choices) producing a material object that gives itself up to the spiritual realm and its accompanying revelatory enlightenment. It is precisely for this reason that painters vie for status as liberal artists and why creative artistic genius, with its exceptional ability to open the sensible world to a sacred excess, is pivotal to the theological enterprise of painting.

Jean-Luc Marion has theorized precisely this aperture through what he names "saturated phenomena," objects that contain an excess that can be understood only as revelation, with painting considered a well-vested medium. If traditional phenomenology has largely insisted on the requirement that objects obtain their status as objects only when they make themselves fully "visible" (i.e., when submitted to the principle of reason), Marion dwells on how subjects can access phenomenologically the "invisible," that which cannot be proffered to reason:

> The saturated phenomenon must not be understood as a limit case, an exceptional, vaguely irrational ... case of phenomenality. On the contrary, it indicates the coherent and conceptual fulfillment of the most operative definition of the phenomenon: it alone truly appears as itself, of itself, and starting from itself, since it alone appears without the limits of a horizon and without reduction to an I. I will, therefore, call this appearance that is purely of itself and starting from itself, this phenomenon that does not

subject its possibility to any preliminary determination, a "revelation." And I insist that here it is purely and simply a matter of the phenomenon taken in its fullest meaning. (*The Visible and the Revealed* 45–6)

Speaking to the saturated phenomenon in its capacity to communicate truth beyond the I's limited horizon, and using Augustine and John of the Cross as his framing references, Marion privileges an excess that "turns its light upon" and counteracts the truth of "the one whom it affects":

> Here, where the truth concerns the unveiling not of a common-law phenomenon (one that is objectifiable within the limits of my finitude) but of a saturated phenomenon, one has to pass from *veritas lucens*, the truth that shows and demonstrates in a straightforward fashion, to a *veritas redarguens*, a truth that shows only inasmuch as it remonstrates [remontre] with the one who receives it ... This text does not concern the demand to love the truth already seen or even the requirement to love the truth in order to see it. Rather, it concerns loving the truth so as to bear it ... (*The Visible and the Revealed* 140–1)

Painting enjoys a distinct status as spectacle precisely because our relationship with it depends on one of the senses, which for Marion is an important determinant in our experience of a saturated phenomenon. Visibility is not easily contained or exhausted, given that, "due to excess of intuition [versus intention or signification], [the painting] cannot be constituted but still can be looked at" (*The Visible and the Revealed* 47); neither the "successive looks" of a single witness nor the "combined capacity of all who come before it" can dissipate its excess or revelatory facility (Horner 126).[16] A painting thus gives itself to be seen as a saturated phenomenon: "The excellence of phenomenality of the painting ... therefore always surpasses a particular moment of contemplation, a particular empirical look borne on it. The intensity it deploys would demand an almost indefinite succession of looks of which each would do justice to any radiance of the painting and would receive the effect (rather than the emotion) that results from it" (Marion, *In Excess* 71).

Marion's thinking on the status of the saturated phenomenon has seen an evolution from theology to strict philosophical phenomenology, and the examples he offers in his later work are almost exclusively of abstract expressionist and cubist painting. Nonetheless, for our purposes, Marion offers a parallel perspective on the connection between the image, the status of the painter, and the sacred. The critic's conceptualization of the saturated relationship between painting and viewer allows us to conceive better how the *pintor cristiano* of the Spanish Counter-Reformation could have understood his practice as one pregnant with a sacred excess that was made "visible" and yet beyond the full understanding of the faithful viewer or witness. Additionally, on the subject of painters, Marion advances an account of the artist as a genius who bears "the impact of the given revealing itself" (*In Excess* 52). Early modern art treatise writers sought to be thought of as liberal artists and painter theologians; Marion, in a parallel fashion, elevates the status of the painter to that of "king" in his/her ability to produce a visibility of saturated excess:

> The painter is king, as much and certainly more immediately than any philosopher, and none of our kings ignored it. The painting offers us a saturated phenomenon – but it saturates as well all the natural visibles that our look imagines it sees by itself, although in fact it only sees something there starting from a painting and in the frame ... (*In Excess* 70)

The arguments in favour of painting as a liberal art in the early modern period were equally motivated by the economic and social interests of its practitioners. In Spain, as in the rest of Europe, painters sought equal cultural and social recognition to their literary counterparts. Karin Hellwig, whose *La literatura artística española del siglo XVII* is the most exhaustive account of all the Spanish documents (treatises, *folletos*, *memoriales*, depositions) in defence of painting as a liberal art, notes,

> The group of works that is concerned exclusively with the foundation of painting's status as a liberal art is particularly well represented in seventeenth-century Spain. These texts are written mainly in Madrid's court milieu, in which the painters showed a greater concern than in other cities for the social revaluation of their work. The texts were the result of events in which artists did not feel that they were treated according to their status as people who practised a liberal art.[17]

As a matter of station, but also of social and economic necessity, artists asked to be exempt from taxation, both the *alcábala* (sales tax) and the annual *servicios* (emergency tax), as well as the burden of military levies or *repartimientos*. The history of litigation around taxation is telling specifically insofar as it was organized around the claim that painters, as liberal artists, had to be exempt. Mary Crawford Volk explains how, despite the many petitions and rationalizations for the recategorization of painters, success was at best modest:

> When the *Consejo de Hacienda* ruled in 1633 in favor of tax exemption for painters, it granted freedom from the ruthless sales tax, the *alcábala*. This legal victory can hardly be overestimated in the artists' striving for

recognition as practitioners of a liberal art, since the *alcábala* identified its constituents as members of the mercantile class. But although the *alcábala* was administered through the guild system, it was entirely separate revenue from the annual *servicios*, or emergency taxes, which were imposed in connection with the military levies. In short, the successful litigation pursued by the painters in 1628–1633, though a significant advance, did not remove them from liability to guildsmen's conscription. (83)

When obligated to either serve in the military or pay an emergency tax instead, guilds and their members found themselves trapped between abandoning their source of income and paying away much of their profits.[18] Even painters of the stature of Diego de Velázquez, despite their position of privilege and contact with the highest echelons of society, found themselves bound by the civic responsibilities required from ordinary members of the painters' guild. As Volk documents regarding Velázquez's specific case, "Indeed, [his] ... success and favor at court seem only to have increased his liability: his assessment of 150 reales in the levy of 1641, for example, was higher than that of any other painter in the capital" (84). Despite religious images serving Counter-Reformation ideology, painters remained bound to a guild system – grouped with sculptors, potters, carpenters, and other craftsmen – diminishing their ability to climb in social rank, their economic standing, and their freedom from conscription.[19]

The defence of the painter as a liberal artist finds one of its earliest formal proponents in Italy's Leon Battista Alberti's *On Painting* [*Della pittura*], a seminal theory of art recognized for its systematic description of the mechanics and pleasurable effects of one-point perspective construction.[20] As a logical extension of the elevation of these new techniques, Alberti argued for an equal standing of painters with poets, a logic stemming from the humanist recovery and reinterpretation via Simonides, Aristotle, and Horace of the notion of *ut pictura poesis*: painting, as poetry, deserved careful examination in its imitation of human nature in its noblest forms.[21] Yet, as Carroll W. Westfall notes, Alberti's claim goes beyond simple comparisons between the sister arts and is rooted in the fundamental requirement for any liberal art:

A liberal art was a theoretical and systematic method for acquiring and conveying knowledge; God's revelation was the proper source of that knowledge. In producing an *istoria* a painter is not investigating a source of knowledge but is conveying knowledge he has discovered. Alberti therefore emphasized first the investigation and then the production that conveys the discovered truths. (495)

The overall design of *On Painting* focuses on a reformulation of perspective from conical to planar projections; in other words, on how to interpret and translate mathematical and optical knowledge to the picture plane. However, the core of the treatise reproduces a theological premise that two centuries later the Spanish treatise writers, in a Counter-Reformation context, would summon in their own attempts to secure the place of painting as liberal art: the painter translates the Divine within the visible realm conveying and, as in Marion's formulation, revealing through the image sacramental knowledge that would otherwise remain invisible. It is at that juncture that the intellectual/theological import of painting and the economic/social interests of painters need to be jointly understood as responding to and congruent with the promotion of painting and of the painter above the level of craft.

Moreover, opposite to what has been typically assumed, the outcome of the Tridentine injunction structurally facilitates both the religious and the secular rationale for painting as a liberal art. Gabrielle Paleotti – councillor to the papal legates in the final phase of Trent – in his *Discourse on Sacred and Profane Images* offers a textbook example of the representational logic after 1563. Cognizant of the significance of the image (both historically and theoretically), Paleotti ends his treatise with an address to painters as "mute theologians": "[W]e said that just as orators have it as their office to delight, teach, and move, so painters of sacred images, who are like mute theologians, must do the same, and that pictures will be more or less perfect to the degree they approach this mark" (309). This "mark" can only be achieved by "design" (as it regards artistic skill) and "true knowledge of the things to be imitated," which in turn has two principal results: "stimulate the senses and excite spirituality and devotion" (310). What is formulated is an instructional injunction that requires the painter to decode, analyse, and interpret for the viewer the essential knowledge needed from a biblical or hagiographic account. The painter is thus ascribed a role as exegete of sacred texts so as to render them intelligible in visual form, an intellectual practice that underpins the claims for an elevated artistic state. His analytical and spiritual capacity offers the faithful a way to comprehend *and* sense in visual form the narratives and mysteries of their faith, and religious painters understood themselves as working in this double domain. To this point, John W. O'Malley has remarked how "sense knowledge" was assimilated by Counter-Reformation theology and aesthetics, following Aquinas's declaration *"Nihil in intellectu quod non prius in sensibus* – there is nothing in the intellect that is not ultimately dependent of sense knowledge" ("Trent, Sacred Images, and the Catholics' Sense of the Sensuous" 41).[22] Moreover, images had been confirmed by the councillors at Trent as necessary and proper vehicles for devotion and veneration, separating the true Church from Protestant heresy. Thus identified, the figure of the painter as theologian (as one who possessed the faculties to rationally study, interpret, and contemplate the mysteries of the sacred texts) gave ample ground to treatise writers and painters to advance the case for painting as a liberal art.

On the side of contemplation – "exciting spirituality and devotion" – the painter taps into qualities of the sacred that cannot be elucidated through words, and which lead to or intimate a realm that cannot be explained in purely rational terms. The desired effect is for the viewer to experience the Divine, or to get as close as possible to the Divine, while still bearing sin. This potentiality in the visual form was validated by theologians such as Alvise Lippomano, who, as a councillor in the 1540s at Trent, declared that through the religious image the faithful are led "from the visible to the invisible" (qtd in Barbieri 211).[23] It is in this respect that painting can be understood to move the emotions, and positions the painter in the realm of revelation as one who makes available through faith and grace the experience of the invisible and inscrutable. Unlike the visual-sensuous knowledge that facilitates the didactic function of painting, contemplation allows for a super-sensuous intuition of the sacred. At this point, we are also entering the terrain of apophatic theology and expression, since what comes across in the contemplation elicited by a painting is precisely that which cannot be said or known directly, and yet is expressed even if not positively articulated.[24] As explained by William Franke, in the Thomistic tradition God is a Cause that transcends all Being, yet at the same time beings participate (as causes) in the substance of God (17). The contemplative experience in the apophatic register is thus defined as a movement between a divine transcendence that cannot be breached and a coextensive experience of/participation in the unknowable or invisible Divine. Painters of sacred images can indeed claim a space for their work in this interstice between the materiality of the canvas and the correlative, contemplative, "saturated" experience of the holy, and for themselves as privileged facilitators of this aperture to the experience of the unknowable Divine.

There is an additional conceptual factor that is fundamental to an understanding of scriptural interpretation in a Counter-Reformation context: the four senses of scriptural hermeneutics defined by the medieval theologians as literal, tropological (i.e., moral), allegorical, and anagogical. This system allowed multiple simultaneous interpretations of the Scriptures based on the premise that the sacred text was a repository of the Divine, which could only be approximated

via multiple pathways of exegesis and contemplation, i.e., an understanding of the Scriptures as containing revelation. Initially concretized
by Hugh of St Victor in the early twelfth century, the methodology was
highly debated amongst theologians and saw many variants that were
generally précised as follows:

> To be sure there are many insights revealed in many different ways,
> when the sword that is the word transfixes the soul ... In the first place,
> the examples shown by the saints are communicated when it strikes, and
> it transfixes the soul with history. Secondly, the truth of the faith is re-
> vealed, and it touches the soul with allegory. Thirdly, morals are built
> up, and it strikes the soul with tropology. Fourthly, the joys of heaven are
> revealed, and the soul is sweetly smitten by anagogy. (Adam Scotus, qtd
> in Lubac 100–1)

The anagogical, which is what most interests me here, is thus associated
with the knowledge acquired through contemplation, "which leads the
soul upward" (Robert Poulain, qtd in Lubac 102). Or, as proposed by
Hugh of St Victor, a movement from the visible to the invisible: "Simple
allegory is when the visible fact signifies another invisible fact. Anagogy is a certain leading upward, when an invisible fact is indicated
by another invisible fact."[25] Despite a venerable lineage that included
Church fathers such as Augustine, Origen, Jerome, and Aquinas, the
potential pitfalls of this hermeneutical system were singled out by
the Protestants (including Luther), who feared multiple, partisan, and
opportune interpretations.[26] As explained by Henri de Lubac, Catholic
theologians predictably rejected this criticism, calling on the truth that
"sprung from Tradition that is Divine itself" (9). We can easily see how
this hermeneutical system is contained within the idea of the painter-theologian who explores the possibilities found in a pictorial, narrative, iconic, and symbolic interpretation of sacred texts unified in the
visual image, as well as by the Catholic audience who is witness to the
saturated object pregnant with concurrent and profound meanings to
be received, apprehended, and contemplated.

In the Tridentine injunction and its rearticulation in art treatises,
the emphasis is placed on the acquisition of interpreted knowledge,
"didactic and contemplative," through the act of looking at paintings;
this act of visual hermeneutics is fashioned, of course, in opposition
to what was perceived as the Protestant rejection of the sacred image,
a heretical stance against which treatise writers situate their defence
of painting as a liberal art. Through the visual sense, art facilitates
intimate knowledge and experience of the invisible Divine through the

eyes of the mind (theology) and the eyes of the soul (contemplation) – a position that intentionally counterbalances the Protestant claim for exclusivity in the realm of spiritual immediacy. Given these coordinates, the painter would not only have to be classified as a liberal artist but, even more significantly, like Saint Luke the Evangelist, as a key figure in the exemplification and defence of the one true Catholic faith. As I will now show, Vicente Carducho, Francisco Pacheco, and Jusepe Martínez follow precisely this logic and frame their discussions in favour of painting as theology. Their propositions have important implications that go well beyond the stature of painting, and allow us to rethink the signifying potential of immaculacy. In other words, any account of the representation of the Immaculate Conception as political, communal, and individual propaganda should also consider what is at stake in terms of the period's theological imagination, the individual's (painter, viewer, writer, reader) visionary experience, and the resulting multilayered construction of individual and communal Catholic selfhood in early modern Spain.

III. Saint Luke Was an Evangelist and a Painter: Spanish Art Treatises and the Theological Stature of Painting

Carducho and his fellow treatise writers were largely invested in the elevation of painting to a liberal art, a task that predictably includes (although not in all three treatises to the same degree) a discussion on what defines painting, on the preparation and skills that painting requires, on the difficulties involved, and on the great practitioners from antiquity to the present who are worthy of imitation. I will here focus on aspects that touch directly upon the concept of art as theology and of the artist as a "mute" theologian.

Carducho's "Seventh Dialogue" ["Diálogo séptimo"], as previously mentioned, delves into the topic of sacred paintings, emphasizing both in its title and its first sections the topic of decorum, mostly focusing on a rather perfunctory discussion of suitable religious topics for specific spaces, such as a convent, the queen's dormitory, and the king's audience hall, among others, as well as on the proper decorum to be followed when painting portraits where social and spiritual hierarchies are to be observed.[27] The debate, for my purposes, becomes more interesting when the Disciple and his Master turn their attention to the status of painting itself, a long exchange that reproduces and develops the idea of the painter as theologian. The initial claims are rather modest, staying close to the customarily assumed ability of the image to inspire and elicit the imitation of virtue, "to motivate the imitation of those virtues with which they were adorned."[28] Still, even in this preliminary argument, the special role of the painter as liberal artist is brought to the fore in that these virtues are essential to, but also exceed, the core narrative or iconographic elements; to be precise, virtues are not simply visually represented but intellectually and spiritually conceived so that they can take their effect on the soul of the viewer and move it to a higher plane. The rest of the "Diálogo séptimo" is, consequently, occupied precisely with the requirements and qualities that allow sacred paintings to be thought of as *Arte*, which, even if it is not explicitly addressed in this manner, includes the notion of images as theology, both exegetical and revealed.

The question of interpretation is key to the entire segment: should the painter faithfully reproduce the biblical or hagiographical elements as (sometimes very sketchily) described in the source texts, or can s/he adjust or add aspects so as to make the image more inviting? Carducho lobbies for the second option. What we would today ascribe to artistic licence is identified as the painter's interpretation of what is essential versus what is accidental (a category drawn from the Aristotelian tradition) to the biblical narrative or sacred event symbolized. For example, the essential core of the redemption story is that Christ died on the cross. The particulars of how the crucifixion is represented, the specifics of the setting, the players included, the number of nails used, etc., have to be evoked by the painter in order to produce a visual text whose composition will instruct and move the viewer. Interestingly, Carducho connects the accidental with the divine mystery, insofar as the painter's choices and interpretation of these added elements open the canvas to the revelation of the sacred mystery in ways that uniquely unveil the devotional potentiality of its referent: "they are considered accidental, with respect to the principal facts and works, and these circumstances can be altered in painting, especially to better achieve their intended purpose, which is to help inspire devotion, reverence, respect, and piety, and declare more than what is expected."[29] In this respect the painter is equated to a translator, who conveys the holy in an immediately identifiable and affective visual language for the viewer, who seeks a spiritual bond:

And not only do I not consider him [the painter] guilty, but I praise him for the prudent act of adorning and explaining the substance of history by adding the circumstances and most fitting, appropriate, and important accidents known [to us today], because of the spiritual nourishment these circumstances and accidents provide and the mysteries they reveal. The [original historical] circumstances and ancient ways are neither practised today nor will they arouse devotion, making it necessary to replace them with others that, although materially different, attempt to be the same, as in language, offering the phrases that are proper to the translated language.[30]

The role of translator-interpreter explicitly links the painter to an elite group of thinkers and spiritual guides who do God's work on earth, the "Preachers and Writers, enhancing and dressing the essence of the story with elegant words and phrases, proper and known, and with momentous examples."[31] The painter, like the preacher, has to make use of rhetorical and interpretative flair in order to reach the desired effect. The comparison is indeed prescient, given, as Fernando Bouza Álvarez explains, the power attributed to the spoken word in the early modern period, both as a rhetorical device and as a vessel for the transmittal of non-material reality:

> The idea that saying something was not far removed from invoking whatever was being named is reflected in the power that people attributed, for example, to curses, blessings, prayers, and incantations ... Because of its expressive power and alleged truthfulness, the spoken word was expected to persuade immediately, making it especially useful for pastoral missions in Spain aimed at moving large audiences. (21–2)[32]

The association made by Carducho is, thus, founded upon the belief in the transcendence assumed by words and images. Like the theologian (from a religious perspective) and the poet or writer (from an artistic one), the painter works upon the essence of the sacred text, enhancing the religious imaginary in the choices made through the aesthetic imaginary. Furthermore, by establishing the artist's ability not only to reproduce but also to better "declare," through the visual image, "what is intended," Carducho makes the two imaginaries one, treating the act of painting as a religious act, as conduit to and revelation of the divine mystery. This leads us to a separate implicit claim in the positioning of the painter: s/he, as theologian artist, has the intellectual and spiritual capacity to perceive and transfer to the canvas the saturated kernel of the sacred mystery or "the substance of the mystery."[33] And it is for this reason that the painter is undeniably an Artist.

As previously mentioned, Carducho systematizes this visual translation of the Divine into three categories: same, similar, and metaphorical. The function of the metaphorical receives the most attention, since it is there that the abstract and the ineffable are brought to the level of the image, and, therefore, where claims regarding the representational status of the image are most risky. The "Diálogo séptimo" approaches the metaphorical as an instrument that renders accessible radical alterity: "and so when one offers to paint a particular thing, in which there is something incompatible with our capacity, and with our understanding, we use that kind of metaphorical painting, to explain and to label our concept."[34] The artist as exegete performs in the field of revelation, offering via metaphor what otherwise had remained ungraspable by and invisible to our limited understanding.[35] Painting is thus termed a "miraculous medium ... that at the same instant shows us and makes us capable of things that, through reading, it was obligatory to spend much time and leaf through many books to learn, given that they were said with a multitude of words, with much erudition and Theology to announce themselves, and very possibly afterward were less understood."[36] The metaphorical translation of the sacred, as executed by a master painter, provides a clear, immediate, and revelatory apprehension of the Divine.[37] It is at this precise point in his argument that the Master reiterates the status of painting as a liberal art. Citing Seneca's definition of *Arte liberal* alongside the ability of decorous paintings to promote virtue and stave off the Devil, he declares: "And if Seneca says that liberal Art has the power to make men virtuous and good, which more than Painting?"[38] The logic is infallible, for how can one be convinced of the sacred nature and power of the decorous image and yet deny it, and its executor, an elevated status?

Up to this point I have not addressed the debate on the differing quality of painters and the, for Carducho, closely related topic of decorum. On the one hand, fearful of accusations of instigating idolatry – in other words, cognizant of the danger of idolizing the material image rather than adoring the sacred referent – Carducho suggests that quality is trivial. Instead, what matters is the content of and what is elicited by the image: "it does not matter that the image for which the prayer is made, or the sacrifice, is made with great skill, or without it; because neither the form nor the material is relevant (but what it represents, and no more), and for this it does not matter if it is done with perfection, or without it."[39] And yet, even though the Master here seemingly favours religious content over considerations regarding the level of artistry, the argument that follows this statement is manifestly partial to "good painting":

One well supposes how effective good painting is, that God shows himself to make sure that his images, and those of his most holy Mother, and of his Saints are such that what they represent is shown with propriety, and similitude ... so as to arouse greater devotion, and move the spirits to the affects of greater fervour, love, and ignited desires so as to act in virtue.[40]

With God's preference made manifest, the association between content and quality is secured. The effects of good painting are said, no less, to have greatly influenced the, by this time, immensely prominent figure of Saint Teresa of Ávila: "Although the painting that was not well made would not cause such effects, nor would the paper image, and because of this the Saint felt quite disillusioned."[41] The Master's conclusion on the matter, despite his initial claim, is to endorse the importance of an elevated style and skill in the painter: "What has been said is enough that one can infer how differently the affects of devotion and disposition are moved by Painting executed with greater perfection than by those painted crudely or in an uncultured manner."[42] Not just any painter but good painters are to make the sacred visible, lead the viewer to it, and keep the devil "at bay with such paintings."[43] Hence, it is also the most accomplished – the ones who truly represent the liberal arts – who are best able to represent the divine mystery both masterfully and within the proper bounds of decorum: "What is owed to this Art, as such mercies and devotions are gained through the images, that in making them miraculous, many times God shows his gratitude for the devout and religious zeal with which they were made, no less than for the careful and scientific hand."[44] Equally moved by the painter's devotion and skill, God responds to the painting and by his grace allows it to be a conduit for the extraordinary, for a revelation that exceeds the limits of human reason and understanding.

The painter-theologian responds to a divine calling that posits as its model a most holy of predecessors, Saint Luke. As the "Diálogo séptimo" draws to an end, the Master vehemently calls on painters to follow in the footsteps of their patron saint:

And it is very true that Saint Luke was an Evangelist, and a Painter, in whom we see indexed all our value, for it seems that God did not want to trust this Art except to someone who had trusted his holy Gospel, and made portraits of our Lady, and of our Lord; and that he [Luke] brought with him these portraits, with which many people were converted, and many miracles occurred; and of this there is nothing to doubt: and so in the whole Church he is recognized and called Painter; and all the Academies hold him as an intermediary, honouring him as Patron of all Art. We imitate him in life, and in our way of painting devoutly: on the outside [his actions], and on the inside [his spirit], for without any doubt, just as he brought in his company those holy painted images, he also held a portrait of the holy Trinity in his soul, contemplating its sovereign attributes, which he sought to copy; as well as [a portrait of] the most pure Queen of the Angels, attempting to imitate her holy virtues.[45]

The painter, like Saint Luke before him, carries within and brings forth the "image" of the Trinity and of the Virgin of the Immaculate Conception, or, recalling Damascus and Bonaventure, a trace of the eternal, that which came before time, the mystery that lies beyond comprehension but is opened, made available, through the sacred and skilled painting. The logic and devotion (reason and spirit) that sustain the Master's arguments are presented as incontestable, and the Disciple, moved and encouraged by his own role in God's plan, closes the "Diálogo séptimo" with a final dictum: "I venerate, and I revere the image: first for what it represents, and then for the brush that painted it with such excellence. God bless you."[46]

Francisco Pacheco – considered a minor painter whose larger claim to fame comes from his apprenticeship to Diego Velázquez, Francisco de Zurbarán, and Alonso Cano – begins to write his *Art of Painting* [*Arte de la pintura*] soon after being appointed Overseer of the Office of Painters [*Veedor del Oficio de Pintores*] in 1616 by the municipal government of Seville and Overseer of Sacred Paintings [*Veedor de Pintura Sagrada*] in 1618 by the Inquisition Tribunal. The work appeared posthumously in 1649 (four years after Pacheco's death), in his lifetime eclipsed by the publication of Carducho's *Diálogos*. During its composition, the project was supported and encouraged by the humanist circle in Seville who included the collector Fernando Enríquez de Ribera, Third Duke de Alcalá, the poet Francisco de Rioja, the antiquarian and collector Rodrigo Caro, the Jesuit man of letters Juan de Pineda, and the painter-poet Juan de Jáuregui.[47] Not unlike his paintings, the *Arte* is often judged as mediocre in its prose and deemed highly derivative.[48] Even in the best of scenarios, the *Arte* is interpreted as subjugated to and aligned with the overbearing pressures imposed within a Counter-Reformation milieu and by the Inquisition: "Pacheco was not uncompromisingly orthodox; his vital reaction in the face of his social environment is manifested in differing levels of compliance with a reality imposed by the religious power and its most representative and repressive element, the Inquisition."[49] What this assessment misses is how the *Arte* brings together four aspects of Pacheco's experience that are pivotal to his (and our) understanding of the painter as theologian and the relationship of this category to the liberal arts: his sensibility as a painter, his experience as the master of his painters' guild, his intellectual training as a humanist, and his official position as a theologian and censor. For Pacheco the "art of painting" was the site where the loftiest spiritual and intellectual knowledge came together and was made manifest by way of the genius of the painter. In a much more concerted manner than Carducho and Paleotti before him, Pacheco offers a comprehensive rationale for the elevated stature of painting as theology and the image's sacramental bond. Along with its purpose as a manual on technique, an iconographical catalogue for painters (following Alberti), and a biographical account of painters' lives (following Giorgio Vasari), the *Arte* traces a path that considerably expands on Trent, presenting art and artifice as privileged manifestations of the holy in the realm of human experience.

The *Arte* commences with a chapter titled "On what painting is and how it is a liberal art, its definition and explanation" ["Qué cosa sea pintura y cómo es arte liberal, y su definición y explicación"], where, as it is immediately evident, Pacheco tackles the topic of the stature of painting head on. Presented in the first person, the main arguments reproduce many of the tenets established by Pacheco's predecessors (Alberti, Vasari, Paleotti, and Carducho included), with mainstays such as the correlation of the painter to God (as they both create images) and Horace's dictum aligning painting with poetry in their shared liberty to interpret and create anew their referents. Reflecting Pacheco's own sensibilities and expertise as a painter and teacher, his definition and defence of painting primarily focus on the science of the practice, the various knowledge sets that have to be mastered in order to produce images akin to those seen in nature and produced by God: "painting is art, for it has as an exemplary objective, and as a rule of its labours, nature itself, always attempting to imitate it in the quantity, relief, and colour of things, and this is done using geometry, arithmetic, perspective, and natural philosophy, with infallible and certain reason."[50] The painter thus imitates God's wise design in nature, for "natural things ... are made by God with supreme wisdom."[51] Of the twelve chapters that follow in book 1, and which are chiefly invested in substantiating the superiority of painting to sculpture (a debate fuelled in Seville by Pacheco's guild's competition with that of the sculptor Juan Martínez Montañés), I will focus on those where painting is framed as a divine practice and as a sacred medium.

Despite its title, "Saints who practised painting, and some marvellous effects that originated from it" ["Santos que ejercitaron la pintura, y de algunos efectos maravillosos procedidos de ella"], chapter 9 first offers an account of noblemen, princes, and kings who not only supported painting but undertook it themselves as a practice; "They were honoured in professing it, and practising it with their hands and preferring it to other liberal arts."[52] The category of "saints who practised painting" is thus widened to include the Habsburg kings, Christ, Saint Augustine, numerous ancient and contemporary religious figures, devout painters such as Albrecht Dürer ("Catholic painter and saint"),[53] the Valencian Juan de Juanes ("he prepared himself for painting by giving confession and taking communion"),[54] and, predictably, Saint Luke. This broad grouping not only secures the privileged position of painters but also makes of Philip II, Philip III, and Philip IV fellow practitioners of a liberal and holy art:

> But this profession's most remarkable greatness is (as I see it) that our Philip II and III (as is the opinion of many) were not without the pleasure and practice of drawing. And from our great monarch [Philip IV], fourth of this name (being a prince), I have a young Saint John the Baptist in the desert, embracing the lamb, from a very elegant and skilful brush, sent to Seville by the great royal adviser, the Count-Duke, in the year 1619.[55]

Admittedly, we can understand this statement as a ploy to exempt painters from taxation and forced conscription. Philip IV (with his father and grandfather before him) is transformed into a masterful creator of sacred images, his position as king-painter refuting any claim that would marginalize this art to a craft. However, there is a second level of interpretation readily available. In a religious and social imaginary where monarchs represented God's will and grace on earth, the king's creative practice reinforces the correlation between the painter and the Divine.

It is this relationship that chapter 9 features with multiple examples that insist not only on the capacity of the religious painting to interpret for the viewer the sacred narratives but also on painting as a bridge between our earthly experience and the spiritual realm, where the image is a site for the miraculous. The most salient example, an apparition of the Virgin, uses Lope de Vega's 1604 *Peregrine in His Homeland* [*Peregrino en su patria*] as its source. According to the *Arte*, a famous painter (Leonardo Da Vinci), while executing his "devout artifice" on the ceiling of a church, finds himself clinging to falling scaffolding and calls out, "Virgin, take a hold of me."[56] The image was only partially drafted, with Mary's face, half her body, and one arm completed, and her second arm, with which she would hold the Christ child, in process. Despite the incomplete pictorial representation, the painter's cry provokes the Virgin's full physical presence:

> The distressed tongue barely uttered these words, when the pious Lady drew her painted arm from the wall, took the painter's, and held it firm. The scaffolding with the vessels and paints came to earth with great noise, so that all those who were there, believing that the ceiling of the chapel was coming down, raised their eyes and saw the Virgin, not yet painted,

with one arm outside the wall, holding the fortunate man, and they cried
out for mercy, praising the mother of all mercy: and with stairs placed,
having lowered the painter to the floor, the image once again tucked in
her arm.[57]

Numerous minefields come to mind, especially the potential risk of
idolatry that examples such as this may encourage. If the image painted
by Leonardo is the Virgin Mary herself – i.e., if the visual *signum* can
be called upon as the holy *res* and the painted hand is in fact the hand
embodied – Trent's admonitions that "not any divinity, or virtue, is
believed to be in them [images], on account of which they are to be
worshipped; or that anything is to be asked of them; or, that trust is to
be reposed in images, as was of old done by the Gentiles who placed
their hope in idols" seem to matter little. Consciously or unconsciously
ignoring the implication of his examples, Pacheco is seduced by the
power of painting and the sacred space that he fervently believes is
unlocked when the devout brush in the hands of a master touches
the canvas. What we find here, therefore, is far from a subjugation of
painting to the assumed prescriptions and limiting injunctions of Trent
and Inquisitorial censors. Instead, the *Arte*'s logic traverses art, artifice
(technique), and the bonding of image and faith. In doing so, Pacheco
temporarily sets aside the didactic function of the image and explores
at length the contiguity between the canvas and the spiritual realm,
proffering the image as the site where visuality functions as revelation
and where the object becomes a saturated phenomenon.

Saint Luke's artistic practice provides an exemplary template for
Pacheco. Admittedly, the patron saint of painters had the benefit of
knowing Christ and Mary firsthand, witnessing in the flesh the image incarnate drawn by God in human form, and of asking the Virgin
directly about "many things regarding the sacred mysteries,"[58] while
copying her countenance in person and with her approval. Luke, as a
theologian would, studies and ponders the conditions of her life and
the mysteries she holds, reproducing them in word and in image. While
some of the images are produced from direct observation – "he watches
and paints her while she is enwrapped in contemplation" – others are
extrapolated: "If he did paint, as it is true, the other images with the
baby Jesus in her arms, it was not because he could make portraits of
Christ in that age of childhood, having him present as he had the Virgin;
but rather in the likeness of the Mother, and from information provided
by her or with particular favour and using the first portrait, he made
other images."[59] The task is to interpret and create, not to mechanically
copy; this is an artistic practice that serves as the highest example for

all painters and that perfectly explains why the images of the Virgin drawn by Saint Luke and spread around Rome are not replicas, one of the other. They depict a holy mystery that, in its unknowability, cannot be captured in or defined by one singular image or representation. The potential crisis of exactitude is, therefore, avoided as a result of Saint Luke's theological/artistic practice. As a painter-theologian, he illuminates differing aspects of Mary's sacred essence in each of the paintings, filtered through divine inspiration and artifice: "illustrating her with such holy artifices."[60]

Reproducing a claim made by many theologians before him, Pacheco finishes this chapter by pointing to creation, our bodies and the entire universe, as the canvas on which God practised his art. For example, quoting Hermes Trismegistus's *Pimander*, Pacheco relates God's creation of man as a "painted" image:[61] "If what you want to investigate [is beings and their] mortal customs, whether those from the earth, or those from the depth of the waters, look, son, at the man made in the womb, and carefully examine the art of this composition; and learn who formed his beautiful and divine image. Who painted the eyes, who opened the noses and ears, who the mouth, who attended to the nerves and bound them."[62] God's *arte* reaches its highest manifestation in Christ's incarnation, with the Son's body positioned as the most sacred of canvases, where the Divine and the material are perfectly indistinguishable: "dressed in our flesh he found it, to exalt the painting, as a wonderful and new way."[63] Through the Incarnation, God comes to us in a form that is wholly unknowable, and yet reproducible. Christ, as a part of the Trinity, is manifested in a human figure wherein the sacred mystery is contained.

Pacheco further focuses his argument by describing the three instances in which Christ offers his image in pictorial form: the Mandylion of Edessa, the Veronica, and the shroud of Turin. The first example is, in my opinion, the most compelling, for it deals directly with the figure of the painter and painting as a sacred practice. In the version of the Mandylion that Pacheco cites, the envoy Ananais is a court painter entrusted to bring Christ to the ailing King Abgar of Edessa.[64] The delivering of Christ to the king may happen in two coextensive forms, either in the flesh – a flesh painted by God – or on a canvas painted by Ananais. When Ananais reaches his destination, the crowd is too large for him to be able to approach his target; instead, he decides to climb a rock and start painting, an act that proves futile, given the blinding light that emanates from Christ's face. Ultimately, Christ (aware of the painter's plight) calls Ananais forth and reads Abgar's letter. Cognizant of the king's faith and need, "he washed his face on the canvas, oh admirable thing which he rinsed in the water, and stamped [on it] his image, [and it was] taken to the king, where great wonders and miracles happened."[65] In this tale, the painter's ability to approximate the sacred is simultaneously denied and confirmed. On the one hand, Christ's divine image cannot be captured and translated onto the canvas by Ananais; its splendour and mystery refuse materialization. On the other, Christ enters the category of painters by imprinting his semblance on Ananais's canvas, an image that will represent and substitute for him in Abgar's eyes and which will cure the king. Pacheco elides this contradiction and, as should be expected, focuses on the manifestation of Christ as painter and on the power of the image to manifest the Divine. It is Christ who creates and admits the miraculous to be contained in the image; but it is also Christ who, through his image making, "authorized and honoured the painting of sacred images with the miraculous events that we have told."[66] Pacheco's intention is to confirm the stature of painting, establishing a confraternity of practitioners that includes all "Catholic painters," Christ the Son, and God the Father (166). Even if not stated directly, the denial of painting as a liberal art and the rights and privileges merited by painters goes against divine design and is sacrilegious; more precisely, to deny Pacheco (and his fellow Catholic painters) their due stature is to go against God himself, and his incarnated Son, as a *Dios Pintor*.

In the following chapter Pacheco shifts the defence of painting as a liberal art to more earthly matters through an appreciation of its nobility and utility, blaming opposing views on ignorance. Pacheco's initial arguments and citations echo those of his predecessors, who cite Horace's comparison of painting to poetry, Aristotle's dictum regarding the didactic capacity of images, and Pliny the Elder's inclusion of painting as one of the arts that serves both active and contemplative philosophy (169). Nonetheless, even in this secular context, Pacheco insists and enthusiastically remarks on the sacred nature of painting, most especially in a Catholic context, where "much more illustriously and excellently can a Christian painter today make works than Apelles or Protogenes."[67] The divine origin of painting secured in the previous chapter, Pacheco asserts that the image achieves its highest nature when its composition is accompanied by charity and the pure intention to serve God (172). The brush and the devotion of the painter become one instrument, and the practice of sacred painting is conceived as charity itself: "not having another, he looks at all the sacred images ... that unite men with God; given the goal of charity, clearly it follows that the practice of forming images was reduced to charity itself, and because of this will be a most worthy and noble virtue."[68] In fact, if measured in regard to the level of utility and good achieved, painting is the most holy of all mediums with all other arts and crafts far inferior, a fact proven by God's proclivity to communicate with us mostly through images (173–4). Moreover, images lend themselves to the taking in of the sacred through the eyes, into our souls, leading to salvation:

> Painting, as divine work, enters through the eyes as through the windows of our soul while it is enclosed in this prison, and represents in us that light in its nature immortal. And so, it penetrates into the most secret part, which makes it ache, rejoice, desire, and fear, according to the variety of things that by good painters are represented in lines and colours ...[69]

Recalling Christian Neoplatonic notions about the relationship between external beauty (matter) and the image (imago/forma) grasped by the soul – which may be conceived as a meeting point between the material and the Divine – Pacheco insists on the contemplative nature of painting and its singular capacity to move the viewer. The description of the experience is similar to that of the mystical encounter; if the visionary sees the holy image revealed by God, the viewer of a painting sees the sacred in the form of lines and colours drawn by the *pintor cristiano*.

Having reached this high point in his presentation, Pacheco returns to a much more schematic defence of painting, transferring Quintilian's rhetorical categories to the origin and continued production of images: need, utility, pleasure, and virtue. Images fill the semantic gaps left by words, bestow visibility on what can otherwise not be seen or imagined, teach, dazzle us with optical illusions, and above all – or because of all these things – offer virtue (175–8). This last benefit is the most important as it validates the proposition of the painter as theologian and liberal artist. Like Plato before him and Augustine after him, Quintilian associated virtue in a text with the "pre-existing state of virtue in the speaker" (Enos 244). Augustine takes this position further by considering inner piety to be tied to the possibility of communicating truth: "In Augustine's *De doctrina* (c. 396), the discussion of ethos focused on the importance of piety in the preacher. Without piety, the preacher cannot interpret the Scriptures; without being able to understand God's word, the preacher cannot explain it to others" (Enos 244). Pacheco's deployment of Quintilian's categories is fundamentally an effort to equate letters to painting as a liberal art. It also fixes the ethos of the good painter as a man of great virtue and as a communicator of truth:

> It remains, as the conclusion of this discourse, the final cause attributed to the origin of painting, which is born of virtue: because it often happens

that men, because of the benefits received or because of the great esteem held for others, feel an ardent desire to make known these noble and just thoughts, and not understanding how to do this in words alone, attempt to join together other more lasting and glorious demonstrations. From this originated many topics of great respect (in their opinion worthy of memory) to form the images and statues in honour of others: manifesting what they had conceived in their spirit ... As it was a way to honour the sovereign Lord in his heavenly hierarchy and illustrate his holy Church. But this belongs to the sacred images that it is relevant for us to address separately.[70]

It should be noted that Pacheco's claim is double. He proclaims the permanence of the image, as well as its elevated ineffable status, and relegates words to a lesser status. He also, and no less importantly, presents the painter as a pious believer, theologian, and visionary, and therefore, undeniably, as a liberal artist.

Virtue remains central to the discussion in chapter 11, "On the painting of images and their results, and the authority they have in the Catholic Church" ["De la pintura de las imagines y de su fruto, y la autoridad que tienen en la Iglesia Católica"]. The chapter commences by describing the typical distinction between the goal of the painter – to gain fame and give pleasure – and the function of painting – to represent, through imitation, with bravery and propriety (183). And yet, because Pacheco is here interested specifically in the conditions of production and reception of sacred art, this division is presented only to be immediately denied. In his guise as *artifice cristiano*, the painter creates something much loftier, the means for a sacred practice: "raised for holy things, he is not satisfied in his operations with looking so lowly, attending only to the praise of men and temporary comfort; before raising his eyes to heaven, he proposes another much greater and more excellent purpose, delivered in eternal things."[71] Pacheco intrinsically connects the spiritual virtue of the Catholic painter to the "supreme end"[72] of the image as a noble medium in the pious union between the viewer and the holy. The initial division between the desire for personal recognition (presumably based on skill) and the moral and religious content of the work is elided in the figure of the *pintor divino*, a human site where the perception and imitation of the material world and the workings of divine design intersect in favour of the representation of the holy mystery. If we recall Marion, the painter is king amongst all artists and thinkers precisely because he alone can offer an object that gives itself to the viewer, saturated with meanings that cannot be fixed or exhausted.

In the *Applied Discourses on the noble art of painting* [*Discursos practi-cables del noblísimo arte de la pintura*], Jusepe Martínez adopts a similar strategy to describe "the philosophy of painting."[73] Honoured with the title of *pintor del rey ad honorem* in 1644, Martínez finished the *Discursos* around 1675.[74] Like so many of his predecessors, including Carducho and Pacheco (who was a friend), Martínez dedicates the bulk of his treatise to painting theory – the knowledge base and skills necessar-ily related to drafting, perspective, and colour – with an added long section on the lives of exemplary painters. Hellwig has noted how the *Discursos'* main thrust is centred on establishing a three-tier hierar-chy amongst painters: those who simply imitate what they see, those whose imitation is enhanced by mastery of drafting and colour, and those whose "understanding and speculation"[75] allow for the highest mode of inventiveness and mastery of technique: "This is caused by the heightened ingenuity with which they work and meditate, and the gallantry of their discourse is such that they make everything easy, showing in their works that they seem to do it all at once, and with-out any hindrance."[76] Despite these skill-based distinctions, there is for Martínez an additional consideration regarding the "philosophy of painting," or specifically how the practice of painting is an extension of divine wisdom and virtue. According to Martínez, the truly great paint-ers possess an equal command of natural philosophy (*filosofía natural*) and moral philosophy; more precisely, they hold an equal command of the rules and symmetry observed in the natural, material world and those of the moral order underlying what is represented (45). In the context of the Counter-Reformation, Martínez's proposition intention-ally showcases the privileged relationship between the *pintor católico* and Christian virtue. For this very reason, the potential for a superior ethical/religious component does not come about from a tenacious practice or as the by-product of innate talent; rather, it is made possible through the painter's spiritual enlightenment and granted by divine grace – God's influence, inspiration, blessing, and strength. The *pintor católico* is the proper repository (both a source and a warehouse) of divine philosophy: "This comes through divine grace, and that's why it was said, seeing the works of great subjects: this is a painter with divine philosophy."[77] Contrary to the inducement of vices that classical think-ers, such as Seneca, saw as intrinsic to the visual image, the painter with divine philosophy raises the material world and triggers for the viewer an experience of the sacred. Moreover, the close relation between paint-ing and the sacred, "between aesthetic representation and miracles," places painters (as in Carducho and Pacheco) alongside the work and the mystery of God: "Seneca would make the opposite judgment if he saw what has been painted and is painted under the Catholic religion, and not only that painting was taken as a liberal art, but as a very divine one ... he would say the opposite, seeing that it induces all virtue and veneration in the sacred images through which the Highest Lord has worked and works marvellous miracles."[78] As shown, the category of liberal arts is brought up and validated only to be overshadowed by an even higher moral and revelatory criterion. Painting, more than any other liberal art, is the vehicle through which the sacred makes itself manifest in our world. And therefore, for Martínez, the argument of whether painters should be considered liberal artists is secondary to what is truly at stake, the artist's capacity for *filosofía divina*.

The designation of the painter as a liberal and divinely inspired artist, as a man of skill and as a theologian, underlies the pressures, negotiations, and representative decisions (both conscious and unconscious) that mark the vast production of religious painting throughout the Spanish Counter-Reformation. The following questions thus become relevant: Regarding the didactic function of the image, which aspects of biblical and hagiographic narratives are made visible and which are repressed? What are the appropriate coordinates for the contemplation of the sacred? What is the relationship between the visionary experience represented within the frame of the painting and the potential visionary response of the viewer? And, finally, how is the revealed, both visible and invisible, personalized and politicized? These are some of the questions that will guide our study of the Virgin of the Immaculate Conception paintings of Velázquez, Murillo, and Zurbarán that follows.

Chapter Four

Visiones Imaginarias: Pacheco, Velázquez, Zurbarán, and Murillo

Those who made those paintings were the ones who lifted contemplation to its highest flight, and with certain Philosophy considered that what they painted was not subject to the corporal sight, but to imaginary visions, or intellectual apparitions, represented for our understanding or imagination.

Francisco Pacheco, *Arte de la pintura*[1]

The vast proliferation of paintings and sculptures of the Immaculate Conception in early modern Spain clearly demonstrates the value the doctrine held for patrons and believers; at the very least, these images visually signify the attachment to Mariology and the fervent religiosity, both official and popular, that accompanied the defence of the *tota pulchra*. Even today it is almost impossible to visit a sacred space in Spain without encountering an image of the Virgin of the Immaculate Conception.[2] Art historians, most prominently Stratton, have well documented the evolution of the image from the fifteenth to the late seventeenth centuries. Stratton, in fact, goes well beyond the technical and painterly aspects and grounds her reading of the image in the relationship between popular religiosity and the political propaganda machine of the Spanish Habsburg court: "The closer study of the subject undertaken here reveals that the cult received enormous impetus from on high – the court of the kings of Spain – and that its frequent manifestation in Spanish art was initially and primarily in the service of propagandizing the devotion" (*The Immaculate Conception in Spanish Art* 4). This is a critical approach to which my argument owes a great deal. I have addressed in previous chapters the political and popular incentive for the promotion of the image, especially as it relates to the proliferation of individual Catholic identities. Along the same line, I will now examine the ways in which paintings of the Immaculate

Conception equally participate in and bear (both assume and support) the differing and competing interests of the spiritual and cultural geographies inhabited by painters, individual viewers, and the communities in which they were produced.

One way to focus the discussion of these images is the rubric of visual hermeneutics – or how the doctrine of the Immaculate Conception is variously interpreted, weighed, mediated, and deployed in the image. Several aspects have to be considered. Visual exegesis was fundamental from the eleventh century on in the transmittal of biblical knowledge, especially as systems of meaning evolved from a straightforward literal-allegorical division to a multilevel proliferation of systems of interpretation within Scholastic centres of learning. For example, diagrams in texts such as the *Speculum Theologiae* demonstrate the efficacy of illustrations when presenting onto-theological concepts and doctrinal prescriptions that required (or benefited from) the concurrent understanding of a variety of related and yet distinct concepts:

> Visual depictions transcended the limitations of textual learning. When the student viewed a diagram, he was able to take in all meanings attributed to it in one glance. Thus, he was liberated from the temporality of text, where what had already been read was past and what was to come was still unknown. Diagrammatic presentation unified the exegetical process, enabling the viewer to learn more quickly and more assuredly the three or four levels being presented in the lesson. (Noell et al.)

This hermeneutical tradition not only extends to the early modern period but also, I would argue, frames the expectations for reception of post-Trent religious painting. Like its medieval diagrammatic predecessors, sacred art intends all at once – in the immediacy of visuality, mostly unscathed by the burden of time, and congenial to differing degrees of erudition – to make accessible compound levels of meaning and a variety of experiences of the holy, subject to the didactic *and* contemplative injunction. This takes us back to the hermeneutical system of the four senses – literal, allegorical, tropological (moral), and anagogical – which artists of the period claimed as constitutive to their work.[3] Executed by the painter theologian or *pintor divino*, as described in chapter 3, the religious image offers an exegetical commentary on the Scriptures through which a multiplicity of interpretations could be simultaneously discerned and a visionary experience located. The painter of the Immaculate Conception is representing an image following the prescribed theological tenets that framed the doctrine, but also, and no less, offering a space where the excessive exceptionality of Mary's immaculacy may be anagogically contemplated and spiritually revealed to the faithful.

Perhaps precisely because of this conceptualization of the interpretative field, visual hermeneutics is qualified by a doubling. Both the religious painter and the viewer-witness of the religious image possess two sets of eyes, those present in the physical body and those of the soul, generating the faculties of sight and vision, one immanent and the other transcendent, which are, in turn, engaged in literal/allegorical versus anagogic hermeneutics.[4] Following this logic, these two sets of eyes each were understood to possess distinct and multiple capacities and propensities. In the early modern period, sight was often associated with the realm of science, perspective, and the painter's technical skill – what the eyes physiologically perceive in the encounter with the visual image. In addition to its biological duties, sight also informs the cognitive apprehension of the scriptural or hagiographic account. It is through sight that the viewer receives and decodes the didactic import of the image. Vision alternatively is linked to the spiritual capacity of the soul to "see" the Divine; it functions in the realm of what Marion (as we saw in the previous chapter) would call the excessive or saturated or what the councillors at Trent indicated as the site of contemplation. It is this faculty that makes possible, in turn, the pictorial representation of the mystical experience. As Bernard McGinn notes: "Whatever one's attitude toward the mystical dimension of religion, the study of mysticism has revealed a rich tradition of artworks that continue to intrigue us by their paradoxical effort to make the invisible somehow accessible to our gaze" (134).

Paintings of the Virgin of the Immaculate Conception – a theological doctrinal concept (the absence of original sin) *and* always already a pictorial narrative offered by God to John of Patmos – provide a fertile site to examine the dialectics of visual hermeneutics, what sight and vision perceive and produce and how what is "seen" results in the formation and substantiation of Counter-Reformation Spanish identity (individual and communal). In what follows, I examine vision and sight and the proliferation of meaning in the paintings of the Immaculate Conception by Francisco Pacheco (1564–1644), Diego Velázquez (1599–1660), Francisco de Zurbarán (1598–1664), and Bartolomé Esteban Murillo (1618–82). Given the many artists and the hundreds of paintings that treat the subject in the Spanish early modern period, limiting myself to a few compositions from four artists may be interpreted as reductive. My aim, nonetheless, is not to cover the same ground that Stratton and other specialists have already done so well. Instead, I am interested in focusing on the potentiality of the religious imagination and its relationship to the dialectics of sight and vision. My goal is to apprehend better the multiplicity of meanings, inherent paradoxes, and identitary mechanisms that images of the Immaculate Conception represent for early modern Spanish artists and viewers in the broader context. The painters I here discuss are contemporaneous, and their years of production largely overlap. I do not trace an evolution from Pacheco to Murillo. Instead, I examine how each of these Spanish masters singularly imagines the signifying possibilities contained within the visual representation of John of Patmos's visionary encounter with the Apocalyptic Woman.

In his groundbreaking study of Spanish religious painting, *Visionary Experience in the Golden Age of Spanish Art*, Stoichita focuses on the visual vocabulary of the mystical or visionary – the "rhetoric of the inexpressible" (79) – and its relationship to representation and experience. The art critic examines the subject from a technical point of view (the pictorial representation of an undeterminable liminal space between the human and the sacred) and considers the ways in which the Church paradoxically promoted and, yet, held suspect these mystical images. Later in this chapter, I respond in more detail to Stoichita's position regarding the interpretative and experiential limits of visionary paintings. For now, to better set out my own interpretation of visionary paintings, I will briefly delineate the two contradictory premises that underlie his propositions. On the one hand, he argues that it is in Spanish early modern religious art treatises and painting where the most earnest attempt is made to "find the point of contact where 'sight' and 'vision' meet" (78). Pacheco – as is well reflected in the epigraph to this chapter – clearly illustrates Stoichita's claim, starting his treatise precisely with a consideration of the intersection of the two faculties:

> The bodies whose images are represented in painting are of three genres: natural, artificial, or formed resulting from the thought and consideration of the soul ... The bodies made from thought are those that the imagination forms: dreams, dalliances, the grotesque and the fantasies of the painters. Similarly, we have those that are figured by the intellect forged from wise consideration. Angels, virtues, good deeds, hieroglyphics, emblems; and imaginary or intellectual visions that were perceived and revealed by the Prophets, and that painters often represent in their paintings.[5]

Following the arguments made in the previous chapter, we can see that Pacheco privileges the capacity of the painting, and most especially of the visionary painting, to stir the soul and bring it closer to the omnipotent and omniscient nature of God as the image touches and provokes (as cited in chapter 3) the "most secret part." The lines and colours applied by painters – a materiality that renders form (idea) – are translated by the soul into the truth of the divine light revealed. For Stoichita, therefore, visionary experience paintings engage with a sacred mystery that theologically and spiritually frames and yet exceeds their representational and signifying capacity (both for the visionary individual within the frame and for the viewer/witness outside of the frame). This is an elusive mechanism that must somehow be accounted for and theorized, which is precisely why Stoichita alludes to painting's phatic capacity, or what Bronisław Malinowski first coined as phatic communion, an exchange of utterances or codes (linguistic or visual) that lack a stable referent or a given meaning.[6] Following this logic, visionary experience paintings can be understood as fundamentally phatic precisely because they represent a singular and ineffable experience through pictorial codes that are intelligible and repeatable.

On the other hand, for Stoichita the representation of the unrepresentable simultaneously manages to contain the radicality of the individuated mystical experience, placing it in an institutional context that delimits its scope: "thus [the viewer] experiences this ecstatic state at the very center of a consecrated area – the church – and as a consequence, never finds himself completely alone before the manifestation of the sacred become visible" (Stoichita 26). In other words, the phatic function of visionary painting is curbed by the Church's censoring oversight of the content, the imposition of orthodoxy, and the resulting authorizing of the validity of the mystical representation; or what, in the final analysis, Stoichita characterizes as the "taming of the visionary experience" (26). Stoichita thus concludes that sight must ultimately impose itself over vision, the imaginary and singular potentiality of the visionary experience foreclosed by a codified, shared, and duly authorized representational mode.

What the religious imagination of the period in general, and the painters I analyse in particular, understood was possible in the realm of this "saturated" phatic communication is the primary concern of my inquiry. And yet, even though my interpretation of the Immaculate Conception paintings is largely indebted to Stoichita, my own analysis demonstrates that he overestimates the control that the Church as an institution and its censors exerted over the painters and, even more, over the viewers' singular reception, their sight *and* their vision. As is made clear in the art treatises I discuss in chapter 3, Pacheco, Velázquez, Zurbarán, and Murrillo – as *pintores teólogos* and liberal artists – conceptually and ideologically positioned their religious paintings as a practice bound to prophecy and revelation. It is my contention, therefore, that the painters

I here analyse are deeply engaged in the representation of the visionary as a phatic communion on its own terms – revelatory, apparitional, and ascetic; more precisely, their aim is to simultaneously iconographically represent, pare down, *and* blur the boundaries of the encounter with a saturated phenomenon – the vision of the Immaculate Conception – for the viewers of their paintings.[7] This is an argument that has been signalled already by art historians, such as William A. Christian, Jr, who, in an analysis of images and sculptures used in processions or associated with miracles in early modern Spain, states the following: "While bones or other relics had previously been the means for accessing the power and grace of divine figures, by the sixteenth century pictorial or sculptural representations had long since become the principal interfaces between humans and the invisible ones ... The net effect was that certain images became hypercharged" (75). Miguel Morán Turina and Javier Portús Pérez make a similar point in their *The Art of Looking: Painting and Its Public in the Spain of Velázquez* [*El arte de mirar: La Pintura y su público en la España de Velázquez*], when they state,

> Painting, in a theocentric epoch like the early modern period, gained its ultimate justification given its condition as an instrument that facilitated the cult and communication between the faithful and the divinity ... This is why it is very significant that it is in the relationship with religious paintings and sculptures where we best can examine the characteristics of the ineffable; what allows us to better understand up to what point the ineffable ... appeared as a fundamental aspect of the conception of art in the period.[8]

Following a parallel logic, I posit that visionary paintings can both represent and unleash for the viewer as a witness – a beholder of and a participant in – the experience of the sacred mystery; in other words, the status of the image moves beyond being only representational and functions also as a conduit between the immanent and the transcendent duplicated within and beyond the frame of the painting. As my analysis will show, we should read Immaculate Conception paintings as a reproduction and contemporaneous reinstatement of John of Patmos's visionary experience. The viewer stands in the apostle's place, is witness to (or physically sees and spiritually recognizes) the saint's experience, and is himself/herself made worthy of this experience, called forth by the painting and interpellated as a mystical and privileged participant in the mystery of immaculacy.[9] In this binding movement from the image to the viewer and back, the frame ceases to be a fixed threshold; to the contrary, it acts as a conduit through which the viewer – sustained by a religious imagination aligned with the *via mística*'s experience of the self as an emptied purified vessel – functions as a form filled by the visionary content phatically coded on the canvas.[10] Moved by the *pintor teologo*'s artistic mastery and exegetical representation of the ineffable, the viewer receives the visionary image of the Virgin of the Immaculate Conception for her/his own imaginary consumption.

Additionally, we must account for the community of witnesses constituted through the viewership of these paintings in a context where the visionary experience is folded into a larger propagandistic agenda that brings together individual religiosity, the shared identity of believers, the supremacy of the Catholic faith, and the Spanish state as its most fervent defender. Building upon a privileged Spanish *Pietas Mariana*, the paintings I here examine call upon a shared sense of physiological resemblances, identifiable geographies, local community, and national identity (as it was understood in the period under the concept of *nación*) that visually indicates and propagandizes the exclusive relationship between God's design, the Virgin's absolute purity, the Spanish people, and the Spanish lands. Despite this commonality – which relies on an immediately recognizable iconographical program – I argue that the visual and spiritual effects of Zurbarán's and Murillo's paintings of the Virgin of the Immaculate Conception differ in ways that define each of their particular religious imaginaries and how they apprehend the relationship between the sacred and the human as made patent in the visionary experience of Mary's mystery. An initial examination of Pacheco's and Velázquez's incursions into the topic serves as a summary examination of the contrasting dialectics between sight and vision deployed by Zurbarán and Murillo.

I. Becoming the Seer: Pacheco and the Visual Narrative of the Mystical Experience

In his "On Painting the Purest Conception of Our Lady" ["Pintura de la Purísima Concepción de nuestra Señora"] (found in his *Arte de la pintura*), Pacheco instructs the painter tasked with representing the immaculate mystery on how to go about resolving potential confusion and conflict for the individual viewer of the painting and the broader Catholic community. In his instructions, Pacheco strips the representation of the Virgin of the Immaculate Conception of most of the elements that form part of the apocalyptic narrative; more precisely, he interprets and condenses John of Patmos's vision, narrowing what he deems necessary and not accidental to better communicate the concept of eternal purity.[11] She is to be imagined as a childless young woman, remarkably beautiful, with golden hair. Dressed by the sun and crowned with twelve stars, she stands on a crescent moon descending onto the earth. God the Father and the Holy Spirit may appear on the top plane of the painting and putti may provide adornment. The allegorical symbols enumerated in the Lorettan litany (*Letanías de la Virgen de Loreto*) that symbolize the purity of the Virgin may be strategically placed so as to codify immaculacy appropriately; but, to make their appearance less distracting, they should be painted in a subtle manner amongst clouds. The dragon and the narrative crushing of its head are catalogued last, and Pacheco makes a point of this late and near omission: "We almost forgot the Dragon, our common enemy, whose head the Virgin crushes, triumphant over original sin, but how could we forget. The truth is that I never willingly paint it, and I will hide it as much as possible, so as to not hinder (or make repugnant) my painting with it."[12] Immediately after this statement, Pacheco ends his typology with the concession that each painter has the liberty to imagine the combination of elements as he wishes: "But as regards all I have said, painters have the liberty to better themselves."[13] The *pintor teólogo* is encouraged to interpret and visually represent the visionary, but also, and no less significantly, to properly channel and strip the representation of the doctrine of its more controversial aspects in a context in which a full attachment to the apocalyptic narrative, and its theologically unresolved details, could endanger the desired promotion to dogma.

As we should expect, Pacheco's Immaculate Conception paintings follow these prescriptions, methodical in their inclusion of iconographic and symbolic elements explicitly meant to offer a "didactic doctrinal image" (a phrase I am borrowing from Stoichita's analysis of a painting by El Greco, 110).[14] Some examples showcase the sole presence of the Virgin and pare down to the bare minimum the visual representation of the mystery, even excluding the typical multitude of adoring cherubs.[15] Pacheco's Conceptionist corpus also includes three versions where the mystical experience is mediated through the sight and vision of donors who take the place of John of Patmos within the frame, as well as stand in for the viewer without.

In the 1619 *Immaculate with Miguel del Cid*, the portrayed visionary is a pivotal figure in the Immaculist movement in Seville, a poet whose couplet in defence of the doctrine became the city's most popular anthem upon Paul V's dictum of 1617 disallowing the promulgation of Maculist notions (figure 4.1). In the 1619 Miguel del Cid had been dead for four years, making the painting's dialectical negotiation between sight and vision ever so much more complicated.[16] We, the viewer, see on the canvas a vision of a spirit – Miguel del Cid holding his poem – experiencing a vision of the Immaculate Conception; as such, the

Figure 4.1. Francisco Pacheco, *Immaculate with Miguel del Cid* (1619).
Seville Cathedral.

painting offers a double vision, one which brings back the beloved
Cid alongside the sacred image of the Virgin. Surely, we can read the
painting as the representation of a past scene, the moment when, in
the throes of inspiration, the poet sees the Virgin with the eyes of his
soul; it also explicitly elevates and commemorates the stature of a
well-known civic figure. And yet, if thought of as related to the passage between sight and vision that so much concerned Pacheco in his
Arte, the Miguel del Cid painting stages a multi-level visionary narrative, unlocking the didactic and contemplative potentiality triggered

when sight and vision are deployed simultaneously. To be more precise, the spirit of Miguel del Cid – as it appears to the viewer – reflects
upon and writes about the doctrinal attributes of the Virgin *and* simultaneously experiences a vision that confirms her positionality as
a sacred mystery. As charged in the *Arte*, the didactic attributes of the
litany surround the Virgin. Moreover, the geographical setting is Seville,
transposing the local geography to a liminal space between the familiar
here and the Divine there – a representational choice of which I speak
further later. Most importantly, the painting presents the beholder
with the possibility of sharing in this double experience, of inserting
him- or herself into the narrative of the visionary, both as a protagonist
(seeing the spirit image of Miguel del Cid) and as a receiving vessel
for the sacred mystery of immaculacy (taking the place of Miguel del
Cid). This dynamic is further made possible because the Virgin does
not look towards Miguel del Cid but out of the frame aslant towards
the viewer, her gaze making it possible for us to imagine ourselves as
direct addressees of her presence alongside the commemorated poet.

A similar, although more conventional, imaginative pathway is
present in the 1621 *Immaculate with Vázquez de Leca*, a painting that has
often been deemed one of Pacheco's highest technical achievements
in portraiture (figure 4.2). The identification of Vázquez de Leca –
archdeacon of Carmona and one of the representatives sent by the
city of Seville to defend the doctrine in the courts of Philip III and
Philip IV – is nevertheless currently in doubt, and thus we are unsure
of the precise relationship with the intended audience at the Convent
of Santa María del Valle (where the painting was originally placed).
What we can be sure of, nevertheless, is that the viewers saw in the
religious figure portrayed an example of and a conduit for the visionary experience of the Virgin of the Immaculate Conception; she makes
herself present to "Vázquez de Leca" and to us (as she had in the past
to John of Patmos), the mystery of immaculacy revealed in the act of
contemplation.

Of the three examples, the most interesting from my perspective is
the *Immaculate with Donor* (circa 1619) (figure 4.3). The donor, who has
at times been identified as Bernardo de Toro, head of the Congregation of the Pomegranate [*Congregación de la Granada*], looks out from
the frame directly at the viewer, formally inviting him/her into the
visionary experience as a full participant.[17] As in the Miguel del Cid
painting, the Virgin also looks out, summoning the viewer to join the
donor (and John of Patmos before him), become the seer, and be filled
with her revelatory presence, thus removing the purpose of the frame
as a threshold. As such, this painting offers a dual invitation, a double
dare, if you will, for the beholder of the painting to imagine himself/
herself as seen and called upon to be a spectator and a partaker, vision
made possible through sight. We see the donor and the Virgin looking

Figure 4.2. Francisco Pacheco, *Immaculate with Vázquez de Leca* (1621). Private Collection, Seville.

Figure 4.3. Francisco Pacheco, *Immaculate with Donor* (circa 1619). Granados Collection, Madrid.

Figure 4.4. Bartolomé Esteban Murillo, *Immaculate with Friar Juan de Quirós* (1653). Archbishop's Palace, Seville.

upon us, and we are consequently asked to imagine ourselves as fellow witnesses. In this dynamic representation, the narrative split between immanence and transcendence – what Stoichita calls the "verticalization of the visionary experience" (28) – is evidently dissolved.[18] The Virgin of the Immaculate Conception stands almost side by side with the donor (and not high above him in an exclusionary upper half of the composition), both subjects looking out onto the viewer in a triangular and contiguous line of sight *and* vision that extends from the mystical image to the viewer, to the donor, and back to the Virgin.

The narrative of sight and vision, represented within the painting by a donor or other religious observer, is not exclusive to Pacheco. Murillo plays with this narrative visual pattern in his 1653 *Immaculate with Friar Juan de Quirós* (figure 4.4), the Franciscan friar shown writing his *Glories of Mary* [*Glorias de María*], looking at the viewer, with a large painting of the Immaculate Conception hung behind him.[19] Juan de Roelas also composed an early example: the 1612 *Immaculate with Hernando de Mata* (figure 4.5), which Pacheco must have known and imitated. Zurbarán further develops the representational schema in a unique direction with his *Immaculate Conception (with Two Boys)* of 1632 (figure 4.6), where two

Figure 4.5. Juan de Roelas, *Immaculate with Hernando de Mata* (1612). Staatliche Museen, Gemäldegalerie, Berlin.

Figure 4.6. Francisco de Zurbarán, *Immaculate Conception (with Two Boys)* (1632). National Museum of Catalonia.

unknown schoolboys, kneeling and flanking an apparition of the *tota pulchra*, recite verses of the *Ave Maris Stella*.

The idea of including within the frame both the person experiencing a vision and the mystical revelation itself is not uncommon and is used for a wide variety of biblical and hagiographical accounts. Nevertheless, as I have demonstrated, it is Pacheco who, within the corpus of early modern Spanish Immaculate Conception painting, exemplifies a fundamental move towards the opening of the frame to the viewer as an active participant in a fluid passage between sight and vision, straddling the imaginary space between immanence and transcendence.

II. Sight and Vision in Velázquez's Pendants: *Saint John the Evangelist on the Island of Patmos* and *The Immaculate Conception* (1618–19)

Executed when Velázquez was still a young painter (around nineteen years old) and had just graduated from the workshop of his tutor and future father-in-law, Pacheco, *Saint John the Evangelist on the Island of Patmos* and *The Immaculate Conception* (both 1618–19) (figures 4.7 and 4.8) are generally contextualized as a response to the fervour surrounding the doctrine, brewing in Seville, and Philip IV's calling the third *Real Junta* to legislate for the elevation to dogma.[20] Unlike Zurbarán and Murillo with their numerous versions, Velázquez only executed one additional *Immaculate Conception* (also of 1618), a painting that in fact only recently, in 2010, was recognized as his (figure 4.9).[21]

These Carmelite companion pendants have, nonetheless, elicited numerous detailed studies, amongst the most interesting being those of Stoichita and Tanya J. Tiffany. Stoichita points out how these paintings move from "the act of vision and its medium" (*Saint John the Evangelist*) to "the vision as painting" (*Immaculate Conception*) (115). Tiffany, alternatively, grounds her analysis in Carmelite doctrine, the social geography of the Carmelite monastery within Seville, and the psychology of the friars who served as these paintings' original intended audience. In her estimation, the pendants concretize and "give shape to the ineffable quality of the divine revelations," placing the vision of the Virgin in the landscape of Mount Carmel, mediating the reception of the Virgin as a "site of devotion and desire" for the friars, and offering John of Patmos as an example of how to receive a vision and translate it into its "symbolic meaning: that the Virgin was conceived without the 'stain' of original sin" (26). Thus considered, Velázquez's companion pendants delimit the mystical experience of John of Patmos and the doctrine that

Figure 4.7. Diego Velázquez, *Saint John the Evangelist on the Island of Patmos* (1618–19). National Gallery, London.

is its product within the social and religious early modern Spanish and Sevillian context (as Pacheco had instructed and already done). They also mediate specific needs and desires – individual, local, and communal. In his imaginative decoupling of the visionary event and its symbolic product, Velázquez successfully tailors, for his Carmelite benefactors and audience, divine revelation and devotion in the narrative and symbolic representation of the Immaculate Conception.

Following Stoichita and Tiffany, a straightforward analysis could lead us to interpret the John of Patmos painting and its Immaculate

Figure 4.8. Diego Velázquez, *The Immaculate Conception* (1618–19).
National Gallery, London.

Conception companion piece as a clearly decoupled representation of
sight versus vision: one shows the happening of the invisible revealed
and the second its symbolized and sanctioned configuration, both didactic and contemplative. For this very reason, one could argue that
Velázquez's pendants are amongst the most restrained pictorial representations of the doctrine in the Spanish canon. In his depiction of
John of Patmos's spiritual encounter with divine revelation, Velázquez
delimits the scope of the contact with the ineffable; in other words, his
visual representation of the mystical experience materializes the event
for the Carmelite friars, displacing and substituting for the possibility

Figure 4.9. Diego Velázquez,
Immaculate Conception (1618).
Velázquez Centre, Focus-
Abengoa Foundation.

of an individual, and thus unrestricted, visionary experience (real or imaginary). Vision – seeing with the eyes of the spirit – is concurrently transferred into a fully codified visual object, filtered and stripped of its potentially disruptive capacity. This curtailing of the visionary aspect would then be further confirmed by the representation of the youthful Virgin accompanied by the appropriate iconography, which symbolizes her eternal purity and sublimates the potentially objectionable details of her apocalyptic story. This reading would place Velázquez's *Immaculate Conception* well within the legacy of Pacheco, a fact supported by the two painters' familial relationship as well as by the impact that the *Arte* had upon the school of painters in Seville at this moment. And it would lead us to read these paintings, despite their explicit referent being John of Patmos's mystical experience, as skewed in favour of sight – moral and allegorical in its leanings – and pushing aside the realm of revelation. Velázquez's *Immaculate Conception*, rid of the dragon and the celestial battle represented in miniature in the upper right corner of the *Saint John the Evangelist* pendant, illustrates Pacheco's dictum: the two images together offer a visual bridge between the ineffable and the symbolic, a digested and coherent representation of doctrine – didactic, moral, and allegorical. In sum, the pendants can be said to perfectly exemplify the interpretative translation that visionary experiences go through to communicate an intelligible and authorized meaning that serves the requirements of instruction and propaganda.

And yet, in my opinion, this interpretation of the pendants is not entirely satisfactory, given the anagogic potentiality of vision and sight. To be clear, the above-offered analysis stands, but it is not enough. I would argue that it is impossible for Velázquez to avoid the dialectical relationship between the mystical and the doctrinal, and that therein remains an excess that cannot be adequately symbolized and contained. Velázquez takes to heart Pacheco's final suggestion to "better oneself" or "mejorarse," and he does so in two important ways regarding vision and sight. First, the *Saint John the Evangelist* painting prominently features the apostle, quill in hand and book in lap, ready to narrativize the image that presents itself both as a revelation and as a mystery. José López-Rey and Odile Delenda describe this moment as a "contemplative pause needed to put the [Revelation] into words" (45), a reading that subscribes to the delimiting and taming of the visionary experience that Stoichita suggests. Second, Velázquez nonetheless insists on including in the upper right corner of the painting the uncensored, apocalyptic vision, a winged pregnant woman standing on the moon and attacked by a seven-headed dragon. As noted by Tiffany, the revelation is "painted on a small scale with loose brushstrokes and almost bleached colors, which make her figure indecipherable" to the viewer, especially if we consider that the pendant was meant to be hung above eye level (43).[22] From my viewpoint, it is precisely this almost illegible presence of the Woman of the Apocalypse in the *Saint John the Evangelist* painting that exploits the indeterminacy of the sight-vision interaction. Even if the viewer can physically (with his eyes – sight) identify the indistinct contour, it would have been hard to make out all of its details. The revelation is there to be seen, but only as a trace that leads to what is formally represented in the *Immaculate Conception* pendant. Still, in *Saint John the Evangelist* this trace insists on a revelation of the invisible Divine, opening the canvas to a vision and transforming the painting into a saturated phenomenon. Given the context offered by the pendant, the Carmelite friars would have immediately understood the blurry contours of the Immaculate Virgin as correlating to the narrative of Revelation 12; there are enough codes around the figure of Saint John of Patmos (the eagle, the natural setting, the rusticity of the male figure) to instigate this recognition in tandem with the accompanying image. By signposting the unmediated vision as described in the biblical account – accurate in its painterly details while simultaneously almost obscure to the naked eye of the viewer – Velázquez promotes the spectator's individual *encounter* with revelation. He posits the sacred mystery as immediate and open for the perception and singular imaginative interpretation of the viewer alongside John of Patmos. In sum, within the *Saint John the Evangelist* pendant the image persists, as Hugh of St Victor would have it, as an anagogic "invisible fact," accessible to vision and experienced as a revealed excess.

Velázquez's naturalism, evident in the representation both of the mystical experience and of the symbolized doctrine, also plays into the dialectic of sight and vision. This is an element typically brought to light in the analysis of the *Immaculate Conception* pendant, specifically in that Velázquez represents the Virgin as a brunette with olive skin, resembling the familiar Spanish physiognomy, and sets aside Pacheco's abstracting typological suggestion of a pale blond Mary in his *Arte*.[23] Fleshy rather than sculptural, Velázquez's pictorial choice humanizes the Virgin and allows for a (comparatively speaking) undemanding identification by the viewer with the holy other as an exalted self, which I contend underscores for the viewer Mary's contiguous immanence and transcendence.[24] Much of the same must be said about the representational choices made with John of Patmos: ruggedness was part of the set iconography for this religious figure, but not a natural-looking dark Spanish countenance, a difference which a survey of Flemish, Dutch, German, and Italian examples quickly confirms. I will return to the effect that naturalism has on the interaction of immanence and transcendence as taken up by Murillo and Zurbarán. But for now, if it is possible to say that by pictorially representing John of Patmos at the moment of his vision – mouth open, eyes lost in a gaze towards the heavens – Velázquez contains and tames the mystical encounter (as Stoichita would have it), it is also possible to envision that the familiarity of his figure would invite and encourage the Carmelite friars who prayed in front of this painting to imagine themselves transposed in the image of the visionary apostle. Without a doubt, Velázquez's naturalism in religious paintings and the identificatory mechanisms it activates serve the didactic and propagandistic interests of the Sevillian municipality, the Church Militant, Philip III, and the *Reales Juntas*.[25] But the naturalness of the Virgin and John of Patmos in these pendants also makes possible a multiplicity of relational positions and meanings for the viewer within the continuum of sight and vision. The visionary experience – contemplative, anagogic, and mystical – is represented through the figure of a man who looks as if he could be a fellow friar or neighbour. The mystery of Mary's eternal unstained grace and her apocalyptic past are pictorially translated into a young girl who resembles a native Sevillian, crowned by a halo of stars and standing on the moon.

As I see it, Velázquez's pendants fix the site of immaculacy – as a sacred mystery, mystical revelation, and doctrine – in the interstice between the self and the Divine. Moreover, the Carmelite coding included in the paintings (as demonstrated by Tiffany), as well as Seville's (and by extension the Spanish Habsburg) geography, speak to a religious imaginary that is imbued with institutional, local, and political concerns. The pendants stage, as Stoichita has asserted, the "written text ... transformed into the pictorial image" (116). As I have shown, these pendants equally galvanize a multiplicity of meanings that straddle the allegorical and the anagogic, made present in the figuration of John of Patmos and the Virgin as familiar Spanish nationals, Carmelite icons, protagonists in regional-Habsburg-papal politics, and conduits to a divine revelation. More than any of the previous examples of the representation of the doctrine, Velazquez's *Saint John the Evangelist* and *The Immaculate Conception* invite the viewer to see with his physical *and* his spiritual eyes (all at the same saturated moment) himself, his community, the doctrine, and the ineffable in the divine mystery – sight and vision simultaneous and excessive. This is where the power of Velázquez's pendants resides and what Zurbarán and Murillo take as a point of departure for their translation of the mystery and Immaculist doctrine.

In the following sections I examine key examples of Zurbarán's and Murillo's Immaculate Conception paintings, first looking at vision and spiritual identity, followed by sight and national identity, then conclude with a section where I examine together these two ultimately inseparable terms. Although not ideal, this division allows me to offer a more nuanced examination of the dialectic of sight and vision in the work of two master painters who dedicated much of their output to imagining the possibilities and properties of immaculacy visualized.

III. A Gateway to the Transcendental: Zurbarán and Murillo

Zurbarán and Murillo together executed over forty-eight Immaculate Conception paintings between 1630 and 1680.[26] Broadly speaking, both painters follow Pacheco's and Velázquez's leads, making use of the recommended iconography and Marian symbols, portraying the Virgin as very young and with Spanish features, and in most paintings suppressing the dragon. None of their paintings include John of Patmos within the frame of the canvas, although they occasionally incorporate additional human and divine beings – defenders of the doctrine, scriptural figures, angels, God – whose presence shores up the visionary

Figure 4.10. Francisco de Zurbarán, *Immaculate Conception* (1661). Church of Saint Gervais et Saint Protais, Langon.

and iconographical elements of the representation.[27] It is also the case for both Zurbarán and Murillo that the more mature paintings tend to distil the iconography to a few definitive markers that exclusively pertain to the Immaculate Conception. In Zurbarán's last known *Immaculate Conception* (1661), for example, the iconography is reduced to the image of the young Virgin standing on the moon, rounded out by the profiles of only two putti, the blue robe fluttering in the wind, the light of the sun dimly framing her body, and an even fainter halo of twelve stars floating above her (figure 4.10). Murillo's last, the *Immaculate Conception of the Venerable* (1678), shares a similar scaling-down of

Figure 4.11. Bartolomé Esteban Murillo, *Immaculate Conception of the Venerable* (1678). Prado Museum, Madrid.

the symbolic apparatus with only the crescent moon, the blue robe, the diffused light of the sun, and a cascade of putti that offsets the need for the halo of stars (figure 4.11).

Familiarity with the doctrine and an accompanying immediate recognizability of the iconography – by this point in seventeenth-century Spain ubiquitous and woven into the fabric of Counter-Reformation official and popular religiosity – explain from a socio-historical perspective why Zurbarán and Murillo would minimize or completely omit elements of the litany and the narrative and symbolic details of the Apocalyptic account. Instead, the mature paintings focus on the anagogic and visionary core of the representation of Mary Immaculate.

And yet, it is equally evident that there are important interpretative differences between the approaches that these two painters took towards the subject, and which in my opinion can be best analysed following Stoichita's "rhetoric of the inexpressible," hermeneutically rich and aligned with the visionary and the contemplative. Each in his own way, Zurbarán and Murillo figure a gateway for the visionary experience of immaculacy, moving far beyond formulaic representations of the Virgin of the Immaculate Conception.

Zurbarán is often compared to Caravaggio for his use of the *chiaroscuro*, but also noted is the naturalism of his images in service of the visionary. His corpus includes numerous "retratos a lo divino" (portraits of the Divine), saints and martyrs whose devotional potency is rooted in the seeming intimacy and candid familiarity expressed by their countenance.[28] The Virgin of the Immaculate Conception paintings are understood as forming part of this tendency towards naturalism, with specialists such as Delenda (who is author and the editor of the most important and recent books and catalogues on Zurbarán) framing the terms for analysis as follows: "His painting, clear, monumental, and perfectly legible, as well as his simple naturalism put to the service of didactic discourse, may explain without a doubt his extraordinary success in Seville in the second quarter of the seventeenth century."[29] Delenda's approach, which is typical of the critical field at large, is, therefore, to simultaneously speak both to Zurbarán's realism (the expression of the faces, the light, the folds of clothing, the precision of the still lives) and to the visionary; what Alfonso E. Pérez Sánchez calls the "invasion of the supernatural" into the naturalistic or familiar (38) and what Stoichita prefers to describe as "unreality irrupting into reality" (199).[30] The insistence on this distinction, which admittedly holds true for much of the Counter-Reformation visual canon, reinforces an understanding of the human world and the divine invisible as opposites, radically separate realms often pictorially construed as distinct visual planes (our world in the bottom half, the holy in the upper half of the canvas), a split of which art historians make note and that is understood as one of the hallmarks of Counter-Reformation religious aesthetics: "At the time of the Counter-Reformation, the icon/unreal/sacred/transcendence inhabited the top of the painting forming from that time on an upper level in the representation" (Stoichita 199).

I would propose that there is an important aspect of the early modern religious imagination that is obscured or skirted by this type of overarching assessment. As is made evident in the multitude of discourses and accounts – formal, anecdotal, and literary – the relationship of the human and divine was comprehended in the early modern period (and especially within the scope of theology and popular religious belief) as

a system of resemblances, similitude, and symmetry, as a continuum
that was characterized, as Foucault states and as I have previously
cited, "by the solid and secret bonds of resemblance and affinity" (*The
Order of Things* 64). As I noted in chapter 1, these affinities are also ripe
for the hyperbolic excesses of the religious imagination, singular and
capacious. In regard to our limited human understanding of the sacred mystery, there is a here and a there that is constitutive of the visionary experience: the mystic here sees in images (built on repetitions,
resemblances, and similitudes) what is manifest in the there of God's
infinite knowledge and omnipotence.[31] The truth of the divine mystery
is ultimately (and necessarily) obscure and unknowable (paradoxically
invisible), and the mystery of immaculacy stands out in its resistance
to a final exegetical determination. Still, the Virgin as Immaculate appears to us as analogous. She is the most exalted example of human
redemption, embodying what we once were and what we hope to once
again become in the heavens: immanent in her body, transcendent in
her spiritual existence, human *and* excessive in her purity. It is for this
very reason that the continuum between sight and vision, between
what we see, what is revealed, and what remains invisible, makes itself indispensable in the interpretation of seventeenth-century Spanish
Immaculate Conception paintings, which, in turn, explains the sense of
the familiar-strange that Zurbarán's canvases profile so strongly.

Zurbarán's paintings tend to linger upon the visionary experience
of the Virgin of the Immaculate Conception, wavering between that
first apparition to John of Patmos and later assigned iconographic
values, exploring and exploiting the excesses and saturated indeter-
minacies revealed and made visible. As is immediately evident when
surveying Zurbarán, the Virgin of the Immaculate Conception is rendered as a child or as a young girl, the visual translation of the absence
of sin. As such, she is simultaneously accessible and otherworldly, rich
in meaning and yet emptied of life content, mediating an encounter
between the similar (she is a familiar child) and the extraordinary
(she is a revelation). Zurbarán – as a *pintor divino* – invites the viewer
to occupy the place of John of Patmos and look via the frame as if
through an open window to the apocalyptic vision. In other words,
there is an investment on the part of Zurbarán (and we shall see below
how this plays out for Murillo as well) in the imagined immediacy
of the revealed, resulting in the coupling of sight and vision that, as
I argued above, was already at work in Pacheco's donor paintings and
Velázquez's pendants. In Zurbarán the vision is at once recognizable
and strangely excessive, seen in this world but not of this world, contiguous with our experience, a saturated phenomenon both meaningful

Figure 4.12. Francisco de Zurbarán, *The Virgin of the Immaculate Conception as a Child* (1656). Collection of Plácido Arango. Prado Museum, Madrid.

and yet ultimately inscrutable. That is why, for the religious imagination of seventeen-century Spain, a painting such as Zurbarán's *The Virgin of the Immaculate Conception as a Child* of 1656 – in which the Virgin is probably modelled after Zurbarán's eight-year-old daughter, Manuela – is instantly decipherable through the iconography of the Apocalyptic Woman (Virgin standing on the moon, halo of twelve stars, blue robe, the army of angels/putti surrounding her) but experienced as the vision of an innocent child-Virgin, identifiable and enigmatic at the same time (figure 4.12).[32]

Regarding visual hermeneutics, Zurbarán here (as in most of his corpus) favours the side of vision and anagogy, offering his viewer a Virgin of the Immaculate Conception whose representation seeks the contemplation of the mystery of immaculacy in the symbolic guise of a child. It serves us well to recall Stoichita once more, who has described the visual representation of the "ecstatic vision" as an image of the inner workings of the soul of the mystic: "Hence the ecstatic vision takes place in the soul of the chosen one. In one sense it is this soul – become transparent – that the visionary painting depicts" (27). If we account, as I do, for transference of the mystical experience from the purely representational to the participatory, Zurbarán's *The Virgin of the Immaculate Conception as a Child* posits this vision as incorporated into the spiritual life of the viewer and, by extension, into the larger Spanish Counter-Reformation collective spiritual experience.

A late painting titled *Immaculate Conception with Two Allegorical Figures* (early 1660s) is another salient example of the coupling of the known with the strange and of the painting as ecstatic vision, denying the possibility of a simplified didactic functionality. Unlike most of Zurbarán's late Immaculate Conception paintings, the iconographic program includes the fundamental elements for the Immaculate Conception (young Virgin standing on the moon, blue robe, halo of twelve stars, putti), as well as the customary symbols of the litany (the palm, cypress, fountain, tower, and the city of God). Its innovative particularity resides elsewhere, in the presence of two enigmatic figures at the foot of the Virgin and leaning on the moon (figure 4.13).

The opacity of the two figures can be contrasted with the 1632 *Immaculate Conception with Two Boys* mentioned above (figure 4.6) and the 1638 *Immaculate Conception with Saint Joachim and Saint Anne* (figure 4.14), both of which offer a straightforward invitation to contemplate and receive the mystery of immaculacy from the perspective of innocent children, who venerate the Mother, or from that of her own parents, who marvel at the mystery embodied in their progeny. Competing interpretations of the allegorical figures have led to varying conclusions, summarized by Stratton in her examination of the painting (*The Immaculate Conception in Spanish Art* 94). In the most prevalent, the two figures represent the theological virtues of Faith and Hope, thereby inviting an interpretation of the Virgin as illustrative of Charity. This reading is possible because the figure on her left holds an anchor, which in period emblems was symbolic of Hope; that the figure looks comfortingly and signals invitingly with his hand at the viewer would seem, therefore, to support this reading.[33] In addition to having her eyes covered by the Virgin's robe (echoing the image of the Catholic faith wearing a blindfold that had been current from the twelfth century),

Figure 4.13. Francisco de Zurbarán, *Immaculate Conception with Two Allegorical Figures* (early 1660s). National Gallery of Ireland.

Figure 4.14. Francisco de Zurbarán, *Immaculate Conception with Saint Joachim and Saint Anne* (1638). Scottish National Gallery.

the second figure stands on the right side of the Virgin and clutches her chest as is customary for the symbolic representation of Faith.[34] Nevertheless, as Rosemarie Mulcahy and Stratton have pointed out, upon further consideration the final meaning of these figures is not so easily decoded. Stratton, aided by Cesare Ripa's *Iconologia* (1603), interprets the blindfolded figure as *Peccatum* (sin), which was often iconographically associated with the Jews' indifference to the Messiah and which Stratton here extends to "the blindness of the Maculists to God's revelation of the Immaculate Conception" (94).[35] Another possibility found in Ripa is a resonance with the emblem of *Incredibilitas*, who like *Peccatum* is blindfolded and suffers from ignorance of the truth. Following these cues, Stratton reads an allegory of the debate over the elevation of the doctrine to dogma, one figure blind to the truth of immaculacy (the Dominicans and the Protestants) and the other (the Franciscans) inviting the viewer to have faith in its mystery and the hope it provides.

Despite its meritorious logic, from my perspective this reading seems insufficient, given the level of abstraction deployed by Zurbarán. Typically, paintings of the debate over the doctrine explicitly portray the opposing sides, serving the function of religious-political visual documents to the detriment of the visionary or anagogic level of interpretation.[36] In other words, there would be little sense in masking the direct contrast between the faithful and the faithless in a propaganda painting. On the other hand, there are undeniable hurdles to a straightforward allegorical-emblematic reading of these figures. Regarding the figure on the left of the Virgin, even if it is true that in this tradition Hope is recognized by the presence of an anchor, none of the other characteristics found in the customary pictorial grammar of period emblem books and paintings are present – the figure should be a woman, her vestment should be green, and her gaze should be directed towards heaven. The same is the case with the figure on the right, who, if interpreted as Faith, should be dressed in white, wearing a helmet, and reading a sacred book; alternatively, if the figure is echoing the visualization of faith as blind, we have to admit to the fact that the Virgin's robe is not exactly a blindfold (it can also be visually read as flying cloth) and relinquish the need for other customary accompanying emblematic elements, such as the chalice and cross. Even more, in books circulating at the time, such as Sebastián de Covarrubias's *Moral Emblems* [*Emblemas Morales*] (1610), the Catholic faith is represented with the papal crown and the keys to the celestial gates, altogether moving away from the blindfolded female figure (centuria I, emblema 4). If otherwise interpreted as *Peccatum* or *Incredibilitas*, we should expect the figure to be rather ugly, with a serpent biting its chest or a donkey's ears, respectively. When we look at Covarrubias, the figures of a gluttonous dog and donkey are deployed to portray folly and sin (centuria I, emblema 92 and emblema 93 respectively).[37] In sum, Zurbarán's lack of precision in the use of symbols would make it almost impossible for his audience to distinguish the religious-political figurative significance as proposed by Stratton. The emblematic tradition and its translation to art need an explicit and closed codification of the message; given the vagueness in these figures, I am hard pressed to think they meet this threshold. We should also note that amongst the three paintings of the Immaculate Conception in which Zurbarán includes additional figures, the *Immaculate Conception with Two Allegorical Figures* is singular in its composition, with the figures facing the viewer directly and calling upon her/him both as a witness and as an interlocutor; more precisely, these figures are a constitutive part of the visionary experience itself as presented within Zurbarán's canvas.[38]

How then can we, and more importantly the religious imagination of the period, interpret the *Immaculate Conception with Two Allegorical Figures*? I would propose that a productive and plausible explanation is to read them as representative of the bond of sight and vision.

If, as I argue, the Spanish faithful are invited to experience most Conceptionist paintings as a visionary continuum between this world and the sacred, then these figures can represent the hermeneutical doubling of seeing with the eyes of the body through the figure looking out onto the viewer, and the eyes of the soul through the figure looking inward and up in the midst of a mystical experience enraptured in the Virgin's robe. Sight and vision are mapped onto immanence and transcendence, dialectical attributes that are bridged by the Virgin of the Immaculate Conception as an eternal spirit and a woman, as an immaculate human, as doctrine *and* visionary experience. Read in this manner, the *Immaculate Conception with Two Allegorical Figures* invites the viewer to confirm his faith through the renewed knowledge of the doctrine – its symbols and theological tenets – guided by sight and vision here present as embodied figures in the contemplation of the mystery of immaculacy.

Again playing with the viewers' imaginary horizon of expectations, Zurbarán is known for including in many of his canvases a *cartellino* – a small piece of paper incorporated on the visual plane that offers the illusion of substance – bearing his signature and the painting's date. His last two known Conceptionist compositions – the *Immaculate Conception* of 1661 (figure 4.10) and the *Immaculate Conception* also of 1661 (figure 4.15) – include the note prominently displayed on the right side of the Virgin. A seemingly extraneous element, the *cartellino* (with its corners bent, casting a shadow upon the clouds that surround the Virgin) asks the viewer to consider this strange object introduced into the pictorial field of the visionary experience. The question then arises of how to measure the significance of this gesture if we consider these paintings as open windows to the transcendental in the context of the dialectics of sight and vision, allegory and anagogy, and immanence and transcendence.

Stoichita has linked the use of the *cartellino* in these specific paintings to the idea of God as painter and the painter as *pintor divino*, coupled with the baroque play between *engaño* and *desengaño*: "Zurbarán is an (almost) 'divine' artist, since he makes the spectator standing before his painting a doubter: the *cartellino* is a technique that befits the poetics of the *engaño/desengaño*. It deceives the spectator's eye while at the same time announcing that this picture, which might otherwise appear to have emerged from God's brush, is in fact a personal creation" (120). Convincing as it may seem, the premise behind Stoichita's statement is that, by inserting a *cartellino* in these Immaculate Conception paintings, Zurbarán is reclaiming his place as sole creator-painter, and that, through this act of self-assertion, he is displacing the immediacy of the visionary in the painting. If we follow through on the implication of

Figure 4.15. Francisco
de Zurbarán, *Immaculate
Conception* (1661).
Szépmüvészeti Múzeum,
Budapest.

Stoichita's argument, by highlighting the deceptive nature of realism
and illusionism in art, Zurbarán is showcasing the canvas as canvas,
the painting as object, and the image as image and not as icon, contained, not saturated or excessive. The painting is not a celestial vision,
the painter is not Godlike (despite the critic's use of the *pintor divino* category), and he is not a man whose hand and brush are analogous to the
hand and brush of God; the painter, as indicated in the *cartellino*, would
be Zurbarán as *pintor engañador* or deceiver. The drawback of this logic
is that it positions the *cartellino* as a pictorial element that categorically
breaks the continuum between the self and the holy vision that the painting performs, rejects the bond between the painter and God, and seems
motivated by a type of paradoxical secularization of the viewing experience necessitated by Zurbarán's desire to be singularly recognized.
Zurbarán flourishes as an artist in the transition to modernity, and thus
the *cartellino* is comprehended as sign of things to come, the excision of
the ties between God and painter in favour of a conception of the artist
as an independent genius – the liberal artist I discuss in the previous
chapter but without the need for justification in a system of similitudes
and correspondences with God as the supreme painter-creator.

If we reject this assessment, then how do we read this extraneous object that makes its presence felt in the field of the visionary? Within the frame, the *cartellino* exists in the realm of the liminal, floating on the clouds, a man-made object that is instantly familiar and strange: a condition that correlates with the Virgin, a recognizable child with rosy, rounded cheeks, floating on a moon, immaculately conceived, absolutely pure, and eternal. Contrary to the logic of *engaño/desengaño*, I would argue that, for Zurbarán and the early modern Spanish spectator of these paintings, the *cartellino* visually indicates, instead, the link between immanence and transcendence. On the one hand, notwithstanding Stoichita's conclusions, the *cartellino* can be read as reiterating the fellowship between God and the *pintor divino*; Zurbarán adds his signature to the image that reproduces God's original, and together they offer the viewer – through the similitude of the image and the saturated nature of the divine mystery that the Virgin of the Immaculate Conception represents – a window to the anagogic visionary experience. Moreover, thinking of its effect as a pictorial illusion, the *cartellino* offers an imaginary space for the faithful viewer to add his signature. To be more precise, parallel to John of Patmos, who inscribes his vision in the Book of Revelation (as we see clearly in Velázquez's pendants), Zurbarán inscribes on the canvas his own visual account of the Virgin of the Immaculate Conception – this is his version *here* of the Divine *there*, and the paintings perform as a gateway between the two. Just as importantly, the viewer is provided an imaginary surface upon which to add her/his own name as a participant in the visionary experience of the Virgin of the Immaculate Conception. The *cartellino*, signed and dated, offers the spectator the certainty that she/he, like Zurbarán and indebted to his divinely mediated genius, can stand at the threshold between what is seen with the eyes and what the soul recognizes, the bridge between immanence and transcendence confirmed.

Within these interpretative parameters, I will now return briefly to the *Immaculate Conception with Two Allegorical Figures*. The painting famously also includes a *cartellino* fixed on the globe to the right side of the Virgin below the hand of the figure whose eyes are covered by the Virgin's robe. Unlike other examples, the paper this time appears with no discernible signature showing. If we decipher, as I propose, the blindfolded figure as a stand-in for the viewer's spiritual vision and the faith it requires, then the unsigned *cartellino* can only be understood as a surface for imprinting, as a summons for the spectator to imagine his/her name inscribed as a participant in the anagogic experience.

As I now turn my attention to Murillo's Immaculist paintings, a parallel investigation of a visual hermeneutics grounded in the dialectics of sight and vision holds true: the painting understood as a site for the viewer to stand in the place of the visionary, faithfully recall the doctrine, and experience the mystical event that motivates, cognizant of the analogies and mysteries the image holds.[39] The distinctiveness of Murillo's corpus resides in his specific approach, which retains the immediacy of the apparition while eliding the strangeness that populates Zurbarán's corpus. To be more precise, as I demonstrate, Murillo strategically deploys naturalism and vitality in his Immaculate Conception paintings to envelop the viewer in what Enrique Valdivieso has called "a dynamic and celestial vision."[40]

John Jervis, taking an alternative analytical pathway, has recently given Murillo's naturalism a particularly interesting interpretation, arguing for an examination of the "Madonna" paintings in which naturalism weighs heavily on the side of immanence. Basing his judgment on Murillo's alleged use of live models for the images of Mary, who for Jervis manifest an "individual personality" (29), and taking his cue from Stratton's general assessment that Murillo's "religious narratives had an immediacy, a genre-like quality, a feeling of everyday reality" ("Murillo in America" 94), Jervis concludes: "Whatever their traditional trappings, those Madonnas do not point us 'beyond,' towards the transcendental; rather they emphasize the manifestation of the transcendental in the here and now, in the embodied materiality of a specific person. This is not body transfigured by spirit, already rising toward the ethereal, but spirit as immanent in the materiality of the body" (29). Jervis is ultimately interested in the connections between naturalism, the representation of innocence, and sentimentality – the way in which one value system gets mapped or coded by the other in painting. This is an approximation that clarifies, for example, the tendency to represent the Virgin of the Immaculate Conception as a familiar-looking child. Nevertheless, from my perspective, Jervis neither considers the intricacies of Conceptionist thought nor recognizes that the Immaculist paintings are thematically and theologically distinguished from the (admittedly thin) biblical narrative of Mary's life, a lapse that leads him to read all the "Madonna" paintings as part of the same nomenclature. One striking slip is that Jervis does not distinguish the Immaculate Conception from the Ascension, and thus assumes that all of Murillo's paintings of the Virgin floating in the air refer to the body of Mary being transfigured from its material form to a spirit transcended to the heavens. We could easily forgive this confusion, given that in the early modern period the iconography of the Ascension of the Virgin (a specific moment in the life narrative of Mary) was in fact often muddled with the contemplation of immaculacy. The bigger problem is that Jervis's keen intuition of what is at stake in the naturalistic representation of the Virgin results too quickly in the closing of the passage between immanence and transcendence; and this is a tendency that is probably shared by many twenty-first century spectators of his paintings. The Virgin is represented as an everyday girl, and for the critic this familiarity "prefigures" an identificatory sensibility or all-too-human "sweetness," calling forth a modernity where transcendence is abandoned in favour of a selfhood of the here and now (29):

> For all this to work, both naturalism and the hint of the sacred have to be present together; yet the sacred, as manifest only in and through the innocence of the ordinary, the humdrum of the everyday, can simultaneously hint as its absence, at its withdrawal as a transcendent source of power or signification – and this, in turn, adds an element of nostalgia, a sense of "homeliness" as an origin that may need to be precariously recreated in the permanent context of its own threatened disappearance. (30)

Jervis understands the transcendental as something that, when materialized or embodied, is foreclosed, denying any visionary quality to Murillo's Immaculate Conception paintings.

As my analysis up to this point makes clear, I propose that we examine Murillo's naturalism instead as deployed in favour of the visionary, and consider how it promotes (rather than severs) the ability of the viewer to see in this here and now the mysterious transcendence marked by Mary's purity. As with Zurbarán, examining the bond between sight and vision serves us well. In Zurbarán the visionary effect resides in the simultaneity of sight and vision – the viewer sees a familiar Virgin girl-child made strange by the liminality of her setting and the foreign figures that accompany her. Alternatively, in Murillo's Immaculate Conception paintings, sight and vision are coextensive, almost inseparable, and the viewer is thus made privy to a naturalized access to the visionary. It is through sight, by way of seeing the Virgin as a recognizable face and in an easily identifiable setting, that the viewer is summoned to experience the ineffable, the image simultaneously resonant with both material existence (sight) and the divine alterity that resides inside and beyond the self (vision).

As already noted, Murillo's Immaculist paintings mostly eschew the iconography that would lead to a didactic doctrinal reading in the strictest sense; almost none of them include symbols from the litany, for example. Moreover, even though these paintings are often examined in the context of Seville's religious fervour, Murillo does not include pictorial references to the city where most of them were commissioned and placed. In the *Immaculate of the Half Moon* (1665) he further reduces the iconographical elements, representing just her head, the moon brought up to her waist, and only the blue robe and the cherubs that surround her coding the image as the Virgin of the Immaculate Conception (figure 4.16). This contraction is even more pronounced in the *Immaculate Conception* of 1675–80 with the moon and the cherubs expunged, and only the luminosity offered by her being dressed by the sun and the blue robe denoting her identity (figure 4.17).

Some of Murillo's paintings include additional figures, most prominently the early 1665 example that was commissioned for the church of Santa María la Blanca and which today is in the Louvre. But the vast majority, and definitively his entire mature production, reduces the representation of immaculacy to its barest essentials. Murillo is, most certainly, influenced by Pacheco's advice against narrative distractions in the representation of Mary's sinless state; as mentioned before, Pacheco's *Arte* specifically singles out the dragon in an attempt to expunge from the image – in a painterly imitation of God's making Mary *tota pulchra* – any ugliness or unseemly elements. The effect in Murillo is to distil – condense and decontaminate – the image's contemplative capacity. And it is this reduction that is pivotal to the contemplative and visionary potential of an image such as the *Immaculate Conception* of 1675–80. In the most economic translation of the doctrine and John of Patmos's vision that serves as its foundation, Murillo accomplishes an immediate passage from sight to vision, from the immanence of what is familiar and human in the lifelike fleshiness of his young Andalusian Virgin to the visionary experience of the mystery of immaculacy, now unburdened of the pictorial gestures and scriptural codes that detract from focusing on the Virgin as a *pure* image. In fact, I would argue (and here I am echoing Jervis but making the opposite point) that Murillo's late Immaculate Conceptions best offer the viewer saturated transcendence precisely because they show absolute purity through the Virgin's familiar (i.e., similar) and yet excessive humanity – a resemblance that is bound to a sublime difference, immanence in the service of transcendence, sight as a conduit to vision.

Murrillo's most mature *tota pulchra*, the *Immaculate Conception of the Venerable*, wholly encapsulates the ways in which the familiar and immanent visually communicate transcendence (figure 4.11). The Virgin's face invites the viewer to look at her and recognize her as a Sevillian girl – long brown hair, brown eyes, full lips, olive skin, round cheeks. There is nothing sculptural or ethereal about her face and hands – naturalism reigns in a figure that could look down upon the viewer and walk out of the frame without having to change any aspect of her appearance. But

Figure 4.16. Bartolomé Esteban Murillo, *Immaculate of the Half Moon* (1665). Prado Museum, Madrid.

Figure 4.17. Bartolomé Esteban Murillo, *Immaculate Conception* (1675–80). Sotheby's, Private collection, London.

this young girl, in all her material familiarity, is also, and not without effect, floating in mid-air, standing on the crescent moon, her blue robe flowing in the midst of clouds with more than two dozen putti swirling and surrounding her from all directions, hands crossed on her chest, and gazing upward contemplating her immaculacy as well as her role in the heavenly drama. There is no architectural feature or extrinsic element to tie her to an earthly narrative and distract from what is clearly coded as a manifest vision. The Virgin comes upon the viewer in the guise of the Immaculate Conception, pure revelation, surrounded by a darkened emptiness that points towards the apophatic no-thingness of transcendence, luminescent with no identifiable source of light, admired by the angels, beckoning the viewer to venerate her but also join her in the contemplation of the sacred mystery and the invisible and unsymbolizable background that surrounds her. The visionary transcendence of this sacred mystery can thus be easily perceived and received, even if not rationally understood. There is nothing to interpret, no radicalized difference, only contiguity, proportionality, analogy, perhaps even more so sympathy between the spectator and the image: "The identity of things, the fact that they can resemble others and be drawn to them, though without being swallowed up or losing their singularity" (Foucault, *The Order of Things* 27–8). Each viewer, in his/her contemplation, can singularly imagine the particular coordinates that make possible the experience of resemblance with the Virgin as both human and sacred. To be clear, the point is not that the viewer can assume the position of being identical to the Virgin of the Immaculate Conception; that would be sacrilege. Mary, in her unstained perfection, maintains her status as a saturated phenomenon. But she is, nevertheless, identical with us in so far as she is singularly similar to us, her sight is familiar to us, she represents a holy version of us, created by the same inscrutable God. In her spiritual, heavenly state (as revealed to John of Patmos first and now to the viewer through Murillo's painting) *and* in her exceptional humanity lies the realized promise of the ineffable as a passage to eternal redemption. Following Foucault, we can say that the canvas offers the sacred "form" of immaculacy (signifier and invisible signified) through the figure of the Virgin, transmitting a visionary knowledge that "can only follow the paths of similitude":

> The form making a sign and the form being signalized are resemblances, but they do not overlap. And it is in this respect that resemblance ... is without doubt the most universal thing there is: at the same time that which is most clearly visible, yet something that one must nevertheless search for, since it is also the most hidden; what determines the form of knowledge (for knowledge can only follow the paths of similitude), and what guarantees its wealth of content (for the moment one lifts aside the signs and looks at what they indicate, one allows Resemblance itself to emerge into the light of day and shine with its own inner light). (*The Order of Things* 32)

Putting it in terms of the "rhetoric of the inexpressible" through which Murillo achieves Mary's immanence, the Virgin is filled with the spiritual knowledge of divine transcendence (simultaneously showing what is most visible *and* most hidden). The relationship between her materiality and her sacred positionality – between the Virgin's natural

Figure 4.18. Francisco Pacheco, *Immaculate Conception* (1610). Archbishop's Palace, Seville.

humanity and her natural sacred perfection – is visually presented as anchored in a resemblance that calls upon the self-recognition of the viewer. Murillo became the most sought after of the *pintores divinos* precisely because he perfectly understood the parameters and horizons of the religious imagination of his time, in which the anagogic and visionary potentiality of devotional painting was counted on and welcomed by those who commissioned and those who viewed these images.

Given what I have asserted up to this point, I would like to add a brief discussion of how the potentiality of the religious imagination as evinced in Zurbarán and Murillo intersects with issues of identity – communal and national. As discussed in previous chapters, the political implications of the connection between Immaculist thought and Spain as *nación* are substantial. It is not surprising, therefore, that Virgin of the Immaculate Conception paintings often include topographical and architectural elements that literally place her as a connecting body between the heavens and specific places, such as Seville. Sometimes the visual cue is explicit, as in Pacheco's *Immaculate Conception* (1610), where the Guadalquivir is used as a stage for the iconographical program that anchors the representation of the Virgin (figure 4.18). Mulcahy, in her examination of Zurbarán's *Immaculate with Two Allegorical Figures*, remarks on the generic inclusion of the identifiable autochthonous geography in the Conceptionist corpus: "Set in a lush Sevillian landscape with a view of the city are her symbols" (90). The effect is intentional and explicit, placing the visionary experience within the distinct and familiar landscape of the Spanish cities and countryside. I would add that the visual referencing of the Andalusian geography is an extension of the Spanish-looking countenance of the Virgin in the paintings I have discussed. The viewer is presented with the pictorial representation of the sacred and transcendent in the local and immanent, given a form within the boundaries of a Spanish geographic and physiological identity. In other words, the recognizable and domestic geography of immaculacy in these paintings bolsters the movement towards the anagogic and visionary. The logic is identical to what I argue regarding Murillo's naturalism in his depiction of the Virgin. The goal is not to mire the Virgin of the Immaculate Conception in the immanence of the Sevillian countryside. To the contrary, the religious imagination of Counter-Reformation Spain is bolstered by the premise that the *here* can be made to resemble and be contiguous with the *there*; what is seen and recognized by sight (familiar and didactic) is simultaneously opened to the anagogic and visionary, which has as its horizon the experience of the transcendental mystery of the *tota pulchra*. In a context of religious fervour, these paintings offer the image as mediating vehicle and strive to deliver the viewer a pathway to revelation.

IV. The Persistence of Excess (Against Stoichita's Taming of the Visionary Experience)

In the first chapter of *Visionary Experience in the Golden Age of Spanish Art*, Stoichita remarks on the status of the mystical vis-à-vis the personal and the institutional:

> [T]he first [point made by Saint John of the Cross in his *Subida del Monte Carmelo*] relates to the Church's jurisdiction over the visionary experience

and the second to the necessity to have the vision interpreted. These had to have been accomplished before a vision could be committed to painting. Only visions whose authenticity had been verified and whose holy interpretation had been accepted were allowed to become a pictorial representation. The latter was their final certificate of authenticity. (25)

Undeniably, the mystical experience – comprehended as a revelation of the Divine – was deemed in need of oversight, and only visions that had been sanctioned as legitimate could make it to the level of a reproducible image. Following this logic, Stoichita's concluding summary remarks in his "21 Theses on the Representation of the Visionary Experience" focus on the separation between the two planes of experience, the earthly and the sacred, with one irrupting into the other: "The visionary painting is a double painting: it presents unreality irrupting into reality" (199). Again, there is little to debate in this assertion if it is taken as the general condition of representation of the ineffable, or what the critic calls the "paradoxical rhetoric" of visually translating what is singular and indescribable (199). But Stoichita's larger claim is in fact far more constrictive, privileging the limits imposed on the experience of the viewer by the Church, both as an institution and as a physical space: "Far from inspiring uncontrollable mystical activities, the contemplation of the vision-painting is equivalent to 'taming' the visionary experience ... thus [the viewer] experiences this ecstatic state [of the visionary-saint] at the very center of an area – the church – and as a consequence never finds himself completely alone before the manifestation of the sacred become visible" (26). As presented by the critic, the spectator's visual experience – contextualized within a controlled public space, observed and measured, removed from the particular and immersed in externally regulated rituals – is successfully precluded from her/his own distinctive imaginary experience. It is for this reason that Stoichita's overall assessment of the Immaculate Conception paintings falls heavily on the side of a "rhetoric of the inexpressible" that disappointingly leads to orthodoxy and away from a singular and imaginative religious experience.

And yet, Stoichita's assessment fails to make allowances for critical aspects that affect the conditions of production and reception of visionary paintings, and specifically the representation of the *tota pulchra*. First, as I have noted in previous chapters, the level of control that the Church Militant officially claimed was rarely matched in practice. While it is certain that artists would not be commissioned to paint mystical encounters that had not been considered "true" or "verifiable," they did take the opportunity to distinguish between what they deemed necessary and accidental, and what to incorporate and leave out in the visual translation of the visionary experience. In their roles as *pintores teólogos* and *pintores divinos*, these artists were tasked with singularly imagining and presenting to the spectator the "sanctioned" encounter with the sacred, and the Virgin of the Immaculate Conception paintings are a particularly interesting case in this regard. Despite a fixed iconographical program and a biblical account of the mystical experience of John of Patmos, as documented in Revelation 12, the exact conditions of Mary's spotlessness and eternal existence staunchly remained in the realm of the transcendental. As a result, the myriad of paintings produced in Spain during the early modern period attest to a vast, varied, and nuanced interpretative field for the individual painter and his projected audience in portraying the conditions of Mary's existence. What is missing in Stoichita's assessment is, therefore, the potentiality of the individual viewer's religious imagination and the ways in which the cultural context of the Counter-Reformation encouraged and nurtured this imagination in its injunction for contemplation. Beholders of Immaculate Conception paintings during this period navigated a set of highly contested tenets and inscrutable sacred acts, which must have elicited a level of psychological and emotional engagement not necessarily found in other biblical or hagiographical representations. The act of recognition and contemplation often took place in a public space, but also and very often in the privacy of the home or of a secluded chapel within a larger cathedral or hospital, where the anagogical and the visionary could well be sensuously embraced and experienced.[41] The positionality of the *pintor teólogo* and *pintor divino* as interpreter and producer of visions that would intentionally call upon the sight and vision of the spectator also plays into this cultural imaginary. The point is that if, as stated by Stoichita, these paintings visually enact "the figurative representation of the *unio mystica*" (199), they do not do so exclusively within the purview of a self-containing and exclusionary frame. As previously noted, it is my contention that Immaculate Conception paintings – at least the ones here examined – invited the viewer to see the canvas not as a purely representational threshold but as conduit to the revelation of immaculacy as it had been experienced by the apostle and interpreted by the painter. If Pacheco and Velázquez offer a mediating identificatory figure in the donors or with John of Patmos himself, the mature production of Zurbarán and Murillo offers the image of the Virgin of the Immaculate Conception as a vision proper: the spectator is squarely placed in the position of John of Patmos; he/she is the sole receiver of the image revealed, the frame performing the function of an opening to the imaginary experience of the Divine (and not as an alienating and regulatory filter), sight in the service of vision. The spiritually charged and anagogic relationship of the viewer to these paintings is necessitated by a Counter-Reformation milieu that depended on both the didactic and the contemplative power of images. It is precisely in this dialectical space where the individual's religious imagination, simultaneously conformist and idiosyncratic, can flourish, conditioned by what is sanctioned by the Church and yet free to conceive of the particulars of the visionary experience and its effects in singular terms. Many accounts of the period testify to the way in which individuals took the experience of seeing an image as a conduit to revelation; this was a practice that was, in fact, systematized and encouraged by Ignatius of Loyola in his *Spiritual Exercises*. Teresa of Ávila is amongst the most famous examples of the ways in which this image-driven slippage between immanence and transcendence could be harnessed in favour of a deepening of contemplation and faith. As noted by Bárbara Mujica,

> Human are physical beings, [Teresa] explains, and God speaks to us in a way we can understand, engaging our senses to communicate even the super-sensorial. Teresa's familiarity with Ignatius's *Ejercicios Espirituales* made her acutely aware of the effectiveness of image and imagination (that is, the mental projection of images) to spur spiritual experience. She recommends the use of icons and other sensory stimuli to beginners in prayer to initiate the process of interiorization. (746)

Following the logic of Teresa's practice, the religious imagination of the period looks to draw on the scriptural and theological elements codified by the Church and interpreted by the *pintor divino* in order to forge a singular, interior, and ineffable experience. It is in this manner that Immaculist paintings, as saturated phenomena – excessive and bound with the inexpressible – and as gateways to the Divine have their most prescient roles in the lives of the faithful in Counter-Reformation Spain.

Chapter Five

Concepción Maravillosa: Theological Discourse and Religious Women Writers

I. Women Writers and the Production of Theological Knowledge

A study on the religious imagination and the Virgin of the Immaculate Conception would be remiss if it did not duly focus on the works and other cultural products of religious women writers. The fundamental reason is apparent: one must assume that early modern Catholic women writers, especially those who wrote from religious spaces, found a rich spiritual and conceptual space in the Marian cult, and, in Spain most particularly, in the devotion to the Virgin of the Immaculate Conception. The history of the Order of the Immaculate Conception in Spain, as I indicated in the Introduction, is intimately linked to women such as Beatriz da Silva, who founded the first convent in Toledo and dictated the vestments and rituals that would largely steer the imaginary for the doctrine all through the early modern period. An examination of women-authored texts, nevertheless, quickly proves more challenging than a straightforward approach to the mechanisms of women's identification with Mary as Mother of God may initially suggest. Religious women writers do demonstrate a close gendered identification with Mary, and this connection is pivotal to the study of their texts; but the parameters, dynamics, and effects of this identification within the context of the doctrine and image of the Immaculate Conception are not altogether predictable and offer a fascinating textual topography through which to investigate the expansiveness and investments of the religious imagination in Spain. Spanish early modern religious women authored some of the most significant and imaginative deliberations on the sacred mystery, formally addressing the various scriptural interpretations and exegetical debates that framed the elevation of the doctrine to dogma. As I will demonstrate, the Immaculist doctrine is fertile ground for and motivates much of hermeneutical practice of Juana de la Cruz, Isabel de Villena, Valentina Pinelo, and María de Ágreda. Despite a Church orthodoxy that structurally and ideologically contested their authority – and as it relates to this book, building on what we saw in the women poets of Zapata's *Justa* – these women offer a fascinating lens through which to investigate the gendered religious imagination in their interpretation and production of knowledge about the Scriptures, the theological corpus, and divine revelation around Mary's purity. As I demonstrate, their texts amply and best display the theological and narrative potentiality of the doctrine, and how the faithful understood and related to the exceptionality of the Virgin as immaculate *and* human.

Any discussion of religious women's writing is almost exclusively guided by considerations of context and authority. Critics discuss at length the social and spatial conditions in which early modern women wrote, with convents and other religious spaces deemed environments that afforded alternatively oppression or liberation, or both. To be more precise, for some critics the early modern Catholic cultural and religious framework overwhelmingly subjected religious women – physically, intellectually, and spiritually – to the authority and supervision of men (mostly confessors). For others, the convents provided a site that facilitated a degree (at times substantial) of intellectual and spiritual autonomy within the auspices of a supportive, or at least a like-minded and similarly instructed, female community; or what Ángela Muñoz Fernández identifies as "networks of thought that endorse the notion of a non-univocal feminine culture."[1] In *Nuns: A History of Convent Life 1450–1700*, Silvia Evangelisti focuses as well on the formation of a community that, as she explains, is forged around the conviction and authority tendered by having been chosen as "interlocutors" of God:

> Whilst nuns often celebrated in their works exemplary piety, chastity, and austerity, they also explicitly asserted their spiritual authority and privileged role as interlocutors with God. In recording their life, they embarked on an adventure that implied the possibility to address an audience inside and outside the convent made up of their sisters, confessors, and other devout associates who, in listening to their words and hearing of their visions, found a means to reach the Divine. (75)

Within this analytical framework, we are tasked to examine the multiple strategies that women employed to legitimize and authorize their visions, their hermeneutical practices, and the exercise of writing. Even though religious women writers were formally and in practice often subjected to the supervision and tutelage of confessors and other male

Church officials and relatives, they nonetheless persisted – whether by design or as a consequence of their religious practices – in producing texts and other cultural products where their individually crafted understanding of doctrine, scriptural interpretation, faith, belief, and practices was elaborately articulated. Religious women writers, as noted by Sylvia Brown, functioned and produced their texts through "a dynamic, fluid, and often contradictory discursive system, operating both to challenge and reinscribe orthodoxy" (2). This is a very important point precisely because, when we look at religious women within the context of Spanish religious communities, we must give credence to the possibility of appropriation and self-definition within the limits of orthodoxy, much as Muñoz Fernández defines the activity of founding and living in convents in the medieval and early modern periods:

> Female monasticism was a liberating life framework, even though inside the established order. This means that it was subject to limitations, as it did not allow women to put forward entirely new cultural meanings ... But it is worth relativizing the reach of this limitation because it does not take into account female subjectivity and its capacity to resignify the symbols and values of the common culture and individual experiences. When this practice of signification, unlimited in its horizons, is generated and perpetuated through women's relationships which in turn produce of contexts of meaning, we can there recognize forms of feminine culture.[2]

One could generalize this statement to the religious authors and artists I have discussed in previous chapters; each of them – from Alva y Astorga to Zurbarán – produces within the limits of religious orthodoxy his or her personal imaginative response to orthodoxy. On the other hand, it must also be acknowledged that the carving out of a religious selfhood – whether as a textual or visual interpreter of the Scriptures and Christian doctrine or as a visionary – is also, inevitably, what Brown has called a "gendered procedure" fashioned in favour of "individual or communal purposes" (2).

For my purposes, the best juncture for examining this gendered procedure within the coordinates of women's religious imagination is in the realm of theological discourse or, more concretely, in the interpretation and production of knowledge about the Scriptures, the theological corpus, Church doctrine, and divine revelation. The category has a long evolution in which the merits and aims of theology were debated, contested, and variously institutionalized.[3] Following Aquinas, by the early modern period Scholastic models of theology had fully acquired the methodological character of a discipline that held a close affinity to philosophical inquiry, even if their aims were distinct, and as such had been formalized in universities all across Europe. The Society of Jesus, which by the late sixteenth century significantly determined the parameters to be followed in institutions of higher learning (universities and monastic schools) in Spain, promoted the following course of study:

> After a three-year preparatory study of (Aristotelian) philosophy, the study of theology lasts four more years ... The method follows that of the thirteenth-century commentaries on the *Sententiae*: explanation of the text while indicating the ratio [rationale, reason for proceeding in a certain order] and then after each article, as needed, a more precise explanation of the matter through *quaestiones*. Under no circumstances should the professor merely present different *sententiae*; instead, where applicable, he should defend Aquinas' teaching. (Leinsle 284)

This highly analytical approach to divine revelation saw comparable programs in Scotist (Franciscan) and Thomist (Dominican) institutions and made its way to the monastic setting by way of those who had been appointed to serve as administrators and educators. As described by Ulrich G. Leinsle, "Generally they brought back to their own monastery the philosophical or theological current that they had studied at the university ... Often the entire community was included in a course on positive theology, which also served as continuing education for the priests who had pastoral duties, whereas Scholastic theology had an influence on the clergy in the surrounding areas through the major disputations" (285). As such, the practice of theology with its Scholastic preferences and corresponding sources, methodologies, and programs of study regulated the appropriate approaches and authorized the legitimate experts for its praxes, which were alternatively tailored either to the university and its philosophical and metaphysical interests or to the pastoral field. If in the Middle Ages a firm distinction could still be made between Scholastic theology and "forms of free, spiritual or monastic theologizing" (9), by the Counter-Reformation to be a theologian or to engage in the production of theological discourse implied a certain set of systematic parameters, horizons, and methods. Nevertheless – and this point will prove important for the religious women whose works I examine in this chapter – monastic theology maintained, especially in a Counter-Reformation setting, "the purpose ... to advance personally in the faith, to edify others, who often share the same way of life, or to defend against false teachings or harmful influences" (112).

Moreover, the writings of Bonaventure and Bernard of Clairvaux (1090–1153) offered a well-established foundation for a theological engagement that correlated more closely to the senses and the faithful's capacity to receive divine revelation:

> As for us, we wish to proceed with caution and simplicity in commenting on these mystical and holy words. Let us conduct ourselves as does sacred Scripture, which interprets the wisdom hidden in the mystery with words that are our own; when it speaks to us about God, it depicts him with the help of our feelings and sentiments. Scripture makes the invisible and hidden reality of God, which is of such exalted worth, accessible to the human mind, as though in vessels of little value that are taken from the reality known to us through the senses. (Clairvaux, qtd in Leinsle 113)

Even if, by the early modern period, Clarivaux's rejection of Aquinas had largely dissolved given the authority conferred on Thomist thought and exegetical methods, the practical applications and personal aspects of theology beyond the formal academic programs promoted by universities had not.[4] Anchored in allegorical, tropological (moral), and anagogical (mystical) interpretation rather than metaphysical or philosophical speculative thought, practical or monastic theology favoured symbolic readings of scriptural texts that became a mechanism for an understanding of divine revelation in the context of personal religiosity as experienced in the cloister.

This is ground that, from a different perspective, I covered in chapter 3 and chapter 4 when examining the category of visual artists as mute theologians, *pintores católicos*, *divinos*, or *teólogos*, and the visionary Immaculate Conception paintings they produce. In that analysis, as also in this chapter, the focus is on how the hermeneutical interpretation, defence, and propagation of the doctrine of the Immaculate Conception critically depended on the imaginative leaps made by artists and writers within the boundaries of orthodoxy and theological thought. And yet, there are important differences between the painters who saw themselves as creators of religious art as akin to God as a creator of images (*Dios pintor*) and religious women writers who deployed a discourse and insisted on contributing to a disciplinary field prohibited to them. Unlike other forms of religious practice (mysticism, for example), the Church Militant understood formal theology to be an area that only men could occupy. The proposition that texts produced by early modern religious women can be examined through the lens of theology admittedly presents a challenge, especially when we acknowledge the limitations women in the period withstood in the realm of basic education, university attendance, and the entrenched interpretation of the Pauline dictum on women's silence in religious matters.[5] The dictum, accompanied by scriptural interpretation by Church officials and theologians, seemed to specifically proscribe the role of women as teachers; this was a standard that had been exegetically confirmed by Aquinas, for example, when he declared that, "because of her female sex, [she] is by nature subject to man, or if not by nature, at least by command of the Lord. Therefore, it is not her place to teach in public" (qtd in Howe, "Let Your Women Keep Silence" 124). Renaissance humanists, such as Luis Vives, softened this position from a secular perspective by deeming that women should be able to teach other women, motivated not by the possibility of equality in intellectual capacity and moral rectitude but rather by the danger of exposing young noble girls to instructors of the opposite sex.[6] In the strictly religious arena, however, theological writing remained restricted to educated male elites, a circumstance that was reinforced by the fact that the Judaic, Islamic, and Christian traditions depend, as Emily A. Holmes reminds us, on a large knowledge base appropriate to the study of divinely inspired and sacred texts (3). Moreover, as also noted by Holmes, the conditions for the production of theological discourse by women are burdened by the masculinist framework of the discipline: "finding a writing voice is especially difficult when entering a tradition that expects women, if they are to write at all, to mask the particularities of their lives and to write like traditional theologians, that is, as educated, ordained men" (3–4).

Consequently, the following set of questions is vital to the analysis of medieval and early modern women's theological discourse: What are the specific circumstances that allow a select set of women to introduce themselves into this field? What are the conditions that legitimize their incursion into this type of discourse? How do women writers, against the prescriptions that dictate their exclusion, authorize their theological discourse? How does their positionality (both ascribed by others and self-ascribed) as cloistered women intersect with their exegetical practice?[7] Theology is a discourse that requires authority: the authority given by God in divine revelation; the authority tendered by the acquisition and production of knowledge and the hermeneutical practice that comes from it; and the authority that results from writing and having one's interpretative capacity be subject to scrutiny and commentary. Women had to negotiate their position of authority against ideological, cultural, and personal biases that their male counterparts did not weather in the same manner. Elizabeth A. Dreyer well explains this disparity when introducing her study of four women who, only since 1970, have been recognized as Doctors of the Church (Hildegard of Bingen,

Catherine of Siena, Teresa of Ávila, and Thérèse of Lisieux): "[N]one of these women was a theologian in the formal sense of the term: as indicated by the title of the book, they are 'accidental theologians.' But all were truly exceptional teachers who reflected on and absorbed the Scriptures; lived the Christian life in creative and full ways; and wrote about major theological topics with passion and insight" (1).

In what follows, I focus on the religious imagination of women writers as it is articulated and legitimized in their theological interpretation and defence of the doctrine. What will become clear is that the economy of excess – bound to established parameters of orthodoxy while simultaneously producing a surplus of interpretation, appended "facts" and affect – that feeds the religious imagination is fundamental to these women's hermeneutical practice and the fashioning of their selfhood as writers. If we recall the arguments I made in chapter 1, the religious imagination is in itself always already excessive insofar as it approaches and attempts to translate a sacred mystery and convey divine revelation with mechanisms that are often and even obligatorily extravagant and hyperbolic. In its engagement with the fluid dialectical relationship between immanence and transcendence that defines the relationship between humans and God, the religious imagination is tasked with capturing that which exceeds the limits of our postlapsarian discernment. Additionally, the doctrine hinges on excess, as becomes immediately apparent when anyone (regardless of whether it is Francisco Suárez or Ágreda) attempts to explain its conditions, suppositions, and necessities. Exceeding her fellow humans both in matter and in spirit, Mary is the Immaculate Mother of God, the eternal Apocalyptic Woman, the Virgin without her Child not yet subjected to his presence, and participant in the narration of redemption in her own right. Moreover, women religious writers invested in producing theological discourse cannot avoid being seen as excessive themselves, insofar as both their interpretations and the resulting texts are often considered unwarranted or outside of the sanctioned realm of theology, Scholastic and even practical, by the vast majority of an elite male Church hierarchy. Let's not forget that for the most part, these texts (oral, written, and visual) were created for private consumption (within the walls of convents), and their public dissemination exceeds their original purpose; as noted by Joan Curbet, "the shift from manuscript to print corresponds here to a shift from the monastic sphere ... to the world at large, from its initial enclosure to the public arena" (10). In the context of a mystical revelation, as is the case with Juana de la Cruz and Ágreda, the visionary experiences that motivate writing (and documentation) surpass the parameters of normal human life, and the textual account is inevitably imbued with an excess of words that attempt to convey the strange and the ineffable. Admittedly, the texts I here analyse were not formally composed as theological treatises. They are a mix of genres – *vitas*, mystical biographies, and sermons – that notably and concertedly integrate theological thought and discourse. The point, at least as I see it, is to examine these women's production of theological discourse within the larger schema of the hyperbolic and the excessive as constitutive of a gender-specific late medieval and early modern religious imagination.

Isabel de Villena, Juana de la Cruz, Valentina Pinelo, and María de Ágreda reaped the rewards but also surely paid the price for their incursion into an exegetical practice that was traditionally understood as off limits to women. If they gained fame and stature within their communities and cloisters, they also suffered censure and Inquisitorial interrogation. Villena's *Vita Christi*, because of its proto-feminist tendencies, required the protection of Isabel I of Castile; the manuscript for Juana de la Cruz's *Book of the conorte* [*El libro del conorte*] was heavily annotated by detractors and, once published, was taken out of circulation by Inquisitorial decree in 1568; the delation written against Pinelo's *The Book of Praises and Excellencies of the Glorious Santa Ana* [*Libro de las alabanzas y excelencias de la gloriosa Santa Ana*] soon after its publication exposed the text to Inquisitorial review (although it was never officially censored); and, not to be forgotten, the uneasiness caused by the manuscript of Ágreda's *Mística ciudad de Dios* resulted in the alleged burning of the first manuscript by Ágreda herself and occasioned her second interview with the Office of the Inquisition. Despite the obvious hindrances, these four women produced sophisticated and highly imaginative theological thought that amply displays their authority, through the hermeneutical interpretation of the Scriptures and the divine mysteries they contain, and features the importance of the Virgin of the Immaculate Conception in the story of human redemption.

In view of the authentication of authority (rhetorical, textual, and spiritual) and the censure imposed on women's textual production, I am interested in explaining how these women – from their contexts as cloistered religious writers – imagined and discursively presented the theological logic and the divine mystery that framed Mary's purity. In an attempt to shed light on the intersection between theological discourse and women's religious imagination (i.e., form and content), I analyse exclusively the passages where the doctrine of the Immaculate Conception of Mary is scrutinized, explained, and justified.

II. From Isabel de Villena to María de Ágreda: Theological Thought and Immaculate (Auto)Biographies

As is immediately evident when reading their texts, Isabel de Villena, Juana de la Cruz, Valentina Pinelo, and María de Ágreda straightfor-wardly tackled the controversies around the doctrine. Their texts do not merely praise the exceptionality of Mary as the "intact" Mother of God. Instead, they go much further, producing scriptural and doctrinal interpretations that do not just tell the story of Mary's conception but also intentionally address the divine logic that made her immaculacy possible and necessary. Isabel de Villena and Juana de la Cruz, who lived and wrote towards the end of the fifteenth century and the be-ginning of the sixteenth, serve as predecessors for Valentina Pinelo and María de Ágreda.

The illegitimate daughter of the influential Valencian nobleman Enrique de Villena (1384–1434), Isabel de Villena (1430–90) grew up un-der the protection and mentorship of Queen María of Aragon, which made possible instruction that included Latin and the study of biblical commentary. Once she was interned, as documented by Joan Curbet, Villena's social position and education enabled her to exert signifi-cant influence within and outside of the Trinitary convent where she lived the rest of her life: "What is beyond doubt is that, for Isabel (as she was known), conventual life certainly did not imply social exclu-sion or inactivity: on the contrary, her progress within the monastery allowed her to become one of the dominant figures in the social and ecclesiastic world of late-fifteenth century Valencia" (13).[8] The *Vita Christi*, written in the nun's vernacular Catalan, circulated widely dur-ing her lifetime in manuscript form and was prepared for publication in 1497, seven years after her death, in response to a request by the Catholic Queen Isabel I of Castile. With her *Vita Christi* – a genre that was very well established by the end of the fifteenth century – Villena attained the highest levels of religious, political, and cultural author-ity in late fifteenth-century Spain beyond Valencia. In addition to the intended biography of Christ, the *vita* genre often included scriptural commentaries, examinations of dogma, moral dissertations, spiritual instructions, meditations, and prayers, which exhibited the breadth of the author's scriptural and theological knowledge, as well as her/his ideological investments. Feminist critics – Rosanna Cantavella, Lesley Twomey, Curbet, and Miryam Criado – have correctly emphasized the many ways in which Villena's *Vita Christi* can also be read as a *Vita Mariae*, showcasing the Virgin's and other women's vital participation in the narrative of Christ's life and the redemption of humanity, a focus that reveals Villena's late medieval proto-feminist stance, "considering [in the *Vitae Christi*] the incorporation of the feminine experience, the creation of new models of womanhood, and the importance of women in human redemption."[9] For example, Villena's review of the role of women includes Eve, who, as our first true mother, is deemed necessary to the redemption of humanity. This topic has been examined by Curbet, who contextualizes Villena's valorizing of Eve in a "very specific theological domain: the concept of *felix culpa*," originally developed when Augustine dictated the fortunate necessity of the fall of man in his route towards full emancipation in heaven, possible because only then is Christ able to embrace humanity in his role as the incarnated Son of God (Curbet 33–4). It is precisely within this theological domain that Villena elaborates an interpretation of the doctrine.

Villena's *Vita Christi* does not begin, as would be perhaps expected, with the annunciation of the Virgin. Instead, the first segments of the text are dedicated to an account and defence of the doctrine of immaculacy, starting with the visit of the angel to a grieving Saint Joachim, shamed by the elders of the Temple for his sterility and reluctant to speak to anyone: "dolor meus renovatus est" (50). Chapter 1, like all subsequent sections of the *Vita Christi*, is replete with citations from the Scriptures and the writings and commentaries of Church fathers and medieval theologians – including Aquinas, Bonaventure, and Thomas à Kempis – underscoring not only Villena's knowledge and intellectual capacity but also her intention to follow closely the modality of the genre and introduce theological discourse in the form of a biographical narrative. She chronicles the life of Christ – and before him his grandparents, mother, and father – through the citation of biblical verses and other authoritative texts that corroborate and advance her personal interpretation of doctrine, as well as the history that she constructs as a supplement to the Scriptures. In Villena's account, for example, the angel orders Saint Joachim to return to Saint Anne, "who shall conceive from you a daughter of such excellence and rank."[10] This account makes clear Villena's stance on the issue of copulation and Mary's biological parentage, placing her in an Anselmian theological tradition in which original sin is *not* materially transmitted through the sexual act. Mary had been chosen from eternity – *ab initio* – to be the Mother of God, the holy temple, and "an imperial queen, who is not included in or compromised by any common law."[11] The Virgin's singularity is derived solely from God's will, not from a predictable or predetermined design. Citing the Book of Haggai 2:24, Villena offers God's declaration to the Virgin, "his temple," on the matter of her material conception: "Do not fear, my temple, for although you are descended from the proper nature of Adam's stock, you will not fall under the law constituted by his sin, but rather under that privileged by my grace to a singular degree. *Quia ego elegi te.*"[12] The Virgin's earthly conception is thus framed within the boundless omnipotence of God (not tied to any precedent, pattern, or past formulation) and his ability and will to make Mary an exception – "a singular degree" – from the legacy of Adam's flesh and fall. Villena is here aligned with a Franciscan nominalist theological tradition that privileges above all else divine will and omnipotence over any other imperative or expected design; everything is possible for God, even the conception of an immaculate being through the copulation of maculate parents, despite the categorical injunction imposed in the expulsion from Eden. Moreover, Villena suggests a kind of team effort between Saint Joachim and God: while the first will facilitate the conception of the immaculate body, the other will create the immaculate soul, for, "as soon as her glorious soul has been created and unified to her body, He (God) intends to clothe and adorn her with his grace [in the womb]."[13] Villena's proposition should not be considered strange or unorthodox, but certainly complex from a theological perspective. The remainder of the first chapter of the *Vita Christi* develops a description of Mary as a radically singular being, establishing attributes that would be reproduced by Conceptionists throughout the sixteenth and seventeenth centuries. Exalted and extolled above all other created beings (including the angels), Mary is a temple composed of three rooms – one for God the Father, one for God the Son, and one for the Holy Spirit – where she is tended to by seven handmaids who accompany her "within the womb of her mother and throughout her entire life": Faith, Hope, Charity, Humility, Devotion, Mercy, and Compassion.[14] Saint Joachim, a poor, sterile, and marginalized shepherd, is moulded into the worthy father of the Mother of God and the most exalted of men, a transformation, one should note, that may also have resonated with Villena and her female audience insofar as they may well have recognized in Saint Joachim their own marginalized positionality vis-à-vis the male elite Church hierarchy that kept their contributions at bay.

Chapter 2 of the *Vita Christi* repeats the scene with Saint Anne, who, in the midst of her own unbearable distress, is visited by the same angel who announces the conception of Mary: "Our Lord God wishes you to conceive a daughter so singular that neither original, venial, nor moral sin shall ever be found in her. Pure of all guilt shall you conceive her, and pure shall raise her. And in purity and spotlessness shall her entire life be led ... *Pulchra es, amica mea, et macula non est in te.*"[15] There are two separate aspects of this straightforward presentation of the Virgin's conception that merit attention. First, Villena's emphasis on Mary's singularity not only echoes Franciscan nominalist notions on the divine capacity to forgo ostensibly universal patterns or predetermined design but also allows for the Virgin to be uniquely positioned both in her humanity and in her eternal divinity, breaching the gap between the two. Second, Villena emphasizes the absence of guilt typically thought of as one of the main consequences of original sin inherited from Adam and Eve. In other words, her version of Conceptionist doctrine focuses on the lack of the cause (original sin) and on the absence of its effect (guilt). As such, the Virgin is released from the unrelenting burden of originary shame, habitually linked to Eve, and which largely determined the ways that women (both spiritually and materially) were thought of and thereby restricted. Given the authorial context of the *Vita Christi*, it is not a stretch to think that Villena and her cloistered community would have identified deeply with Mary, and with the potentiality for the absence of sin and guilt that she personifies. To this point, it is interesting to note that in chapter 197, when he arrives in the heavens upon his resurrection, Christ is welcomed by Saint Anne and Eve, who together stand as now eternally redeemed grandmothers. The familial connection notwithstanding, Curbet has correctly observed the importance of Villena's approach to Eve, who in her repentance is elevated by Christ as a welcome participant and "life giving force," necessary in the narrative of redemption and in the elevation of humanity: "One of the crucial features of the misogynist tradition has been confronted head-on and, in a bold revisionist move, it has been dismantled from within and rendered inert" (35). If Mary is the mother of our Redeemer, Eve is the mother of humanity, and Villena imagines a harmonious pair (not opposites) in the narrative of deliverance. It is also evident that the pairing of Eve with Saint Anne establishes a lineage of exalted saintly women for Mary's Immaculate Conception, as well as a female progeny – which evidently includes Villena and the nuns at the convent – that Christ himself recognizes: they are "singular and virtuous daughters when you learn that they are so loved and cherished by me, on account of their great deeds, inasmuch as they surpass men in the strength of their love. And I have given my mother [the Virgin Mary], therefore, as Leader and Lady to these women, in order to protect and defend them from those who seek to speak ill of them."[16] Villena and her sisters (and devout women in general) are analogous to their foremothers (Eve, Saint Anne, and the Virgin of the Immaculate Conception), redeemed from sin, freed from guilt, and recognized as Christ's most cherished servants: the true daughters of immaculacy. It is in textual instances such as these where the gendered religious imagination, in its intersection with theological discourse, is at its most expansive and effective, seamlessly imbricating a defence of Mary's exceptionality with a defence of women in general, from Eve onward. The Virgin's singularity is – retroactively and subsequently – every woman's blessed singularity.

At the end of chapter 2, Villena affirms her theological voice, offering a defence of the feast of the day of the Conception, commemorating the apparition of the angel and the encounter of Saint Joachim and Saint Anne. Not only does Villena paraphrase in Latin Anselm's sermon in favour of the feast, "Quia non est verus amator virginis Mariae qui respuit colere diem eius conceptionis," but she also sternly warns against a lukewarm veneration and love for Mary; those who do not celebrate the feast of the Conception – in other words, those who do not promote the doctrine – risk displeasing the Virgin and finding themselves outside the circle of the blessed. Even more, as Villena states, given that the feast of the Conception "represents the beginning of our salvation,"[17] those who choose to rebuff its celebration ignore and reject as well a divinely traced pathway to redemption. The Virgin is the Mother of God and, as such, it is her spotless body and soul that make possible the incarnation of Christ, his sacrifice, and the elevation of humanity to a state of salvation.

Chapter 3 and chapter 4 offer an account of the birth and early years of the Virgin up to the Annunciation. I will discuss in the following section of this chapter the peculiar representation in Spain (including Villena's) of the childhood of the Virgin in the context of the defence of the doctrine, which sees its best-known examples in Ágreda's *Mística ciudad de Dios* and Zurbarán's paintings. For now, let me note that Villena's infant Mary – from her conception to when she is called upon to fulfil her maternal role – is postulated in the *Vita Christi* as an instructional model for the nuns at the convent: "so as to set an example to her servants that they may follow in her footsteps, if they wish to attain the repose she enjoys."[18] Accepting of penance, in continuous prayer, contemplative, merciful, and modest, Villena's Virgin child is not only exemplary for the nuns but also already a dedicated advocate in their trajectory towards purity and salvation: "Our Lord God caused her to be born in this world so that she may be an advocate for human nature and a sanctuary for all its needs."[19] In this manner Villena refashions the *vita Christi* genre, presenting a theological exposition of the conditions that make Mary's spotlessness possible, accompanied by a narrative of the Virgin as the primary model, advocate, and spiritual sanctuary for her cloistered community. The nuanced representation of women within Villena's text has been noted and examined by Curbet, Criado, and Twomey, among others. I would add that, as I have shown, this focus is anchored in the doctrine and larger implications

of immaculacy as made manifest in Mary and as it figuratively extends
to all other women, from Eve to Villena and her sisters, who share her
female nature, participate in her grace, and follow her example.

Juana de la Cruz (1481–1534), a regular Franciscan tertiary, nun,
and abbess of the convent of Santa María de Cubas near Toledo,
was a mystic who for thirteen years proffered sermons every Sunday in the course of her visionary ecstasies; seventy of them were
transcribed by María Evangelista and gathered in the 1509 collection
titled *El libro del Conorte*. The *Conorte* has been extensively studied
by Ronald Surtz, Jesus Gómez López, Isabelle Poutrin, and Jessica
Boon, all of whom document the context that allowed Juana de la
Cruz, with the protection of Cardinal Cisneros, to publicly present
herself in the midst of her raptures, "with the voice of Christ audible
to the congregation by means of Juana's vocal cord" (Boon, "Mother
Juana de la Cruz" 128). As Boon observes, Juana de la Cruz claims,
as a ventriloquism of God, to offer a more "complete version of the
biblical narrative" than was possible to the scribes and apostles who
composed the Old and New Testaments ("Mother Juana de la Cruz"
129).[20] Additionally, Poutrin has noted how Juana de la Cruz sets an
important precedent for the many nuns (and most importantly in our
case for Ágreda) whose "dominant feature is the affirmation of direct
contact with the celestial world."[21] The "unobstructed" transmission
of sacred knowledge is key to these women's claim to authority; the
message imparted and the experiences related are conferred as incontestable. As such, Juana de la Cruz's visionary sermons form part of
a vast canon of mystical writings, a textual tradition that in orthodox
theology is anchored in the writings of Pseudo-Dionysius the Are-
opagite and shored up by Bonaventure. And yet, I would like to emphasize that for Juana de la Cruz (as later for Ágreda) the knowledge
transmitted is not limited to the path towards mystical revelation and
the textual description of its experience. The *Conorte*, as Boon notes,
is a text in which Juana de la Cruz "addressed such diverse subjects
as the Trinity, angelology, and the Immaculate Conception" ("Mother
Juana de la Cruz" 129). In the absence of a systematic university or
monastic school education, the visionary delivers theological knowledge as revealed to her directly by the source of all knowledge, God
in his manifestation as Christ. The *Conorte* displays a voice authorized by celestial logic and reason that emanates through Juana de la
Cruz from the Word itself. No less significantly, as again documented
by Boon, "Juana's entire career at the convent was marked by a series of conversations with and visions of the Virgin. Juana functioned
as a go-between for the nuns with Mary, relaying their prayers and

gifts to the Virgin and in turn assuring the nuns of Mary's delighted responses" (Introduction 22).[22] It is also because of the authority bestowed upon her by the Virgin that Juana de la Cruz offers her visionary exegesis of immaculacy.

The sermon on the Immaculate Conception begins with an explanation of why the apostles did not fully clarify Mary's exceptional condition: it was evident to everyone who knew her that she was free of sin, and to say so would be stating the obvious: "they recognized her and knew who she was, whom she had served, and so to them there seemed to be no need."[23] Juana de la Cruz expands this line of thinking by noting that, after all, the apostles were busy documenting Christ's incarnation, miraculous existence, and the narrative of his sacrifice, and could not take the time to elaborate on Mary's apparent purity (16).[24] With this fact established, Juana de la Cruz focuses on the material aspects of the doctrine; in other words, rather than taking the Anselmian route, where the cleanliness of the spirit is privileged over that of matter, she certifies the exemption from stain of Mary's flesh, which could not have been ever touched by sin if she was to bear the holy body (i.e., immaculate matter) of Christ: "Because from God's flesh she became flesh, it was right that she was so clean and so pure and so chaste and chosen among all living things."[25] The implication, and therefore her challenge to those who would dare question the theological stance of the *tota pulchra*, is that Christ's perfect humanity can only be possible because the Virgin was perfect in every way, flesh *and* spirit, what she calls Mary's "saintly humanity."[26] The fundamental thrust of her theological proposition is that the Virgin had to be and in fact always was exceptional not only in her spotlessness but in every aspect of her life: "that is more pure and excellent than all living things, so in her conception and birth as in all other things of her life and childhood."[27] Mary's exceptionality is, in Juana de la Cruz's discourse, the key to her equality with her Son; but, instead of being structured as a quality that makes of the Virgin a remote superior being, it makes it possible for Juana de la Cruz to humanize the divine mystery. In Juana's account of the doctrine, Mary's condition confirms – both symbolically and literally – the nexus between the sacred and the human. Nowhere is this theological proposition more evident than in the explanation for how Mary's (and by extension Christ's) flesh remained materially uncorrupted. Similar to a woman who, when making bread, separates a piece of unleavened dough, "to make a roll, creased and white and glossy and without any bitterness or corruption from yeast,"[28] so did God upon the creation of Adam separate out pure matter, thereby anticipating Adam's fall and the resulting need to preserve uncontaminated substance that could be turned into Mary's and Christ's immaculate bodies:

> And the most holy Trinity did the same; this could be represented as by a woman that kneads dough: when he wanted to knead the dough of man, and even before he sieved it, it is advisable to know, when he wanted to create man, and even before he did, he knew and accepted that man would be corrupted by original sin ... And so he knew that there must be a chosen woman, pure and without leavening and corruption from sin ... and the Holy Spirit says it, speaking on her behalf since before the ages, since *ab initio* I am risen, and until the age to come, I will not perish.[29]

The mystery of the Virgin's existence *ab initio* is addressed in a variety of ways by Immaculists, who cite Revelation 12 coupled with Ecclesiastes 24:9 – "From eternity, in the beginning, he created me, and, for eternity, I shall remain" – in order to explicate God's eternal plan for Mary. As I have previously noted, these scriptural sources are typically taken to signify the timeless existence of Mary's spirit present in the heavens alongside the angels and the holy Trinity. Juana de la Cruz, as is immediately and rather surprisingly evident, offers an alternative route to this theological tenet, placing equal weight on the event of human creation and the material (i.e., bodily) mechanisms through which original sin is passed. It should not escape us that in Juana's account the Virgin and Adam are made of the same perfect matter; in other words, Juana de la Cruz's Mary is a protagonist in the act of creation together with Adam, equally formed from the same originary "unleavened dough" or immaculate substance. Unlike Scholastic (mostly Thomistic) theories of hylomorphism in which the body (matter) is seen as moulded by the soul (as a configurative form), Juana de la Cruz binds the mystery of immaculacy to the original creation of the body itself, as yet uncorrupted. In other words, it is not just that Mary's pure eternal spirit is miraculously implanted at the time of conception (an unsullied form configuring a, therefore, unsullied body), but rather that Mary's body itself (her human substance) had since the moment of originary creation been preserved from all sin: "he created her and chose her and drew her according to his will and understanding and wisdom before he created the first man."[30] This is an important aspect of Juana de la Cruz's theological propositions because it concretely connects the Virgin's absolute purity to human physical existence; Mary's spotlessness is materially linked to God's creation of the human body from the beginning to our present state. Just as importantly, she frames this foundational moment as a feminine act; like a woman who lovingly

prepares dough, God formed and separated the matter of Mary, a sim-
ile which allows her female conventual audience to readily visualize
the intricacies of the sacred mystery, but which also invites it to intimately identify with God as Creator; the nuns, like the Supreme Divine
Being, deal in the dough of immaculacy in their veneration of Mary
and in their own pursuit of purity.

What follows is an account of the holy Family – God as loving
husband of Mary and as Father of Christ – which includes language
that concretizes the symbolic marriage. The analogy of a marital union
between God and the Virgin of the Immaculate Conception is not exclusive to Juana de la Cruz, but what is novel is the emphasis, once again,
on the flesh: "Because our lady was so pure and God had fallen so in
love with her, that he must take her flesh and join himself with her, and
become a man without the seed of man, but by the marvellous work
of the Holy Spirit, which brought him to be in this way: That our Lord
Jesus Christ should have a mother on earth and a father in heaven."[31]
As a loving husband, God takes Mary's immaculate flesh, absent of the
human seed and mediated by the Holy Spirit, to procreate Jesus incarnate. The focus on the body itself as a site of purity is given yet another
imaginative turn in the logic of inversion that Juana de la Cruz offers
when comparing the birth of Eve and the birth of Christ. Adam, before his fall into sin, births Eve from his body, "and inside of the very
first man the woman was enclosed, and then Adam gave birth to her
because from him the Lord drew out the woman,"[32] while the reverse
occurs when Mary births Christ: "And just as Eve was born from a man
without woman, so similarly was our redeemer, Jesus Christ, born from
woman without man."[33] From a gender perspective, this specific comparison is charged, in its use of the language of gestation and birthing
when talking about Adam, producing a narrative in which Christ is not
the first "human" to be created as and born of an immaculate body; in
fact, the lineage of immaculate conceptions and births in Juana de la
Cruz's account is traced from Adam/Eve to Saint Anne/Mary to Mary/
Christ, making the mystery an essential component of God's overall
omnipotent practice. No less, Juana de la Cruz's account of Christ's
lineage stands apart in the interpretation of immaculacy as dependent
exclusively on, once again, the site of the uncontaminated flesh, what
she will later in the sermon call "unsoiled and virginal entrails."[34]

The segment on Saint Anne, whose own spotlessness is both potentially necessary and highly problematic, is in this regard telling (and
the subject will be more so in our examination of Pinelo's text). Juana
de la Cruz does not directly address the controversy of Saint Anne's
retroactive immaculacy, opting instead to interpret anew a verse in the

Song of Songs – *nigra sum sed formosa* – which Maculists had used as proof of Mary's original stain. The Virgin of the Immaculate Conception, as presented in the *Conorte*, paradoxically embraces her "blackness" not as a marker of sin but, just the opposite, as proof of her pure humility:

> I am black, which she did not say because she had any blackness from original sin, neither original, nor actual, nor venial nor mortal ... I am small and I am not worthy that God should remember me, but I am beautiful because the same Lord, in his power, gave and accepted the humility of his servant and still did great things. And therefore, he praised me and he made me the greatest and most beautiful, clean of all sin, and adorned with as many virtues and excellences as there ever were or will ever be.[35]

However, it is Saint Anne (alongside the rest of humanity) who most benefits from the dialectical relationship between *negra* and *fermosa*. Like her daughter, Saint Anne is also "black" and beautiful, and when pregnant visits Christ and the angels in a mystical vision. The visionary experience and its logic (both conceptually and in terms of a congruent earthbound timeline) are rather convoluted and include the spectacle of the foetal Mary floating out of the womb. And yet, what is most interesting is how Saint Anne is figured as an expansion of Mary and Christ. Invited (or self-invited, it is not clear) to join her grandson in praise of the Immaculate Virgin-to-be, Saint Anne has licence through her good deeds and faith to come into the presence of the sacred and carry in her what is exceptional, untainted, and redemptive: "look, my beloved lord and grandson, as I come pregnant and bring here the star of the sea and the glory of heaven."[36] An extension of her daughter, she is solely a human who in her deeds and faith has been made pure. Following Saint Anne, whose "black" humility provides the means for her return to a "white" heavenly immaculacy, the audience is invited to imagine their own return to a state of purity: "And so no man or woman, no matter how ugly and deformed, should be distressed. Because if they do good works and deserve to go to heaven, there they will be beautiful and white and adorned, and there they will not fear any blemish or ugliness or blackness."[37] In the original text, the gendering of the adjectives fluctuates between the feminine and the masculine – "fermosas y blancos" – reinforcing the equal opportunity for all believers, and most specifically for all Conceptionists, that Saint Anne's example provides. The audience, both the nuns of the Franciscan convent where Juana de la Cruz lived and the wide audience that visited every Sunday to witness her visionary sermons, was assured of its purification – a future redeemed return to prelapsarian purity – exemplified in the always singular Virgin Mary. Spiritual and material purity, even if not equal to the sacred mystery that allows for Mary's exceptionality, extends to the faithful and most certainly to Juana de la Cruz and her fellow nuns, who are guaranteed a singular mystical-theological pathway to virtue and salvation.

Juana de la Cruz's sermon on the doctrine of the Immaculate Conception functions not only as an imaginative exposition of revealed truth and scriptural exegesis, but also as an attack against those who would reject Mary's status and who, consequently, should expect to be punished for their troubled intransigence: "And such people are burdened by their restless spirits in this life, but later in the other life some notorious ones will receive sorrow because of it."[38] The final segment of the sermon hinges on yet another analogical turn, this time offering an interpretation of Mary's body as a castle, which in Juana de la Cruz's account is corporally divided into two parts: from the waist down where Christ "dwelt" ["moró"] in her immaculate flesh and from the waist up where God had forever resided in her heart, "by which she was made a very beautiful young woman."[39] The corresponding condemnation of Maculists does away with the poetic and the scriptural. Juana de la Cruz ends the sermon with Christ manifesting his anger against the obstinate and the hardened, who provoke their own "afflictions and tribulations and sorrows."[40] In the face of Christ's disappointment – "so enraged was he against the world"[41] – it is the Virgin of the Immaculate Conception who ironically intercedes in favour of her enemies and favourably sways her adoring Son to cease their much-deserved punishment: "And only because of her does he do more favours than all celestial and earthly beings, seeing that she was the one who made him come from heaven to earth."[42] Christ's debt to Mary and his symbiotic relationship with her eternal spirit and spotless body would merit no less. Crucially, the Virgin of the Immaculate Conception's redemptive role is featured and enhanced in her deliverance of even those who would deny her elevated status; it is only because of her that Christ's anger is appeased.

Juana de la Cruz's theological discourse delivers, as Bernard of Clairvaux had suggested centuries earlier, what is hidden in the Scriptures with words that are her own; her imaginative narrative renders inseparable the immaculacy of Christ, the immaculacy of the Virgin, the sympathetic immaculacy of Saint Anne, and the immaculacy that was lost by Adam but that can be regained through faith and good deeds by all true Immaculists. Against a rich theological tradition – from Justin Martyr to Saint Jerome and Saint Augustine, who professed as fundamental the dictum "Mors per Evam Vita per Mariam" – Juana de la Cruz offers an alternative inscription for the origin and transmission of and exceptionality from the stain of sin within the orthodoxy of the cult of Mary. Sin comes from Adam's corruption of his immaculate flesh, Eve is elevated as the mother of humanity (with the exception of Mary and Christ), and eternal redemption results from devotion to the Virgin as the Immaculate Mother of Christ the Saviour.[43]

Valentina Pinelo, a nun at a convent in San Leandro in Seville, writes the *Libro de las alabanzas y excelencias de la gloriosa Santa Ana* as a deliberate exegetical elaboration on the sacred Scriptures, not the telling of a visionary mystical experience. As noted by Lola Luna, the biography of Saint Anne and her role in the narrative of salvation are anchored in Pinelo's intellectual breadth, "an Augustinian writer of intellectual prose."[44] Insofar as Pinelo is writing a theological treatise on the life of Saint Anne, she also is engaged in writing a theological interpretation of the conception, birth, and sacred mission of Mary in a God-driven universe. The cult of Saint Anne held a central place in Sevillian popular religious life, a fact that is intimately related to the city's fervent promotion of the elevation to dogma of the doctrine. The two sets of devotion go hand in hand for an apparent reason: Saint Anne's unique relevance in the history of the redemption of humanity was effectuated when God chose her to immaculately conceive and carry Mary. It is for this reason that one can read the *Libro de Santa Ana* as a treatise on immaculacy – the immaculacy of Mary, the spotlessness by association/resemblance of Saint Anne as "mother of the Mother" (Prologue),[45] and the present penitential purity and future eternal purity of those who venerate the Virgin and worship her Son; this is a lineage of purity and redemption that, as we should expect, positions Pinelo and her fellow nuns at the Convent of San Leandro as a privileged group.

Pinelo focuses on the event of the Immaculate Conception of Mary in book 2, chapters 1–3, where she narrates the divine design that allowed its fruition. Chapter 1 is, from my perspective, the most interesting. In it Pinelo – in a claim that is parallel to Juana de la Cruz's "dough" metaphor – contends that Mary's immaculacy resulted from God's preemptive omniscient knowledge when, upon the creation of Adam, he foresees the fall and preserves a portion of the "most perfect substance in which there is no inconvenience or dissonance."[46] It is precisely this matter from which the Virgin Mary's immaculate body and soul later emerge, but in Pinelo, it is transported via Adam's loins – "He placed and deposited her in the most important part of Adam's body"[47] – and carried forth through generations of patriarchs until landing in the body of Saint Joachim: "And it is in this way that the sacred substance of which we have been told by the testimony of so many and such serious scholars, so preserved by so many centuries-long ages, and carried by so many Patriarchs by the will of God's miraculous hand, had arrived, and was already under custody of Saint Joachim the Patriarch."[48] With the transmission of the perfect material substance from the creation of Adam on, Pinelo (like Juana de la Cruz before her) offers her interpretation of the concept of *ab initio*, which figured so prominently in the discourses of immaculacy. Nevertheless, Pinelo's hermeneutical claim, I would argue, is, theologically speaking, more sophisticated than her predecessor's and takes an unprecedented imaginative leap. As with Juana de la Cruz, the implicit referent is the Scholastic debate regarding matter and form with the added considera-tion of substance and accidents. Although those debates are drawn-out and complex – tackling numerous nuances depending on the theologian and his specific onto-philosophical engagements – it seems that Pinelo is pointing to the category of primary substance, one which possesses ontological unity, undivided in itself, and independent of and/or prior to the accidents of nature.[49] Notably, in the *Libro de Santa Ana* this meta-physical distinction is folded into a second theological concern regard-ing the specific details of the event of Mary's Immaculate Conception. Contrary to the most prevalent explanation espoused, for example, that Mary was miraculously instantly redeemed upon conception (through the sexual act), which for Scotus evinces Christ's perfect retroactive re-demptive power; or to the miraculous narrative attached to the "chaste" embrace between Saint Anne and Saint Joachim at the Golden Gate and the virginal placement of the fully formed foetus in Saint Anne's womb; or even to Anselm's focus on the wholesomeness of the soul over the body, Pinelo chooses an alternative revealed interpretation for this sa-cred mystery, positing the passing of the original pure material sub-stance into the womb of Saint Anne through the loins of Saint Joachim. Even more so than Juana de la Cruz, Pinelo's theological postulation convenes a copious religious imagination whose gendering of the ide-ological underpinnings of immaculacy and redemption should not be dismissed. Mary is not only immaculate; she is a product of the origi-nal creation, and therefore the perfect vehicle to bring back humanity, alongside the sacrifice of her Son, to its original state. This is all possible, no less, precisely because Saint Anne was an equally worthy vessel, a postlapsarian human being who, enveloped in God's omniscient sacred mystery, receives and carries in her womb the primary substance:

[I]n such a blessed and happy married couple, there was placed a celestial treasure and substance, from which the body of the Queen of Angels was to be formed, in Anne's most holy womb ... and Anne gave birth, the best labour that either heaven or earthly creation has seen or recognizes ... and the glorious Virgin Mary was born into the world, and ... the dispensation had been granted, to marry the divine nature with the human one, and although human, she was to be conceived with singular privilege.[50]

Naturally, Mary's exceptionality is extended to Saint Anne, whose godly favour "made her unique."[51] Framing and legitimizing her discourse through Scotus's well-known dictum on Marian privilege, Pinelo offers an altogether innovative account of the Virgin's exceptional creation, generational transmission, and conception, one in which matter and bodies – including Saint Anne's and Saint Joachim's – carry forth redemption. In an expansive continuation of Juana de la Cruz's visionary analogies, Pinelo here places humanity – as carriers and bearers – in direct physical contact with the perfect creation of God. This is a proposition that takes the *tota pulchra* out of the realm of an abstracted ideal and places her purity, instead, in direct relation to our original perfect and pure substance, what we once were and will return to be.

Having set the parameters for the transmission of the immaculate substance, in chapters 2 through 7 Pinelo continues to narrativize and theologize the physical and spiritual conditions of Mary's conception. The central motive of these chapters is an extensive examination of the Scriptures and revealed divine design, where Saint Anne, Saint Joachim, and the Virgin's exceptionality are foretold and justified. Pinelo promotes not only her own defence of the doctrine but also her own conceptualization of the relationship between the immanent and the transcendent. In generally keeping with, as stated above, Scotus's position on Marian privilege, but with a directness that is rarely seen in other Immaculist texts, Pinelo bluntly broaches the subject of sexual activity between the chosen parents, denouncing the "idiots" and "fools" who uphold Mary's conception under the golden arch through a simple embrace.[52] Pinelo, in a turn that would not be expected from a cloistered nun, insists on memorializing God's design in the procreative act and the miracle of the sexual transmission of the perfect substance carried by Saint Joachim: "As for the parents of the glorious Virgin Mary: I say that they, for their part, proceeded like everyone else, although with a more chaste and pure intention ... because this blood and flesh was to be, with an outstanding reason, with a singular privilege, so that there could be no blemish of sin in her."[53] The logic of Pinelo's assertion is entirely congruent with the scheme that Mary's matter originated in the act of original creation. For this very reason, Pinelo must also honour the passing of the material substance through the sexual act, as it happens with "everyone else." To shore up her point, she rejects a facile opposition between the Divine and the human.

God created humans in his image, and God assumed a human form as Christ the Redeemer; consequently, the human and the Divine, rather than antithetical and distant, are figured as inextricably ontologically and theologically linked. Mary's originary stainlessness confirms the conjunction of the two stations, a human nature identical to God's original design and from which Christ incarnate can emerge without repulsion: "and her sovereign purity complements God, that divine nature is not repulsed by human nature."[54] The design that makes possible Mary's immaculacy and Christ's incarnation is perfectly insular – God is Mary's Father (as creator of her perfect substance at the beginning of time), and Mary is the Bride of God and the Mother of God – and yet, this perfect substance is also contiguous with the matter that constitutes humanity. The Virgin of the Immaculate Conception is, in the *Libro de Santa Ana*, a singular hybrid, perfect human and eternal spirit, conceived by Saint Anne and Saint Joachim, formed of the harmonious substance first produced by God at the time of creation, born a saintly infant but always already the eternal Apocalyptic Woman:

> Here the mother of God received from her son, and from her parents, human nature alone, but as it was her true Father and Creator who was to be her Son and her Husband, raising her in one instant, he created her surrounding her with the Sun, there was no earthly matter in the way, everything was heaven, neither her light nor her impeccable being could be eclipsed: God did not move away from her, from the moment of her conception.[55]

Pinelo's examination of Mary's condition in these chapters navigates the arena of similes and metaphors; Adam and Mary are compared to clay casts, one made brittle and lacking in essential oils, the other bathed in the oils of divine charity and grace (134 A). Producing an analogy that I examined at length in chapters 3 and 4, she names God "supreme artificer and divine painter";[56] in doing so, she adds an interesting turn to the trope by simultaneously denoting both God the Father's original creation of the substance of Mary and Christ the Son's retroactive redemption: "[Christ] painted his mother with that divine essence, such that it was worthy of his mother."[57] Moreover, Pinelo's hermeneutical practice refers to established interpretations of Old Testament verses that support the doctrine of the Immaculate Conception; the theological discourse that arises from it makes use of a syncretic exegetical corpus which altogether refutes any possible negation of the Virgin's eternal immaculate state. In one segment, for example, Pinelo returns to a traditional Scotist justification, reiterating

Christ's perfect retroactive redemption of his Virgin Mother at the moment of her conception: "that upon instilling that soul in that body, came the sin of dressing her in that heavy armour: the Divine Word arose defending her, taking that blow upon itself, sending it to the cross, rescuing her when she was going to be captive, and this way she was not."[58] Even though this theological proposition is not altogether congruent with Pinelo's account of the transmission of the original perfect substance from Adam to Saint Joachim, it expands the exegetical field so as not to diminish or limit in any way God's omniscience and the mystery of immaculacy. From an authorial perspective, the amalgam of citations and scriptural interpretations and references to theological debates throughout these early chapters corroborates Pinelo's breadth of knowledge, shores up her authority, protects her from claims of heresy, and (as is her intention) indisputably promotes the doctrine and the exceptionality of Mary's family. Pinelo deploys this discursive strategy on numerous occasions, such as when she cites Augustine's rebuttal of Pelagius and the assertion of Christ's wholly sinless nature at the moment of conception and through his human life.[59] Pinelo then applies the Augustinian logic backwards to Mary's conception, drawing the conclusion that if the Virgin never sinned in her lifetime it is because she, like Christ her Son, was always already untouched by sin: "the Virgin did not commit either venial or mortal sin, which leads us to confirm that she also did not have original sin."[60] Citing the decrees of the Council of Trent in favour of her theological discourse – "proven by the Council of Trent, as you will see, not only was mortal sin, but even venial sin, impossible for her"[61] – and, furthermore, establishing that all detractors are imprudently going against the certainty offered by the "concept of Theology,"[62] Pinelo tenders what she estimates is a foolproof theologically informed and reasoned, as well as divinely inspired, argument for the doctrine. Pinelo makes these claims much to the chagrin of censors who, as Marín Pina has documented, note that the debate was ongoing and the Church had yet to elevate the doctrine to dogma ("'Cuantas fueren las cabeças'" 49). And yet, what is ultimately featured is not simply a case for Marian privilege, but rather – and this is pivotal from a gendered perspective – a presentation of the Virgin as a supreme and necessary figure in the sacred *and* the human spheres. Unlike Villena, Pinelo does not exempt Eve from fault in the narrative of the fall, "being, as she was, the cause of our pain."[63] But neither does she repeat the dichotomy Eva/Ave, with Mary bound theologically and discursively to a weak and inadequate female figure. For Pinelo, the Virgin's eternal purity – original, venial, and moral – positions her

in an indispensable and equal correspondence with each of the manifestations of the holy Trinity and with humanity:

> This proves the Virgin Mary's nobility and privilege, and her being pre-
> served from sin, and that she is very good for all stations: For heaven, and
> for the earth, for God, and for men; and so, it seems that we are compelled
> to judge she was suited for everyone. For the Eternal Father, to be his wife,
> and for the Divine Word, to be his mother, and for the Holy Spirit, to be
> his tabernacle, and for the Angels, to be their queen; and for the righteous,
> to be their guide, their light, and their intelligence; and for the sinners, to
> be our advocate and mediator. Finally, for all the world's creatures, it is
> right to acknowledge in her the honour and glory of the earth, the joy and
> happiness of heaven, where we all intend to enter by means of her inter-
> cession, through which she grants us mercy.[64]

In sum, the miracle of the Virgin's Immaculate Conception and its fulfilment in Saint Anne's womb goes far beyond the role of serving as a
generative vessel for Christ's incarnation. Congruent with the expansive religious imaginary that sustained the popular cult of Mary, the
Virgin's theologically examined immaculacy in the *Libro de Santa Ana* is
construed as a coextensive element that buoys the celestial and human
orders, all the divine and created beings.

María de Ágreda, abbess of the Convent of the Immaculate Conception at Ágreda, delivers in her *Mística ciudad de Dios* an even more substantial and exhaustive theological interpretation of Revelation and its
implications for the veneration of the *tota pulchra*.[65] *Mística ciudad de Dios* –
published posthumously in 1670 after its wide circulation in two full
manuscript versions – comprises eight lengthy books, each composed
of numerous chapters that offer a detailed account of Ágreda's visions
of the Virgin of the Immaculate Conception. The bulk of the books re-
count the life of the Virgin from birth to her death and assumption.
Significantly, each chapter ends with a question (or set of questions) by
Ágreda regarding the doctrinal consequence of the episode, followed
by a reply from the Virgin (her voice heard in the first person, ventril-
oquized) certifying the correct interpretation and theological import of
the segment. Noting the immense amount of detail and care employed
in interpreting every aspect of Mary's biography (both documented
and imagined), Katherine Risse has read Ágreda's representation of the
Virgin as humanizing and defying the "patriarchal misconception of
Mary's inimitable perfection" (232). According to the critic, what the
reader finds is a new paradigm,

> [A] humanized, authoritative female who nurtures her family while
> simultaneously contributing to religious and civil affairs, thus presenting

a more sympathetic, inclusive, and realized example for womankind. By reinterpreting Mary's perfection, which was traditionally juxtaposed with the imperfection of mortal women, Sor María attempts to significantly alter the Virgin's familiar role as archetype for women in Renaissance and Baroque Culture. (232)

My own reading of *Mística ciudad de Dios* is informed by this proposition; and yet, I find that Ágreda's challenge to the logical trajectory of this new paradigm is, in fact, more complicated and even more radical than Risse proposes. As I have demonstrated, Ágreda's female predecessors had in many and important ways already shifted and challenged the idea of the Virgin as a remote, inimitable, abstracted, and exclusive maternal symbol; or, from a misogynistically informed position, of the Virgin as women's inverse, a perfectly conceived figure of that which we are not and which by opposition only highlights and places shame upon women's immoral nature. In their theological discourse and treatment of the doctrine of the Immaculate Conception, Villena, Juana de la Cruz, and Pinelo are wholly invested in an elevation of the perfection of Mary that has as its logical effect an elevation of all women; in other words, because Mary – in her sacred humanity – is perfectly pure, all women have (through their faith and in their devout commitment to her example) an open path to a holistic redemption that results in their own eventual heavenly immaculacy. Even before the eternal promise is fulfilled, Mary's purity provides a relatable benchmark for the potentiality of perfection in all women, especially the audience of nuns who are privileged readers of these texts. Moreover, it places all women as belonging to the same "kind" that made possible the incarnation of Christ and the redemption of all human beings.

Ágreda takes this logic and the "excessive" or "hyperbolic" religious imaginary that it depends on to a new level in book 1 of *Mística ciudad de Dios*. The humanization of the Virgin that Risse describes entails in this first instalment an apparently counterintuitive but, in my opinion, parallel logic: Mary is figured as wholly and radically exceptional. And yet, in *Mística ciudad de Dios* radical exceptionality does not lead to remoteness and abstraction, or consequently to the demeaning of regular women as the sinful inheritors of Eve. Instead it takes Ágreda, and the readers with her, to a theologically exhaustive and psychologically intimate understanding of the Virgin's singular purity and the ways in which her state of perfection is both radical and yet completely relatable to and compatible with our limited human experience. Much like that of Villena, Juana de la Cruz, and Pinelo, Ágreda's extravagant religious imaginary – in its formal incursion into theological exegesis – positions her (and all women) as worthy sisters and daughters of our perfect mother, Mary.

Book 1 of *Mística ciudad de Dios* includes substantial and detailed (verse by verse) exegetical examinations of Revelation 12 and 21 over numerous chapters, a characteristic that distinguishes it from the previous three women-authored texts I have examined in this chapter. What these lengthy theological incursions display is Ágreda's deliberate intent to provide formal doctrinal guidance on the mystery of immaculacy and to position herself as a theologian. These segments are interrupted, however, by a narrative account that (re)constructs Saint Anne's and Saint Joachim's experiences as they are called by divine intervention to parent the Virgin, as well as an account of the material logistics of Mary's conception, in which the eternal spirit of the Apocalyptic Woman described in Revelation 12 is sexually conceived and yet wholly preserved (matter/body and substance/soul) from sin. The narrative form – alternating formal theological exegesis with an intimate and highly imaginative biographical hagiographical account – is fundamental to the presentation of the Virgin of the Immaculate Conception as an exceptional sacred *and* human woman. Given this fact, I would argue, the text performs as a remarkably inviting vehicle for instruction, identification, and affiliation with Mary for the nuns at Ágreda. The detailed examination of Revelation 12, where John of Patmos documents his visionary experience, keeps Ágreda close to official doctrinal Conceptionist discourses and certifies her hermeneutical capacity and theological orthodoxy. These chapters contextualize the existence of Mary before the beginning of time and the creation of the earth, in the presence of the angels who recognize in the woman dressed by the sun a creature that rises above them in the hierarchy of perfection: "They saw it therefore before the good ones chose the good and before the bad ones had turned to evil. It was as it were a mirror of the wonderful perfection of the handiwork of God in creating human nature ... in a mere creature the most perfect and holy, which, next to the humanity of our Lord, he was to create."[66] Following John of Patmos's vision, it is precisely this perfection and the placement of the Virgin above all other created beings that drives Lucifer to the depths of jealousy and rebelliousness:

A third precept was given [the angels], namely that they were to admit as a superior conjointly with [God], a Woman, in whose womb the Only begotten of the Father was to assume flesh, and that this Woman was to be the Queen and Mistress of all the creatures. The good angels, by obeying this command ... freely subjected themselves, praising the powers and mysteries of the Most High. Lucifer, however, and his confederates, rose to a higher pitch of pride and boastful insolence ... Given that he understood that he was inferior to the Mother of the Word made human and our Lady,

> he resisted with horrendous blasphemies, turning himself with unbridled indignation against the Author of so many marvels.[67]

At this atemporal primary moment, and as it remains for all of time, the Virgin expresses the flawless and unspoilable superiority that exempts her from the tragedy of Adam's and Eve's insubordination and places her as the rare example of God's intended original design. Inserting it in a cause-and-effect narrative, Ágreda will return to this event many times over. One way to interpret the emphasis that she places upon Lucifer's animosity is to consider her retelling of Revelation 12 as a mechanism for placing the creation of a woman, ever pure and a model for female devotion, as the most important event in the narrative of creation, second only to the mystery of the holy Trinity. In turn, Ágreda, another woman, has been singled out by the Virgin of the Immaculate Conception as a conduit for the telling and correct interpretation of this exceptional event. The logical conclusion that must be drawn is that women (i.e., devout women, such as Ágreda and her cloistered sisters) should be regarded and valued as an extension of God's primal design via the creation and elevation of Mary (and not the temptation posited by Eve). Any negation of the doctrine of the Immaculate Conception, as well as any rejection or distrust of women who are positioned as supplements to this exalted figure, is thereby associated with Lucifer's envy and dismissal of God's perfect design.

God's privileging of the Virgin is further corroborated when Ágreda, in what she understands as a theologically consistent description of the divine hierarchy, places the Virgin of the Immaculate Conception in parity with her Son: "Our most pure Mary was, in proportion to her saintly Son, exalted to a dignity corresponding to his. In the length of her gifts and graces, and in the breadth of her merits, in all things she was equally proportioned and without defect as was her Son, and no grace was created in Christ that was not in proportion with his pure Mother."[68] Mary partakes of the same gifts of grace as Christ, and it is to her that we ultimately owe the harmony that is restored through Christ and the resulting triumph of the Church. At the same time – and this is a balance that is not always perfectly kept or sought in *Mística ciudad de Dios* – the Virgin is equally a human being. Exceptional in her purity and her provenance, Mary is an extension of us, what most resembles us, in the Heavens. Given her dual nature, the Virgin is the perfect intercessor between the Divine and the human, even defending those who reject her exceptionality, who will not "fail to attain eternal life if they invoke the intercession of this powerful Lady and Advocate."[69]

As cited above, the Virgin of the Immaculate Conception is repeat-edly named by Ágreda "Mother of the Word made human" ["Madre del Verbo humanado"], a designation that calls attention to the mystery of Christ's incarnation and highlights Mary's maternal role (1.19.293, 92).[70] A construction I have only found in *Mística ciudad de Dios*, this title also conceptually establishes an existential timeline whose origin remains in the realm of mystery and revelation. As proclaimed in John 1:1, "In the beginning was the Word, and the Word was with God, and the Word was God." As such, the Word's state "made Flesh" marks a path from atemporality to temporality, and from eternal spirit to human body. Ágreda's "Madre del Verbo humanado" positions Mary in this atemporal/temporal, spirit/body passage, placing theological weight on her as Mother of the Word both before and after his transition into "humanado." If thought of from the perspective of Aristotelian gen-dered proportions, Mary as "Madre del Verbo humanado" encapsu-lates both the atemporal masculine letter and the temporal feminine maternal body. Perhaps most significantly, Ágreda positions Mary as an extension of the holy Trinity, always already present in her rela-tion to the Word, from the beginning of time and incarnated into time. Congruent with this logic, book 1 of *Mística ciudad de Dios* consistently offers the pair "Christ and Mary" and "Christ and his Mother" as a single and singular entity against which Lucifer forges his hateful and envious rebellion. Through this coupling, Ágreda insists on Mary's ma-ternal function as eternal and independent of the requirements of the incarnation. Moreover, it affirms a contiguous dialectical relationship in Christ incarnated *and* in Mary between transcendence and immanence, not as the proposition of a thesis and an antithesis, or of a synthesis, or a substitution of one term for the other, but rather as poles that remain distinguishable and yet inextricable. Christ and Mary are necessarily always already – excessively and hyperbolically – sacred *and* human, a duality that is fundamental to God's design. *Mística ciudad de Dios* thus reaffirms and expands upon a religious imaginary in which the Virgin's purity and maternity are elevated – both in terms of their need and of the power they command – to the realm of the Divine and constitutive to the narrative of redemption.

This dialectical coupling is also fundamental to and further devel-oped in Ágreda's exegesis of Revelation 21 in book 1, chapter 17. At this visionary juncture, John of Patmos listens to a voice that emerges from a throne announcing the arrival of new day – "Behold, I make all things new" – and a new tabernacle which God will inhabit: "Be-hold the tabernacle of God with men, and he shall dwell with them. And they shall be his people and God himself with them shall be their

God."[71] The emphasis on the new, as interpreted by Ágreda, is symbolic of how Mary – together with Christ – makes possible a fresh beginning in the narrative of creation and reconciliation. More specifically, Mary is "a new earth and a new heaven,"[72] inhabited by the Word incarnate in the making of a new redemptive day. The metaphor of the Virgin as tabernacle visually expresses not only her status as an eternal spirit and as an immaculate human but also her foundational role to the Church and her coextensive relationship with the Trinity:

> Because all these mysteries had their beginning in most holy Mary, and were founded in her, the Evangelist said that he saw her in the form of the holy city Jerusalem, etc., for through this metaphor he spoke of our Queen ... For the mysteries that God performed in the holy City of Jerusalem were proper as symbols of her who was his Mother, and the centre and the map of all the marvels of the Omnipotent. And for this same reason she is also the symbol of the Militant and Triumphant Church, and over each of them extended the vision of John of Patmos's generous eagle, given the correspondences and analogies that are found in the mystical Cities of Jerusalem. Our holy Mary looked intently upon the supreme Jerusalem, where there are encrypted and collected all the graces, gifts, marvels, and excellences of the Church Militant and Triumphant; and all [that] was done in the Jerusalem of Palestine, and what she and her inhabitants signify, it is all reduced to our most Pure Mary, Sanctified City of God, with more admiration and excellency than in all the rest of the heavens and the earth and all its inhabitants. For this reason, she is called the *new Jerusalem*, since all her gifts, her greatness and virtues are new and are the cause of new wonder to the Saints. New also because she came after all the ancient Fathers, Patriarchs, and Prophets, and in her were renewed and accomplished all their clamours, their prophecies and promises; new, because she came without the contagion of guilt and under a new dispensation far from the common law of sin; new, because she entered into the world triumphant over sin, the devil and the first deceit, thus being the greatest new event since its beginning.[73]

Metaphorically configured as the mystical city of God and anagogically new in every respect, Mary is presented once again as the "Mother of the eternal Word,"[74] placed side by side with the Father, her immanent humanity described as an accessory secondary to her "divine" nature (1.17.251, 78–9), or what Ágreda calls "gifts of divinity."[75] This description develops into a discussion of Mary's position as wife and mother of God (1.17.252, 79), accompanied by the necessary defence of the compulsory logic of immaculacy in the fruition of redemption.

It is in this context that Ágreda returns to the topic of the insepa-rability of the Mother and the Son, both theologically and affectively: "having already sent into the world the most holy Mary free from original sin, all that pertains to the Incarnation is already an accom-plished fact, and given that the most pure Mary was now on earth it appeared impossible for the eternal Word to remain *alone* in heaven and not come to earth in order to assume human flesh in her womb."[76] The Word cannot endure the absence of the Mother, or to be "alone," inserting the mystery of the incarnation and the narrative of redemp-tion into a chronicle of filial love. Moreover, Ágreda (who momentarily ventriloquizes the voice of God) presents God the Father's position as Alpha and Omega, and the divine design that accompanies this total-ity, as instrumentalized through Mary and Christ *together*, "through the work [of redemption] of Christ and Mary."[77] Mary's all-encompassing relationship with Christ is ultimately secured through her dual role as mother *and* bride, as told to John of Patmos as part of his vision:

> The angel declares in this passage that the holy city of Jerusalem, which he showed to him, is the espoused wife of the Lamb, referring by this metaphor (as I have already said) to the most holy Mary, whom Saint John saw both as a Mother, or Woman, and as a Spouse of the Lamb, who is Christ. The Queen held and fulfilled in divine manner both offices. She was the Spouse of the Divinity, exceptional and singular, and incompara-ble on account of the unequalled faith and love with which the espousals were entered into and accomplished; and she was the Mother of the same Lord incarnate, giving him his substance and mortal flesh, nourishing and sustaining him in his existence as man, which he derived from her.[78]

Symbolically figured as the new Jerusalem, the Virgin is the perfect woman who supplies all heavenly and earthly needs for the holy Trinity, the spirit, and the human body through which God the Father, God the Son, and God the Spirit can and must display the power of their omnipotence and the grace of redemption.

Chapter 18 declares a further elevation of the Virgin in the contin-uing exegesis of Revelation 21. Although the reader is presented with many well-known tropes and explanations for Mary's exceptional con-ception, the key to this segment is the enhanced justification for the book's title, *Mística ciudad de Dios*. As the reader of the period would have immediately perceived, the referent for Ágreda's text is Augus-tine of Hippo's *City of God*, in which the theologian and philosopher offers a description of the Church as correlative to the heavenly City of God in opposition to the world, redeemed spirit against the material and sinful bounds of earthly existence and eternal damnation. Ágreda offers an alternative (even if not oppositional) interpretation, particularizing the heavenly city by anagogically transposing its purity and clarity to the immaculacy of the Virgin. The new Jerusalem, symbolically revealed to Ágreda as Mary, is the mystical city formed in the heavens, uncorrupted, celestial, sacred: "built up and formed, not on earth, where she was like a pilgrim and a stranger, but in heaven, where the common earthly material was excluded. For though the material of her being was taken from the earth, it was at the same time so elevated in heavenly perfection as to be fit for the building up of that mystical City in a celestial and angelic manner, even Divine and similar to the Divinity."[79] The Virgin is the spiritual heavenly site where the sacred resides, thus allowing Ágreda to claim Mary's coextensive similitude to the holy Trinity:

> Therefore, [Saint John] adds that she had the clarity of God; for the most holy soul of Mary was favoured with such a participation of the Divinity and of its attributes and perfections that, if it were possible to see her in her own essence, she would appear as if illuminated with the eternal splendour of God himself. Great and glorious things are said in the Catholic Church of the City of God (Psalms 86:3) and of the clarity which she has received from that same Lord; but all of it is insignificant and all human words fall short of the truth. The created intellect, entirely overcome, can but assert that the most holy Mary partakes of the Divinity more than can be comprehended; confessing thereby the substance of the reality as well as the incapability of the mind to express in a proper manner that which it would like to explain and which is confessed as truth. She is formed in the heavens and only the Artificer who formed her is able to comprehend her greatness and the kinship and affinity which he contracted with our most holy Mary, likening the perfections he gave her to the same that are found in his infinite greatness and Divinity.[80]

The Virgin of the Immaculate Conception is God's most perfect creature, known fully only to God: eternal and human mother, mystical church, spiritual bride, and collectively an extension of God's perfection.

Chapter 19 is the last instalment in the formal interpretation of Revelation 21, offering a final set of metaphors that profile Mary's singularity and sacred status, and that Ágreda will refer to throughout the rest of the text. Specifically, the chapter expounds upon the materials from which the City of God is built, each of which symbolizes a characteristic of the Virgin of the Immaculate Conception: jasper for strength, sapphire for serenity, etc. With the transcendent

and immanent superiority of Mary now amply described and secured –
the exegetical and visionary "foundation" for the entire *Mística ciudad
de Dios* metaphorically set – Ágreda calls Philip IV to the service of
the Virgin. This personal exhortation to the king (the only one in the
entire text) is both predictable and daring. On the one hand, Ágreda
reminds Philip of what is to be gained in the service of the Mother of
God: "Remember that this great Princess honours those who honour
her, enriches those who seek her, makes illustrious those who praise
her, and defends those who hope in her. I assure you that in order to
perform her services as a singular mother and shower her mercies upon
you, she hopes and desires to have her maternal love be sought and
solicited."[81] Ágreda here figures the Virgin as the Immaculate Mother
of the Spanish Catholic king, a classification that raises Philip IV to the
level of chosen brother of Christ and places upon him immense privilege and a great deal of responsibility. On the other hand, and given the
degree of power and divinity awarded to the Virgin, she warns the king –
with whom she famously exchanged letters for twenty-two years and
for whom she served as spiritual advisor and friend[82] – of what is at
stake if the Immaculate Virgin is not properly served and her cause
duly defended:

> But at the same time remember that God needs no one and that he can
> make stones out of the children of Abraham, if of such great good you
> make yourself unworthy, for he can reserve this glory for those who serve
> him and do not disdain him ... for you should not ignore the service that
> you today owe our Queen, and the Lady of all, amongst many, and this
> will be shown to you because of your devotion and piety; tend to the sta-
> tus of the mystery of immaculacy in all of the Church, and to what is left to
> be done to firmly ensure the foundations of this city of God.[83]

This portentous plea is not issued lightly. Ágreda is fully cognizant of
the line she is straddling: the defence of the Virgin of the Immaculate
Conception motivates her religious selfhood, but it is Philip IV who can,
in very real and practical terms, exert his power and safeguard her and
her manuscript in a context in which her mystical experiences and intellectual projects have made her increasingly suspect. And yet, in her
zeal to have the doctrine be championed by the king, Ágreda dares
anyone – including the king – who would doubt her or the revelation of
the mystery she has presented: "Let no one judge this warning as coming from a weak and ignorant woman, or as founded upon a particular
devotion or because of love of my own station and profession under the
name and religious order of Mary Immaculate; I obey in my exhortation

the Lord who gives speech to the mute, and makes eloquent the tongues of infants."[84] Certainly, she deploys in her argument the weakness of women, false pride, and God's grace towards the damaged and defenceless (the mute and children). Nevertheless, given Ágreda's uneasy relationship with censors and the Inquisition – and the fact that she had much to gain from keeping secure Philip IV's friendship and protection – her boldness in publicly calling for the king's subordination to the Virgin's reign and taunting her censors and critics with the truths she has received through divine revelation is considerable. She only defers to God and the Virgin Mary, who chose her and reveal through her theological truths that had until then remained obscure. This is an authorial position that follows in the footsteps of Villena, Juana de la Cruz, and Pinelo, and which demands recognition for Ágreda as a worthy witness and heir to the immense power and privilege enjoyed by the Virgin of the Immaculate Conception. As with her predecessors, Ágreda's bounteous devotion and identification with Mary's sacred humanity – made possible by an expansive religious imagination – authorize her voice as a visionary and theologian, heir to the Virgin's exalted position, prophet (in the Augustinian sense), and writer.

III. The Virgin Child: Mary's Infancy and the Immaculist Imaginary in Villena, Ágreda, and Zurbarán

As represented in the texts by Villena, Juana de la Cruz, Pinelo, and Ágreda, the Virgin is radically singular in that she alone is (as an extension of her Son) wholly pure – transcendent – even if as a human she exists within the realm of God's material creation – immanent. As I have pointed out throughout this book, these premises are fundamental to the Immaculist imaginary, positioning Mary beyond a purely maternal function and elevating her as a creature that, as Duns Scotus would have it, expresses "the perfection of created beings in fullness, which in lesser degree is participated in by other lesser creatures, angels included" (Apollonio 68). Additionally, as Boss reminds us, Mary's eternal existence and its corresponding iconography signify "that Mary was conceived in the mind of God before the foundation of the world" ("The Development of the Doctrine" 224). This is a theological premise that, as I have shown, is concretized and particularized in the form of a material eternal existence in Juana de la Cruz's "dough" and Pinelo's "divine substance." The theological discourse around the Immaculate Conception thus constructs the Virgin as a being who belongs to and yet exceeds humanity – whose absolute, essential, and eternal purity places her as coextensive to the realm of the Divine, even as she carries her and her Son's material body. These were all important elements of the doctrine throughout the medieval and early modern periods, and they play an important part in the religious imagination of the women authors I here examine. What I would like to explore further in this section is how, precisely, the simultaneity of immanence and transcendence that makes the figure of the Virgin of the Immaculate Conception a strangely singular hybrid of the sacred and the familiarly human is imagined and deployed. Following this line of thinking, I find it particularly interesting how this dialectic is envisaged in the representation of Mary as a young child in Villena's *Vita Christi* and Ágreda's *Mística ciudad de Dios*; and how these representations may inform our understanding of Zurbarán's series of paintings of the Virgin as a young child. More to the point, it is my contention that Ágreda's visionary biography, with its precedent in Villena's *vitae mariae*, most fully delves into an imaginative zone of excess and hyperbole when offering a theologically coherent account of Mary's infancy. What we find in both Villena and Ágreda is testimony of a thoroughly exceptional and yet wholly familiar sacred *and* human child; an inventive theological discourse that, as I will argue, allows us to better read the images of the Virgin as a child that single out Zurbarán's pictorial trajectory and which should be considered alongside these women's religious writings and imagination.[85]

First, it is important to acknowledge why an account of Mary's early life must be formulated as remarkable and excessive. To start with, there is no scriptural account of the life of Mary as a child; the only mention appears in the Protoevangelium of James (7–8), where it is established that Mary is brought to the temple at the age of three, where she takes a vow of virginity and stays put until her marriage to Joseph. Nevertheless, given the Virgin's characterization as the Apocalyptic Woman in existence *ab initio*, the religious imagination of the period lent itself to the following considerations: Was Mary ever – intellectually and spiritually – a child? What was Mary's relationship with the holy Trinity at the very early stages of her material life? Did she remember her past existence in the heavens? How did she understand her present state and her future destiny? How does a rare and sacred human exist amongst lesser mortals? What are the terms of her distinct visionary experience of the sacred while here amongst us? What can an infant Mary teach us about humanity and what does she reveal about our relationship with the transcendent? These are amongst the many questions that those devoted to the cult of Mary, and most especially to the Immaculate Conception, would have needed to ask in order to make sense of Mary's passage from the spiritual to the earthly realm, from eternal spirit to becoming the physical mother of God.

Given the lack of scriptural support, representations of the Virgin Mary as a child are rare and mostly limited to Saint Anne teaching her daughter to read, the exception being the few paintings of the young Mary by Zurbarán. I am not the first to explore the iconographic connection between Conceptionist doctrine, Ágreda's *Mística ciudad de Dios*, and Zurbarán's young Mary paintings; Mindy Nancarrow, Emilie Bergmann, and Charlene Villaseñor Black have traced this path for me.[86] Where I depart from these critics' assessment is in my interpretation of what Villena's, Ágreda's, and Zurbarán's young Mary enacts, what she performs for the reader or viewer: her peculiar indeterminacy, her eternal function as the Queen of the Heavens coupled with her humanity, and her necessary in-between state of transcendence *and* immanence. It is precisely for these reasons that the adult Mary has been considered, as Marcella Althaus-Reid states, "the strangest thing in Christianity" (71). In the adult Mary this singularity, as Althaus-Reid also reminds us, is fundamentally located in and theologically founded upon an intact hymen that is nonetheless permeated by God, an act that is followed by the birthing of God while Mary is still intact in "some unimaginable way" (71). In other words, Mary contains mutually exclusive possibilities: virginity and maternity. This exceptionality is echoed in Mary's labour without pain and her assumption, when she, "having completed the course of her earthly life, was assumed body and soul into heavenly glory."[87] The question of how she exists both in the material world and outside of it, both familiar and incomprehensible, is thus at the core of how Mary is imagined, what she represents, and her sacred potentiality. The Virgin represents a point of contact between sacred mystery and material life; but she, like her Son and unlike her fellow human beings, transcends her physical being. In Mary (as in Christ) a synthesis of two opposites remains ultimately unresolved, and what is left is a powerful singularity: she is alone of all her sex. This is an existential condition that, as shown in the texts and paintings I here analyse, is transposed to her birth and childhood. The coexistence of the immanent and the transcendent at the core of the doctrine of the Immaculate Conception fuels Villena's and Ágreda's accounts of Mary's infancy, and drives what Zurbarán's unusual paintings attempt to visually represent and mediate. If the Virgin is gloriously excepted from the rule of original sin, she consequently must be extraordinary and singular from the moment of her conception and physical formation in the womb.

Villena's account of Mary's infancy in chapter 3 and chapter 4 of the *Vita Christi* is structured as the final proof for the defence of the doctrine; accordingly, she ends it with a citation attributed to Bonaventure from the Office of the Immaculate Virgin Mary, and which she translates as follows: "O Lady, how deeply is the world obligated to laud and praise your father and mother who have begotten you, the memory of whom shall remain immortal throughout all present and future generations!"[88] What precedes this praise of the miracle of the Virgin's conception is a description of a child who is simultaneously humble in her human body and yet eager to go back to heaven and occupy her place alongside the angels. As mentioned above, Villena and her fellow nuns fashion the Virgin as a paradigm for their own religious lives. Villena's narration allows this exemplarity to be first fully realized in the body of an infant whose spiritual and mental capacity far exceeds that of any other human being before her. For example, upon birth Mary communicates with her mother, via an intense glare, that she should refrain from excessive physical affection (kissing her feet and her hands) that would verge on adoration. Similarly, she quickly recognizes the value of a well-ordered life, refraining from the excesses that would derail her purity, and which include feeding herself without measure: "for on certain days of the week she suckled but once, knowing that fasting and penance constituted the life of the soul."[89] Praying almost continuously, hands clasped together, the infant Virgin also contemplates and reflects upon the repercussions of the Fall – "the cruel ailment and affliction passed down by infection from and extending to all his children"[90] – a condition that can only be remedied through the grace of God as bestowed upon humanity through her immaculacy and the resultant incarnation of Christ. And yet, infant Mary's activities are not limited to the act of prayer and contemplation; at the break of dawn, according to Villena, the infant Virgin would ascend to "Paradise," entering God's presence and thus commencing her role as advocate and intercessor for the redemption of humanity, "begging God's mercy to put an end to this exile of Adam and of his children, and to bring them back to his grace and love."[91] The purpose of Mary's spotlessness is, as presented by Villena, consequently not only to serve as a pure vessel for her sacred Son but also, just as importantly, from her very first moments here on earth, to intercede on behalf of the inheritors of original sin. There are additional elements in these chapters that are significant when examining Villena's hermeneutical practice. First, infant Mary repeatedly singles out Adam as the cause of human suffering, with no mention of Eve throughout: "And when she considered that this place of such sovereign bliss was shut and closed on account of Adam's sin, she broke into a flood of endless tears."[92] This bias seems to confirm the proto-feminist import of Villena's text; just like Juana de la Cruz, Villena is here recalling Paul's letter to the Corinthians and integrating the sinful lineage of

Adam and redemptive mission of Christ within the logic of the Marian cult. Second, the value placed on Mary's first words, on her act of speaking, is quite striking and greatly celebrated by Saint Anne, who instructs Saint Joachim to come and hear "the *clever words* of your beloved daughter, and your soul shall flourish by way of the incalculable satisfaction you shall draw from *hearing her speak*" (emphasis mine).[93] When these passages are considered vis-à-vis the exemplarity that the Virgin provides for Villena and her fellow nuns, the celebration of Mary's voice must be understood as significant; this is a model whose virtue is exhibited through speech from the earliest stages of her life, not in silence. Finally, we must consider the manner in which Villena employs sources to develop an original narrative and offer new meanings. Her use of Bonaventure to end the chapter on Mary's infancy in praise of the Immaculate Conception refashions the conventional arc of the Virgin's life, which traditionally zeros in on the miracle of the conception only to quickly skip over to the annunciation, with occasionally a brief mention of Mary's presentation in the temple. Another interesting use of a source is Thomas à Kempis's *De imitatione Christi*, which Villena evidently had carefully read and which she recycles in praise of the infant Mary. In Villena's text, the hopes and actions of Kempis's devout adherent, who prepares himself – body and spirit – to receive the benefits of holy Communion, are transposed so as to communicate the purity of Mary as a holy infant. Unlike Kempis's believer, who furnishes his own "rooms"[94] in order to receive the presence of Christ, the infant Mary enters the rooms of God's palace in Paradise, where she unreservedly joins the divine presence and is invited to contemplate his "joys and sweetness."[95] The infant Mary, an immaculate eternal spirit, is free to inhabit the sacred space, and it is God who orders and offers the spiritual topography for their heavenly communion. The second Kempis citation, which comes from an earlier segment of book 4 of his *De imitatione*, is equally inventive. If in the original the wine of the sacrament of communion is compared to the sweetness of a fountain, in Villena's text it is imagined as and translated to the infant Mary herself, held in her father's arms, with the sweet "fountain" of her newfound voice an exalted vehicle for what Saint Joachim describes as a "unique sense of pleasure in his soul."[96] If in the first Kempis citation the infant Mary is gifted with communing with the heavenly presence of God, in the second she pays it forwards by offering her earthly father the extraordinary gift of her pure and sacred presence and voice. In both examples, the infant Mary is – by way of the use of Kempis's text – analogous to Christ in her purity, unquestioned belonging in heaven, and capacity to offer those who hold her close and hear her voice deliverance from the stained legacy of Adam. In Villena's capacious religious imagination, the infant Mary participates in the same attributes as Christ the Redeemer, offering the cloistered audience an alternative sacred site in which to experience joy and redemption.

As explained in the previous section, Ágreda's *Mística ciudad de Dios* is a tour de force in Counter-Reformation Spanish religious imagination, a 650-page text where the nun relates in great detail the Virgin's life and examines all doctrinal aspects related to Mary's sanctity as told to her in a vision of Mary. It is evident that Ágreda was familiar with Villenas's *Vita Christi*, and her own account of Mary's conception and infancy is highly influenced by this source. For Ágreda, following in Villena's footsteps, the Virgin's singularity provides the ideal conceptual space where doctrine, theological discourse, and (for Ágreda) mystical experience meet. Nowhere is Mary's exceptionality more evident than in her gestation, birth, infancy, and early childhood. From the moment of her conception, the Virgin is described as existing between the spirit world and the earth: "she was the most valued treasure of Heaven, and on Earth the purest creature, inferior only to God and superior to all that has been created."[97] Underscoring the dual human/ sacred nature of Mary, the first two acts she performs upon birth are to acknowledge her parents and, immediately after, to be carried by a procession of angels "body and soul"[98] to her due place by her Creator and her Son, a position she will one day return to for all eternity. It is also already in this initial (even if temporary) visit to the heavens that infant Mary inaugurates her role as intercessor for humanity, addressing her Son and petitioning that he, without delay, fulfil his own role in the narrative of redemption: "Mary pleaded that he accelerate the reparation of the human race, expected for so many ages amid the multiplied iniquity and the ruin of souls. The Most High heard this petition ... and he assured his mother ... that soon his promises should be fulfilled and that he should descend to the world taking on the flesh in order to redeem it."[99] Taking Villena's cue much farther, Ágreda's infant Mary is more than the model of a saintly child; she immediately (re)occupies her position of power in the heavenly realm and commands the attention and respect of her Son and the admiration of the angels, nine hundred of whom will later gather in her earthly abode to venerate her in song (1.23.363–5, 113). It is she who insists on the timely fulfilment of the promise of salvation, an event that is only now possible as a result of her immaculate conception and saintly birth.

Congruent with Ágreda's comprehensive religious imagination and as a confirmation of her singular hybridity, Mary's passage from eternal spirit to perfect human being is simultaneously a strange and yet relatable existence in the womb. The narrativization of Mary's stopover in Saint Anne's uterus describes a trajectory that is equally a characterization of the limitations imposed on her eternal spirit by the adoption of the human state *and* an exploration of a human being fully committed to sanctity and worthy of grace. As told by Ágreda in chapter 16, "Of the habits of the Virtues with which the Most High endowed the Soul of our holy Mary, and the first acts that she performed in Saint Anne's womb" ["De los hábitos de las Virtudes, con que dotó al Altísimo la Alma de María Santísima, y las primeras operaciones, que con ella tuvo en el vientre de Santa Ana"], Mary descends into Saint Anne's womb, "adorned as the Bride, descending from heaven endowed with all perfections and with the whole range of infused virtues; it was not necessary that she should exercise all of them at once, it being sufficient that she exercise those that suited her state in the womb of her mother."[100] As it turns out, the "necessary virtues" Mary demonstrates in her foetal state already epitomize a reformed devout life: the theological virtues of faith, hope, and charity, guided by the acceptance of God's perfect, even if inscrutable, design, rightfully acknowledge God as the desired final end, and see in God the infinite and ultimate good (1.16.226, 71). In the foetal Mary, the theological virtues are complemented by the four cardinal virtues, which "adorn and perfect the rational part of the creature"; the moral virtues, and no less the "infused habit of all these virtues and of all the natural arts, so that she knew and was conversant with the whole natural and supernatural order of things, in accordance with the grandeur of God."[101] Mary is, as Ágreda imagines her and as the logic of the doctrine of the Immaculate Conception suggests, above all other created beings even in her gestational stage: "From the first instant in the womb of her mother she was wiser, more prudent, more enlightened, and more capable of comprehending God and all his works than all the creatures have been or ever will be in eternity, excepting of course her most holy Son."[102]

And yet, what is most noteworthy in this segment, as in the rest of the description of Mary's infancy, is not that Mary already possesses all the qualities that will prove necessary to her singular role as Mother of God; far more striking is that Ágreda – incorporating the doctrine's dependence on Revelation 12 and 21 with the Virgin's material embodiment – animates the foetus, transforming it into a fully sentient and enlightened being. Ágreda explains the transition from pure spirit to immaculate being from a theological perspective. Mary, in her foetal state, "was not united substantially with the Divinity and therefore she did not begin her activity fully comprehending God but entered into life as a pilgrim. However, as the one closest to the hypostatic union, she was endowed with a vision of God proportionate and most immediate to the beatific vision."[103] Even though the Virgin's conception forces a separation from her eternal spiritual existence, she maintains, from the moment of her materialization in the womb, an exalted contiguous connection to the Divine and abstract (as opposed to intuitive) knowledge of the sacred mysteries (1.16.237, 74). Given these existential coordinates, Mary is characterized *in utero* as a fully formed, sentient, and active self. Ágreda, hence, presents a narrative that is coherent with the Conceptionist position. She makes of Mary's foetus something utterly peculiar *and* something entirely familiar, anthropomorphizing and animating a prenatal being that would otherwise have remained remote and inscrutable: "a tiny, animated body not larger than that of a little bee."[104] Foetal Mary reveres God, "beginning from that instant with fervent desire to bless him, love him, and honour him";[105] laments Adam's fall, "although the exterior faculties of her body at the creation of her most holy Soul were hardly large enough to be distinguished ... in perceiving the fall of man, she shed tears of sorrow in the womb of her mother at the gravity of the offence against the highest good";[106] factors in knowledge which leads her immediately to assume her position as advocate and co-redemptress: "at the instant of her coming into existence, she began to seek a remedy for mankind and commenced the work of meditation, intercession, and reparation";[107] and, in her immaculate and remarkable embryonic state, welcomes "the gifts, which she had received with profound humility and with the corporal prostrations that she performed in the womb of her mother, and with such a small body."[108] Foetal Mary embodies an aspirational model of devotion that would have been instantly acknowledged by the cloistered nuns at the convent at Ágreda and that, within the unusual context of Saint Anne's womb, makes of the Virgin a wholly fathomable, familiar, and imitable sacred human being.

Finally out of the womb, in chapter 24, "Of the exercises and saintly occupations of the Queen of the heavens in the first year and a half of her infancy" ["De los ejercicios y ocupaciones santas de la Reina del cielo en el año y medio primero de su infancia"], Mary eats, cries, and sleeps compliant to what she perceives are the exigencies of her suckling physical body and the psychological and cultural expectations of her parents. Working within the hermeneutical parameters of the doctrine, Ágreda imagines a sacred child who deliberately acts like a baby because she inhabits the body of an infant baby. When left alone, the Virgin – conscious of her condition as an eternal and venerable being – continues to seek the camaraderie of her former celestial companions, the angels who have held loyal to her supremacy. Even more significant in terms of her exemplarity, infant Mary immerses herself in sacred revelations and intellectual visions, which result in magnificent ecstasies, what Ágreda categorizes as "the violence of love."[109] Still, as the Apocalyptic Woman, descended from heaven to her sinless body, the infant Mary is a being whose spiritual self logically longs for a return to her true home:

> In such colloquies and many others, too high for our capacity, our holy Mary passed her infancy conversing with the angels, and with the Most High, in whom she was transformed. As her fervour and longing to see our highest Good increased, whom above all else she loved, she was by the disposal of the Lord many times borne bodily by the hands of the angels to the empyrean heaven, where she enjoyed the presence of the Divinity.[110]

Ágreda's child Virgin is a manifold being: human and divine, she inhabits a child's body with the consciousness of an eternal sacred spirit. In kind, at this early stage she finds herself a foreigner, forced by circumstances to conform to the world she now inhabits, and comforted only when she returns to the presence of God; she is in the world, but her world view is attached to her relations in heaven. The theological discourse in this segment is, therefore, fixed on the logistics and logical consequences of Mary, as the eternal Apocalyptic Woman, inhabiting our earthly material realm. Despite the apparent peculiarity of what is being narrated, Ágreda offers a hermeneutically coherent pathway for the trajectory of the Virgin of the Immaculate Conception between the heavenly realm where she defeated the seven-headed dragon before the beginning of time (a subject examined and commented on in the preceding chapters of *Mística ciudad de Dios*) and the material and spiritual conditions of her newly found earth-bound humanity, through which she will fulfil her exceptional destiny and become the Mother of God. Furthermore, and no less importantly, Ágreda reveals for the reader the coordinates of a sacred mystery that is simultaneously exceptional and explicable, singular and yet recognizable and imitable. We, like the infant Mary, should all prefer to be in the company of angels and one day will, as a result of the redemption made possible by her hybrid existence, achieve that destiny in our restored, redeemed, and newly immaculate selves.

From a separate but complementary perspective, the matter of Mary's knowledge – intellectual, theological, and mystical – is a core concern of Ágreda's theological discourse. Along the line of Scotus's exceptionality, Ágreda's infant Mary possesses the capacity for complex thought and speech from the moment of conception, abilities which she hides, "opportunely concealing her science and grace, and evading the astonishment that would have been naturally caused by seeing an infant speak."[111] This innate intellectual superiority might be understood as bizarre only if one does not recognize the Virgin's positionality in Ágreda's religious imagination as coextensive with the holy Trinity and naturally partaking of the sacred knowledge that circulates in the heavens *ab initio*. This point is made clear in the segments where the Virgin, responding to Ágreda's queries, provides doctrinal and biographical clarification. In chapter 21, for example, Ágreda asks the Virgin how and why, if the doors of heaven were closed to all human beings after the fall of Adam, the angels could take her to corporally be with God upon her birth. The core of the answer is predictable: Mary was never stained by the legacy of sin and therefore the doors of heaven need not be closed to her. Nevertheless, in her reply, Ágreda's Virgin of the Immaculate Conception does not perform the role of a silent vehicle for the fruits of God's omniscience, inscrutable will, and perfect grace; instead, she profoundly apprehends and can in great detail theorize and explain the logic and causes of God's design: "As I was not a slave of sin, I exercised the virtues not as a subject, but as a Lady, without contradiction, and with sovereignty; not like the children of Adam, but like the Son of God, who was also my Son."[112] There is no contradiction in her between the perfect humanity that God created (God can only create perfect beings) and the stain that human beings caused by their own corrupted will and desire. Sin is defined as a disjuncture, and in this sense the Virgin, in her perfection, is similar to her Son and unlike Adam; in other words, Mary materializes (as we saw in the previous section) an original prelapsarian seamless humanity and, in the present state of affairs, intercedes in favour of a dissonant humanity (because sin inhabits God's perfect creation). The Virgin is what the "norm" was intended to be and would have been if Adam had not taken the forbidden fruit. She is a perfect (i.e., non-contradictory) human body and spirit, as we all should have been had the incongruity introduced by the knowledge of good and evil, and the disobedience that ushered in that knowledge, not been wilfully taken up by Adam. As exegetically clarified by Ágreda, the wonder of infant Mary – her flight, for example, to heaven in spirit *and* body – encapsulates two aspects of the doctrine. Mary is the eternal Apocalyptic Woman miraculously conceived and birthed in order to fulfil her mission as the Mother of God; she is also, and no less, the original and unspoiled (either by the knowledge of evil or by disobedience) human being, a second unblemished Adam, who conse-quently contains in her the promise (literal, tropological, analogic, and anagogic) of our own restitution to an originary prelapsarian shared immaculacy. As stated above, the nuns at the convent in Ágreda (and any reader, for that matter) could hope for the day where they could also return to their originary created nature, aided by the Virgin of the Immaculate Conception's redemptive intervention. They – as devout women – can also recognize and aspire to Mary's intellectual capacity and doctrinal wisdom, an objective that, although never *de facto* fully achievable, is nevertheless textually attained because Ágreda's vision-ary text receives and passes on this wealth of erudition to the nuns who read it, study it, and interiorize it.

In chapter 25, "How when she was a year and a half old the young holy Mary started to speak and her occupations until she went to the temple" ["Cómo al año y medio comenzó a hablar la niña María santísima, y sus ocupaciones hasta que fue al templo"], the reader is told how at the age of one and a half God deems that infant Mary finally speak; whereupon, despite her apprehension at what may be the sinful potentiality of words – "it is very hard for rational creatures not to fall into the excess of words"[113] – she eloquently asks her parents for bene-diction and starts to walk. Saint Anne and Saint Joachim are enthralled by their prodigy, what Ágreda describes as a "mature girl,"[114] but little do they know that before the age of two she is already well aware of the ineffable mystery of her Messianic maternity: "but she never told Saint Anne the sacrament she held in her heart, that she had been chosen to be the Mother of the Messiah";[115] that she often sojourns with angels: "At times she would retire to enjoy, by herself and with greater liberty of sight the divine colloquies of her Saintly Angels, and to give outward signs of the burning love she had for her Spouse";[116] that she had taken up physical penitence for the sins of humanity: "beginning to use her corporal strength at that tender age, she commenced in works of pen-ance and mortification, to be in every respect the mother of mercy and the mediator of grace, sparing no exertion and opportunity permitted in order to gain grace for herself and for us";[117] and that she cares for the poor: "she began to exercise her special affection and charity for the poor ... she gave to the poor alms, not as if conferring a benefit upon them but as paying a debt due in justice."[118] Despite the breadth of her spiritual and intellectual capacity, she nevertheless indulges her mother's and father's parental role and attachment by sustaining the delusion that they can teach her how to read: "She was instructed in reading and other arts, and she admitted all teachings though she had infused knowledge of all things created, and she was silent and listened to all. The angels were filled with admiration at the unparalleled wisdom of the child, who demonstrated such foreign prudence."[119] As this description makes clear, Mary's singularity is patent even to the angels who witness in awe her capacity to navigate the exigencies of a world she does not fully belong to while in the guise of a human child. Shortly before turning three, Ágreda's infant Mary has a vision that confirms God's plan that she leave her parents for the Temple, a revelation that soon after is also experienced by Saint Anne and which seals the deal, so to speak, for Mary's continued trajectory to become the Mother of God on earth. Ágreda's visionary biography of the Virgin goes on for many hundreds of pages, but the coordinates for exceptionality are set firmly from these very first descriptions of the Virgin as an infant: an eternal spirit and original perfect human, congruent with Christ and the project of redemption, and separate from the corrupted nature of Adam. Ágreda's young Virgin of the Immaculate Conception, "conceived in the mind of God before the foundation of the world," exists between God's design for her Messianic purpose (both in the heavens and on earth) and her material existence; between her physical body and her spiritual self in the cosmic drama of Apocalyptic revelations; between her utilitarian function as the reproductive body who will bear God Incarnate and her sacred state as Mother of God and intercessor; second only to the Trinity and exceptional in her own right, set apart from the legacy of Adam. Just as importantly – deploying a strategy that is paradoxical and yet simultaneously parallel and complimentary – the narrativization and hermeneutical examination of Mary's exceptional passage from eternal spirit to human being offers the reader a recognizable and imitable model for what, from a purely doctrinal and theological perspective, could have remained an abstracted state preceding her mature maternal function.

It is through this same set of coordinates that I take a brief detour to Zurbarán's paintings of Mary as a young child (figures 5.2–5.4), with an emphasis on his debt to the religious imaginary of the women authors I have here discussed. Art historians, such as Delenda, not only remark upon the uniqueness of Zurbarán's work – "The only painter, no doubt, to represent the young girl at such a tender age" – but also interpret these images as a naturalization of "the sublime and the familiar."[120] This interpretation is in essence accurate, and yet – given the correspondences that can be drawn out with Villena and Ágreda – it flattens the complexity of Zurbarán's composition and its potential didactic and contemplative effects. At first sight, the "familiar" image of a child evokes innocence untouched by the trials of time or the ravages of sin, a suitable preamble to the Virgin's adult iteration as *tota pulchra*. The

placement of lilies and roses nearby only further symbolically emphasizes Mary's purity and charity. Moreover, informed by the apocryphal Protoevangelium of James and the Gospel of Pseudo-Matthew,
the young Mary is visually placed next to or holding needlepoint
(symbolic of the shroud she will eventually sew for her Son) and a book
of prayers. In sum, the symbols that are included in these paintings
signify the adult Mary as a devout and sacrificial mother. Not surprisingly, this visual codification of the image perfectly corresponds with
the meanings attached to childhood in early modern Spain as described
by Grace Coolidge:

> The perspective [of Spanish society in general] was ... inherently practical,
> and tended to emphasize children as latent adults who needed to be trained
> and shaped for their future roles ... This vision tended to overshadow child-
> hood, rendering it a training ground for impending careers and imposing
> the distinct gender roles of the adult world on Spanish children. (1)

On the one hand, therefore, we can conclude that the early modern Spanish viewer (putting aside her level of literacy and erudition)
would have read the visual narrative of the young Mary as a preface
to her fully realized adult maternal self. In this same light, Zurbarán
criticism has typically understood these images as representing Mary's
departure at the age of three to the Temple, where she would be protected and prepared for her role as Mother of God. In "Theology and
Devotion in Zurbarán's Images of the Infant Virgin in the Temple,"
Nancarrow offers a slightly different interpretation, keeping the timeline close to Mary's departure for the temple yet positing the possibility of a conceptual association with the doctrine. Following the lead of
Karen Pinkus, Nancarrow argues for a "socio-spiritual ritual" in which
the viewer understands Zurbarán's young Virgin to be in the act of
seeing and communicating directly with God because, as the Virgin of
the Immaculate Conception, "Mary alone of all humanity is united to
God in perfect love and harmony from the first instant of her life and
always after that" (78). Additionally, the critic notes the connection that
Zurbarán's images have with convent and women patrons, indicating
that "they made ... particular meaning for nuns" as an ideal for female
Christian devotion (76).

Echoing a common religious set of referents and imaginary with
Villena and Ágreda, I propose we amplify the import of Nancarrow's
suggestion. I would argue that Zurbarán's young Mary paintings, like
the texts of the women authors we have here examined, are narratively
and conceptually tied to the Apocalyptic Woman of Revelation 12 and 21,

Figure 5.1. Bartolomé
Esteban Murillo, *Immaculate
Conception* (1660).
Louvre Museum.

including the notion of the *ab initio*. This theological context is visually
indicated by the inclusion of the corresponding iconography (blue cape,
halo of angels, dressed in the light of the sun, specific symbols of the
litany), and supported by the fact that most Immaculist paintings codify
the Virgin's purity by representing her as a very young or even childlike woman. In Murillo's 1660 *Immaculate Conception*, for example, the
tota pulchra looks no older than a five-year-old girl (figure 5.1). And yet,
Zurbarán's paintings of Mary as a young child bring to the fore a specific set of referents and religious sensitivities, visually enacting the rich
descriptions of Mary's transition from eternal spirit to human being that
were theologically contextualized and narrated by Villena and Ágreda.

In *The Childhood of the Virgin* (1630–5) (figure 5.2), the infant Mary
sits between her doting parents as she looks up to the heavens.
Zurbarán portrays the family bond within a dialectic of immanence
and transcendence, offering a visual and conceptual bridge between
the quotidian setting and infant Mary's visionary gaze, which conveys
her sustained sacred existence. The viewer can well imagine, much as
Villena and Ágreda had in their writings, the young child spiritually
and intellectually partaking of her heavenly home while she conforms

Figure 5.2. Francisco de Zurbarán, *The Childhood of the Virgin* (1630–5). Colección Abelló.

to her parents' attentions and the requirements of her earthly body. To be more precise, I contend that the early modern viewer would have seen in the *The Childhood of the Virgin* the image of the young Mary as a manifestation of the Virgin of the Immaculate Conception. If Mary has existed in the mind of God before time and is a sacred and singular human being, higher than the angels and second only to the holy Trinity, then an interpretation of this image as solely exhibiting the trajectory of the child towards her sacred maternal role strikes me as lacking. When Zurbarán's young Mary looks to heaven, when she

Figure 5.3. Francisco de Zurbarán, *The Young Virgin* (1640–5). The Metropolitan Museum of Art, New York.

closes her eyes in the midst of a meditative state, what is she seeing? What is she experiencing as her mother and father try to coax her back to an earthly sensibility? What does the viewer believe this child, split between the spiritual realm she just left and the human body she has acquired, is feeling, thinking, doing, experiencing? Within the Conceptionist imaginary, Zurbarán's *The Young Virgin* (1640–5), *Virgin Mary as a Child, Asleep* (1655), and *Childhood of the Virgin, Praying* (1660) elicit a similar set of questions for the viewer, who would not conceptually distinguish the image of this child from the legacy of her sacred prehistory as the Virgin *ab initio* (figures 5.3–5.5).[121]

Figure 5.4. Francisco de Zurbarán, *Virgin Mary as a Child, Asleep* (1655). Galerie Canesso, Paris.

In her analysis, Nancarrow chooses to describe the young Mary's prayer and interlocution with God as an exercise of her free will: "Mary, filled with grace, continued to perform [after her birth] meritorious acts of her own free will throughout the entirety of her childhood and the rest of her life. In the process she accrued more grace through merit than any saint" ("Theology and Devotion" 79). When this is read alongside Villena and Ágreda, I would argue that Zurbarán's infant Mary paintings take on a much deeper level of narrative complexity and meaning. They visually represent a theological space where Mary's exceptionality can be imagined as most striking, when as a child she spiritually

Figure 5.5. Francisco de Zurbarán, *Childhood of the Virgin, Praying* (1660). The Hermitage, St Petersburg.

and physically communes with and commutes to the heavens, sentient of the mysteries in which she participates, and aware of her difference from the humanity that surrounds her. In his infant Mary paintings, Zurbarán's religious imagination is clearly on par with Villena's and Ágreda's: Zurbarán visually codifies these women's theological and biographical discourse. These images confirm the ways in which Mary's unique infancy was imperative to an early modern Spanish religious Immaculist imaginary that required her to be exceptional and yet tenderly familiar; to be born human and yet remain without sin; to occupy her physical body in order to become the Mother of God while simultaneously holding tight to her past as eternal spirit, Apocalyptic Woman, and unsullied sister of Adam from the beginning of time; to be a familiar child and simultaneously exceed the parameters of our own human experience.

The early modern viewer of these paintings – nuns and women patrons and, by extension, believers in the doctrine in general – logically assumed (or at a minimum readily accepted) that exceptionality extended to and defined Mary's youngest years; i.e., the faithful expected her to embody singularity even as a child. This is what the theological imaginary of the women writers I have examined supports and promotes, and what Immaculists seem to welcome without hesitation. In fact, the cult of the Virgin of the Immaculate Conception and the religious imaginary that depends on it cannot exist without the excessive humanity that fuels Mary's preternatural and redemptive stature. It is for this reason that Villena, Ágreda, and Zurbarán embrace the indeterminacy of the Virgin's youngest years. Despite Mary's tender, childlike humanity, she must always already be fully herself: Apocalyptic Woman, eternal spirit, unsullied original matter, and co-redemptress. If the faithful are to be comforted by her humanity – her immanence – it is only in the context of and as an effect of her insistent transcendence. Where her infant body indexes a material return to the original design and creation (image/imagination) of God, her spiritual and intellectual capacities confirm her eternal position in the heavenly realm as the Apocalyptic Woman. For Villena, Ágreda, and Zurbarán, Mary's infancy therefore provides a representational field where the bond of the human and the sacred – as well as the complex trajectory of humanity from the creation to the fall to a return via redemption – is contextualized as congruent with the theological tenets and narrative that frame the doctrine. As such, their texts and paintings amply demonstrate the expansive logic and inventive excess of the early modern Spanish religious imagination.

Returning to the main focus of this chapter, we can draw significant conclusions regarding the ways in which theological discourse and the religious imaginary of the period are retooled by women writers in order to meet specific identificatory needs responsive to their conventual setting. As I have shown, religious women writers reinscribe orthodoxy, producing alternative content for the history of humanity, its redemption, and the place of women in the broader religious and cultural fields. The discourses around the Virgin of the Immaculate Conception, doctrinal and biographical, are a perfect fit for a gendered reflection on the encounter between orthodoxy and the religious imagination. The doctrine, the Virgin herself, and these women writers are all

characterized by excesses, broadening early modern ontological, theological, and cultural boundaries. Even though the patriarchal paradigm
qualifies female nature as akin to a sinful and weak Eve, Juana de la
Cruz, Villena, Pinelo, and Ágreda deliberately provide a counter-model
that features and fashions anew Marian privilege. By showcasing
Mary's exceptionality, these writers raise themselves (and their female
readers) spiritually and intellectually to the level of devout believers
who will achieve their own future heavenly immaculacy via the intervention of the Virgin and the redemptive sacrifice of her Son. And, even
though purity is for them (as human beings born in sin) a future goal to
be achieved by the grace of God, in their present they are the daughters
of a powerful, superior, and immaculate Mary; they are of her kind, and
thus worthy of her intellectual and visionary revelations. Juana de la
Cruz, Isabel de Villena, Valentina Pinelo, and María de Ágreda together
elaborate a coherent hermeneutical and hagiographical narrative that
would – by association and in their claims of direct contact with the
assumpted Virgin of the Immaculate Conception – translate their own
specific existence as singular and exalted. And, just as importantly, by
doing so they fully legitimize each of their own excessive and singular
religious imaginations. Thus understood, and as I have presented in
this book, these religious women writers find themselves in the good
company of innumerable faithful who in their theological and political
treatises, literary writings, art, official and personal letters, sermons,
relaciones, public engagements, and private devotion carve out through
the multivalent sign of the Virgin of the Immaculate Conception a rich
tapestry of imaginative Catholic selfhoods.

Notes

1. The Anatomy of the Religious Imagination

1 "Pero ya la devoción Cristiana, vemos, que se ha inclinado tanto a honrar la Virgen, que tiene el Predicador obligación a huir todo escándalo, y honrarle con sus palabras, y decir que fue concebida sin pecado original, porque son fundamentos de esta divina Ciudad" (10). All translations of original texts, primary and secondary, are my own unless otherwise indicated.

The cult of the Immaculate Conception, although often associated with Seville, was widespread in all of the Spanish kingdoms, a fact that is shown by the prevalence of the image and other cultural artefacts produced in all regions of early modern Spain. Recent books such as Ricardo Fernández García's *La Inmaculada Concepción en Navarra* and Clementina Ara Gil, Francisco de la Plaza Santiago, and María Meléndez Alonso's encyclopaedic *Inmaculada* document the vast proliferation of the cult in all corners of the Spanish Habsburg lands.

2 John O'Malley has noted: "To such historians even religious art of the latter [Counter-Reformation] period reflected the monolithic uniformity of Catholicism at large. It adhered slavishly to the dictates of ecclesiastical authority, which acted on the well-known lines of sacred art from the Council of Trent, and it was programmed as a reaction to Protestantism" (cited by Marcia B. Hall in her Introduction to *The Sensuous in the Counter-Reformation Church* 3).

3 As cited in *Michel Foucault: Key Concepts*, "[T]he word power is apt to lead to a number of misunderstandings – misunderstandings with respect to its nature, its form, and its unity. By power, I do not mean 'Power' as a group of institutions and mechanisms that ensure the subservience of the citizens of a given state [such as characterize many liberal analyses]. By power, I do not mean, either, a mode of subjugation which, in contrast to violence, has the form of the rule [typical of psychoanalytic approaches]. Finally, I do not

have in mind a general system of domination exerted by one group over another [i.e. class oppression], a system whose effects, through successive derivations, pervade the entire social body [as in many Marxist views]. (1990a: 92)" (Taylor 16).

4 "God thus defines himself as the Subject *par excellence*, he who is through himself and for himself ('I that I am'), and he who interpellates his subject, the individual subjected to him by his very interpellation ... [A] subject *of* God, a subject subjected to God, *a subject through the Subject and subjected to the Subject*" (Althusser 134).

5 Numerous religious treatises at the time dealt with the status of the visionary experience. See, for example, Leandro Granada y Mendoza's 1607 *Luz de las maravillas* and Gerónimo Planes's 1633 *Tratado del examen de las revelaciones verdaderas y falsas y de los raptos.*

6 We can think here of Saint John of the Cross's explanatory treatises for his poems or large segments of María de Ágreda's letters to Philip IV justifying her theological thought and mystical experiences.

7 See Greene and Cushman 546.

8 See O'Malley, "Trent, Sacred Images, and Catholics' Sense of the Sensous."

9 For further discussion, see Kappes.

10 "Que Dios predestinó a la Virgen antes de previsto el pecado original, tanto a la divina maternidad como a la perpetua santidad e inocencia que a ella convenía, pudo, sin embargo, comprenderla bajo aquella ley impuesta a Adán; y de nuevo, previsto el pecado de Adán, para que su primer propósito acera de la Virgen permaneciera firme, pudo querer preservarla por Cristo de toda mancha; porque entre estas cosas no hay nada repugnante, antes son cosas muy coherentes y conformes a razón" (74–5).

11 Francisco P. Solá offers an additional detailed analysis of Suárez's theological position on the doctrine of the Immaculate Conception, which tellingly – and given the inscrutability of God's design – wavers between Mary's individual and momentary debt of original sin at the time of conception (*débito próximo*) and the remote debt of sin linked to her only as a descendant of Adam (*débito remoto*). See especially pages 238–40. On the subject of the *débito* see also Alcántara.

12 Jerome mistranslated from the Hebrew text the gender of the actor in Genesis 3:15; the Hebrew text states "He will crush your [the serpent's] head," not as in the Vulgate where this prophecy is perpetrated by a "she."

13 I modernized Francis Xavier Lasance's translation as found in his *My Prayer Book*. The original Latin prayer, which Lasance also documents, reads: "Tota pulchra es, Maria. / Et macula originalis non est in Te. / Tu gloria Ierusalem. / Tu laetitia Israel. / Tu honorificentia populi nostri. / Tu advocata peccatorum. / O Maria. / Virgo prudentissima. / Mater clementissima. / Ora pro nobis. / Intercede pro nobis ad Dominum Iesum

Christum. / In conceptione tua, Immaculata fuisti. / Ora pro nobis Patrem cuius Filium peperisti. / Domina, protege orationem meam. / Et clamor meus ad te veniat."

14 Twomey summarizes the theological debates and how they specifically resonated in medieval Aragon and Castile in chapter 3 of the same book, titled "Good and Evil: Theological Dispute over Mary" (23–46).

15 For a detailed account of the cult of Mary as it developed in Spain, see Linda B. Hall, chapter 2, "The Spanish Reverence."

16 "The association between Santa María, Isabel, and the Reconquest was strong. Another of her chroniclers, Diego de Valera, wrote to her 'that just as our Lord wished that our glorious Lady might be born in this world because from her would proceed the Universal Redeemer of the human lineage, so he determined that you, My Lady, would be born to reform and restore these kingdoms and lead them out from the tyrannical government under which they have been for so long.' Here was combined not only Isabel's achievement as the mother of the new heir but also a reiteration of her responsibility to restore Christian government to the entire peninsula. Just as Mary could be seen both as the Virgin of Battles and as the deliverer from evil, so could Isabel" (Linda B. Hall 43).

17 See Weaver, especially chapter 7, "Maria Patrona Ferdinandi (et Austriae): Ferdinand III's Marian Devotion as Public Image."

18 For a detailed account of the history of royal confessors in Spain, see Leandro Martínez Peñas's *El confesor del rey en el antiguo régimen*.

19 Juan Mir y Noguera traced many of the efforts of the Spanish Habsburg kings and extended family to get the doctrine promoted to dogma in chapter 22, "Devoción de los Reyes Católicos a la Inmaculada," of his *La Inmaculada Concepción*. See also Peinado Guzmán and Magdalena Sánchez.

20 See the Royal Collection Trust's description of Pantoja de la Cruz's painting, https://www.royalcollection.org.uk/collection/404970/margaret-of-austria-queen-consort-of-philip-iii-of-spain-1584-1611.

21 "Porque tu carta ... nos ha mostrado con cuanto estudio te empleas en las alabanzas de Madre de Dios, pues de tal manera escribes, cual si hubieses de llegar a la cumbre de la gloria el día en que las disputas de los teólogos y de los pueblos concurrieran finalmente en una sola sentencia de la Purísima Concepción ... Por el cual conocerá tu Majestad, cuán de veras te deseamos complacer con amorosa propensión, pues te amamos con paternal caridad, especialmente sabiendo que del palacio real trasladaste los ejemplos de las cristianas virtudes a ese santo monasterio, para con la imitación de tu nobleza incitar a esas religiosas Vírgenes ..." (Mir y Noguera 419–20).

22 "Leading French Catholics believed that the pope could not define the Immaculate Conception without convening an ecumenical council. The influence of the Spanish court in Rome was paramount in the sixteenth

century, but the growth of French political power in the seventeenth century would prove to be a thorn in the sides of Spanish emissaries to the holy See" (Stratton, *The Immaculate Conception in Spanish Art* 74).

23 Given the pressure from the papacy and the impasse in which the whole matter seemed to be mired, "Philip III probably would have liked to shelve the matter completely, but he was not allowed to. Soon his advisors, including his aunt the Infanta Margarita (at the Discalced Royal Convent), were reapplying pressure" (Stratton, *The Immaculate Conception in Spanish Art* 82).

24 For further discussion of the Conceptionist campaign in Rome, see Colomer, especially 352–4. See also González Tornel. Thomas James Dandelet's *Spanish Rome, 1500–1700*, especially chapter 5, "The Piety of Spanish Rome," is also very useful.

25 For an examination of the complex evolution of the beliefs on Mary in the Protestant Reformation, see Kreitzer.

26 For a more detailed account of the dealings of the papacy with the doctrine of the Immaculate Conception, see Trevor Johnson.

27 See also Marx.

28 See McDonald.

29 As summarized by Karin Hellwig, "With Portugal's separation from Spain in 1640, the Peace of Westphalia in 1648, which confirmed Holland's sovereignty, and the Peace of the Pyrenees in 1659, which put an end to the hegemonic conflict between Spain and France in favour of the latter, Spain's position as a second-class political power became apparent" ["Con la separación de Portugal de España en 1640, la Paz de Westfalia en 1648, que confirmó la soberanía de Holanda, y la Paz delos Pirineos en 1659, que puso fin al conflicto hegemónico entre España y Francia a favor de esta última, se puso de manifiesto el an de España a potencia política de segunda clase"] (29).

2. An Army of Peers

1 "[S]erá cosa digna de ingenios cándidos, y de corazones nobles, y de voluntades pías, no aguardar determinación de Concilio, o decreto de sumo Pontífice, para seguir la opinión de que hablamos, sabiendo todos los Prelados de la Iglesía, que en honra de ella está lleno el mundo de templos y altares, con grande exceso ... con ser así, que nadie hasta hoy se mueve a labrar, no digo un monasterio entero, o una Iglesia, pero ni una imagen, en protestación, que Nuestra Señora fue concebida en pecado original" (Vicente Justiniano, *Tratado de la Inmaculada Concepción de la Virgen Santísima Nuestra Señora* 8).

2 Translation from *Don Quixote* by Tom Lathrop. "¿Adónde va, señor don Quijote? ¿Qué demonios lleva en el pecho que le incitan a ir contra nuestra fe católica? Advierta, mal haya yo, que aquella es procesión de

disciplinantes y que aquella señora que llevan sobre la peana es la imagen benditísima de la Virgen sin mancilla; mire, señor, lo que hace, que por esta vez se puede decir que no es lo que sabe" (*Don Quijote* 524).

3 I offer a detailed analysis of Ágreda's treatment of the doctrine in chapter 5 of this book. For an examination of Ágreda's relationship with Philip IV, see my article "Friends in High Places."

4 In 1624 Pope Urban VIII approved the institution and statutes of the *Orden Militar de la Inmaculada Concepción de la Virgen María Nuestra Señora*, whose members had to meet a set of criteria and perform specific duties. First created by Carlos Goganza de Cleves, Duke of Nevers, its mission was to protect damsels, widows, and defenceless children, fight in defence of the Catholic faith, and maintain peace amongst Christian courts (Fernández Dueñas 72). An interesting document on the formation of the order is the 1624 *Relación de la institución en Roma, de la Orden Militar, de la Inmaculada Concepción de la Virgen María Nuestra Señora. Por la Santidad del Papa nuestro Señor Urbano VIII*, which includes two letters written by the pope to church officials in Seville on the matter. The original *militia christiana* was called by Paul in his Epistle to the Ephesians, where believers are encouraged to fight with the weapons of faith and God's words against evil. The concept was rearticulated in the *Enchiridion* (1503) by Desiderius Erasmus, who instructed each individual believer, as a soldier, to add to his arsenal of spiritual weapons prayer and knowledge of the holy scriptures and laws.

5 Louvain was one of the most important centres for the Franciscan Order and housed one of the most prominent universities in all of Europe. Established in 1427, the Université catholique de Louvain was the first in Belgium and the Low Countries and became a stronghold against the forces of Protestantism in the region.

6 "Para este fin ofrezco a vuestra excelencia este ejercito de casi seis mil soldados que aunque es escuadrón volante, pues solo se compone de plumas; debajo de su disciplina militar servirán de alas que lleven las puntas de acero al blanco y fin donde se encaminan y derezan" ("Memorial").

7 "Scripsit Epistolam ad Summ. Pontiff ... pro definition mysterij Immaculata Conceptionis, qua incipit: Mei officij atque obligationis" (1006).

8 "Contiene es este tratado lo historial sucedido acerca deste soberano misterio, y es para todo estado de personas" (cover page).

9 "darle la mano para que sea bien recibido de todos y corra con seguridad entre un millón de enemigos, que sin razón y verdad, armados de malicia y sabiduría presumida han querido calumniarle aunque no se han logrado sus ladridos, pues todos han parado en ruido y barahúnda y al cabo salir con nada y saldrán con menos" (43).

10 "propone con llaneza algunas consideraciones dignas de ser ponderadas por los devotos de Nuestra Señora, los cuales (según creo) holgará de hallarlas juntas en este tratado" (2).

11 "D. Pues si la Virgen María no fue concebida en pecado, luego fue concebida por Espíritu Santo? M. No fue concebida por Espíritu Santo, sino
por obra de varón, como todos nosotros pues fue hija de San Joaquín, y
de Santa Ana, y con todo eso afirmamos que no fue concebida en pecado.
D. Luego siguiese que fue concebida en gracia? ... M. Digo que en el mismo
instante y punto, que el ánima de la Virgen se unió al cuerpo (con especial
favor de Dios) fue llena de gracia, siendo privilegiada en este singular don
entre todos los demás descendientes de Adán por natural generación, y
por haberla Dios preservado con esta tan particular providencia, no pudo
tener pecado original, ni hubo para que le tuviese" (3).

12 "hásgome a que es Dios incomprensible y que no le he de tomar yo cuenta
de lo que hace, ni se pueden sus obras del todo comprender, ni podemos
dar razón de todas ... que si Dios fuera comprensible de entendimiento
finito, que no fuera Dios" (37).

13 "[D]esde el punto que comenzó a ser en el vientre de la bienaventurada
santa Ana, fue santa: no fue santificada, si santificada quiere decir trocada
de pecadora en santa, porque ningún pecado jamás tuvo, antes fue siempre
santa. Empero, si santificada significase que fue hecha santa al cual modo
habla alguna vez la santa Escritura, bien se podría llamar santificada: así
como los Espíritus Angélicos que juntamente tuvieron ser y gracia; así
como Adán y Eva que fueron criados en gracia; así como Jesucristo, nuestro
Señor, cuya alma, del instante de su Concepción, tuvo infinita gracia" (41).

14 S1 is titled "It describes how Seville came out to receive the Virgin, who
espouses God, with the lamps of her devotion in her hands" ["Se propone
como sale Sevilla a recibir a la Virgen, que se desposa con Dios, con las
lámparas de su devoción en las manos"]. S10 closes the *Sermón* with "We
exhort the *Cabildos* of this city to continue to ask that the pope declare what
he should hold as a certainty regarding the Conception of the Queen of the
Angels, given that the authority of Seville is so considerable, that with its
pleading and petitioning his Sanctity will be inclined to decide this issue in
the same manner as those of the Seraphic Religion (the Franciscans) who in
their pious opinion offered that the Virgin was conceived exempt of Original sin" ["Se exhorta a los Cabildos desta ciudad, a que traten de que su
Santidad declare lo que se debe tener por cierto acerca de la Concepción de
la Reina de los Ángeles por ser la autoridad de Sevilla tan grande, que sus
ruegos, y petición se inclinará su Santidad a tratar de decidir esta cuestión
al modo que por los de la Religión Seráfica lo trató cuando dio por pia
opinión el ser concebida la Virgen sin pecado Original"].

15 "... advertid que cuando oís decir, que Dios nuestro Señor determinó una
cosa y que después determina otra, que no habéis de hacer concepto que
se muda, porque es inmutable, ni que tiene varios actos de entendimiento,
y voluntad, ni que uno es primero y otro es postrero, y que este deshace lo

que primero ordenó, ni que se contradice y tiene diversos pareceres, como vos y como yo: porque en su majestad todo esto es un purísimo acto y una sustancia indivisible totalisimamente: aunque nosotros por ser corto nuestro entendimiento, no alcanzando comprenderlo lo dividamos en varios actos, y conozcamos unos primeros que otros; para explicarnos y darnos a entender nuestros conceptos ..." (63).

16 "después de cierta revelación que tuvo, apareciéndole la Reina de los Ángeles con hábito y escapulario blanco, y manto azul" (6).

17 "no se puede negar que en aprobación de la Concepción de la Virgen ha habido muchos milagros verdaderos" (9).

18 "que fue muy notorio en toda España, que sucedió por una imagen de la Concepción" (10).

19 "la eficiencia de los milagros ... en confirmación de la verdad que su santísima madre, en el instante de su misteriosa Concepción, fue librada de la culpa original" (1).

20 "De manera que como los milagros exceden los límites de naturaleza, y estos no se hacen según la ley ordinaria; buen fundamento es para tener una verdad por infalible, que en confirmación de ella haya obrado Dios milagros" (2).

21 For a history and analysis of this genre, see Peña Sueiro.

22 "celestial pureza"; "añade aplausos la misma naturaleza" (A 4).

23 "María concebida en pecado original" (10).

24 "en sentido místico y espiritual, como lo entienden comúnmente los Teólogos, y Predicadores Evangélicos, y está en el Oficio Divino de Nogarolis, que aprobó el Papa Sixto IV" (11).

25 "que verdaderamente había azucenas entre espinas" (14).

26 "descubrió debajo una Efigie, o Imagen de la Virgen Maria, como se suele pintar en su Concepción, blanca, y perfectísima" (16).

27 "como a persona que la miraría con sinceridad" (16).

28 "perfecta efigie de la imagen de la Purísima Concepción de la Virgen María, Madre de Dios, con sus ojos, nariz, boca y corona, y sus cabellos tendidos por las espaldas y los ombros" (17).

29 "efecto sobrenatural de la Providencia sobrenatural de Dios" (17–18).

30 "grandísima devoción y exaltación de este devotísimo Misterio" (19).

31 "Y refirió todo el maravilloso suceso de la Azucena de los Valles, con todas sus circunstancias, y quedó tan maravillado todo el auditorio, que se encendieron grandemente en la devoción de este piadoso Misterio" (19–20).

32 "innumerable gente de diferentes estados" (20).

33 "su Magestad, que Dios guarde, con la piedad que suele, la ha mandado guardar, y tener con especial veneración, y decoro, por Imagen de la Virgen Santísima, Madre de Dios. Sea el Señor engrandecido y alabado, y la limpia y pura concepción de María Santísima, concebida sin pecado original en el primer instante físico, y real de su Ser" (22).

34 For another study that focuses on Immaculist *comedias* and Habsburg poli-tics, see *The Comedia of Virginity: Mary and the Politics of Seventeenth-Century Spanish Theater* by Mirzam C. Pérez. I reviewed Pérez's book in *Theater Research International*.

35 Mimesis functions as a mechanism of resemblance and interpretation, not exactitude or a copy: "There is also an important point of difference between how Aristotle understands 'mimēsis' and contemporary thinking around the concept of representation. This concerns the issue of whether a representation must resemble the thing it represents. Some philosophers of art argue that something, x, can be a representation or about something else, y, without x resembling y" (Curran 45). Though much critical reflec-tion focuses on the status of representation, imitation has a significant per-formative dimension as a means to constitute and shape modes of identity, expression, and imagination. See also Greene and Cushman 675.

36 "Tu concepción haría, Con culto reverente"; "Esta prisión se cubre De re-splandor celeste, Los techos se han abierto, Luces el cielo llueve; Millares de querubes Del empíreo descienden; Bien declaran los nuncios Quién á la tierra viene. Aparécese Nuestra Señora de la Concepción en una tramoya. Quién á la tierra viene." There are no page numbers.

37 "Beatriz, desta prisión Saldrás muy brevemente; Á Toledo camina, Si agradecida eres, Donde á mi concepción Harás templo eminente, Refugio universal De devotas mujeres. Preceptos les darás En la edad floreciente; Del hábito que traigo, Vestir mis monjas puedes. De Isabel y Fernando, Los Católicos Reyes, No te olvides, Beatriz, Mira lo que me debes." Lope de Vega tellingly confuses Isabel of Portugal with her daughter, Isabel I of Castile, underscoring the imaginary connection of the Immaculate Conception to the Spanish Habsburgs.

38 "Yo soy la privilegiada, cuya cándida creación hecha por Dios *ab initio*, para su madre eligió" (91).

39 "sacro hijo"; "Saldrás de aquesta prisión a ser Beatriz defensora y primera fundadora de mi Santa Concepción" (111).

40 As noted in chapter 1, the 1619 date is significant. In 1616 Philip III – pressed by the queen, Margaret of Spain, and his aunt Margaret of the Cross, who resided at the Royal Discalced Convent – established the first *Real Junta*, whose mission was to ask the pope to silence those who held Maculist views and to define the doctrine of immaculism as dogma. With little movement on the matter by Pope Paul V (the decretal of *Sanctissimus Dominus Noster* of 1617 only forbade the public defence of *post coitus* sanctification), Philip III sent a second *Real Junta* to Rome (much to the distress of the pope) that demanded again the perpetual silence of the detractors or the permanent definition of the dogma. With no progress made, a third *Real Junta* was assembled and sent to Rome in 1618, led by the vicar general of the Franciscan order, An-tonio de Trejo, who carried with him letters from Philip III and prominent

religious and university figures from all over Spain and its territories. Paul V remained unmoved, letting it be known that he would not alter the decision made by the Council of Trent not to promote the doctrine to dogma, and simply left original sin out of the discussion of Mary's status. Not surprisingly, the debate and resistance at the Papal Court were framed not just as a theological dispute between Dominicans and Franciscans but also as an indication of the waning power of Spanish influence in Rome and the rise of the French. Within Spain, Seville's institution of a municipal vow in favour of the belief in and defence of the Immaculate Conception exerted enormous pressure on Philip III to intervene formally with the papacy. Zaragoza, where the *Justa* was held and published, had a similarly long and active history of support and popular devotion to the doctrine. Given these events, 1619 is a pivotal and almost desperate year in the efforts of the crown and local municipalities to exert pressure in favour of the promotion of the doctrine to dogma.

41 Baranda details how, "Generally, the parameters set in the announcement established the topics and modes of the stanzas, the deadline for submissions, when the compositions would be read, the members of the jury, and the prizes. Once the competition ended, some compositions were selected for inclusion in the account of the celebration, whose printing was sponsored by the organizer as a way to document and perpetuate his prestige" ["Las bases de la convocatoria, por lo general, establecían los asuntos – es decir los temas y estrofas de cada una de las modalidades – los plazos de entrega, la lectura de las composiciones, los miembros del jurado y los premios. Una vez terminada la justa, las composiciones podían ser o no editadas dentro del relato de los festejos, cuya impresión patrocinaba el mismo organizador como medio para perpetuar su prestigio"] ("Reflexiones" 309).

42 For a detailed history of women's participation in literary academies and poetic tournaments, see Osuna Rodríguez.

43 "las cifras revelan un interés de las mujeres por la poesía en un momento de clara efervescencia poética en toda España y en concreto en Aragón" ("Los certámenes poéticos" 149).

44 "las mujeres suelen pertenecer al grupo excluido de la sociedad literaria, a la cual pueden tener acceso precisamente a través de una convocatoria pública" (Baranda, "Reflexiones" 310).

45 "En estos certámenes se borran las diferencias de una socialización marcada genéricamente y no hay distinción entre hombres y mujeres" ("Los certámenes poéticos" 153).

46 "[E]xige por su parte un conocimiento de los modelos y un adiestramiento en el noble arte de contar versos" (Marín Pina, "Los certámenes poéticos" 151).

47 See Marín Pina, "Los certámenes poéticos" 152–3. See also Baranda, *Cortejo* 218.

48 "una habilidad bien vista, un distintivo social en un momento en el que lo literario está alcanzando cierto prestigio social" ("Los certámenes poéticos" 151).

49 "la poesía como tal ocupa un lugar, tiene una función de afirmación o rea-
firmación personal, de pertenencia de a un grupo, de propaganda política
y religiosa, de promoción social, que quieren también compartir" (Marín
Pina, "Los certámenes poéticos" 150).

50 Marín Pina reaches a similar conclusion: "The numbers reveal women's
interest in poetry at a time of clear poetic effervescence throughout Spain
and especially in Aragon, where there is a long tradition in the publication
of poetry ... Women's intervention in this type of contests was well received, and parents, husbands, and friends encouraged them to compete"
["las cifras revelan un interés de las mujeres por la poesía en un momento
de clara efervescencia poética en toda España y en concreto en Aragón,
donde existe una larga tradición en la edición impresa de la poesía ... La
intervención de las mujeres en este tipo de certámenes se veía con buenos ojos y padres, maridos y amigos las animaban a concursar"] ("Los
certámenes poéticos" 149).

51 See Marín Pina, "Los certámenes poéticos" 162–3.

52 See my articles, "The Politics of Exemplarity" and "Reproductive Genesis."

53 "más que la luna hermosa, que escogida / triunfa homicida, en superior
belleza / con la cabeza del dragón postrada / no ensangrentada: porque su
hermosura / nada pudo manchar cosa tan pura" (np).

54 "Si pudo Dios, si Dios desde *ab eterno*, / tuvo el gobierno, así de lo invisible /
como visible, y en su suma esencia / ... / ¿quién dudar podría / que de *ab
eterno* preservó a María?"

55 "Estandarte, y no rendido, / llamó a la virgen san Juan, / que cual fuerte
capitán / dejó al contrario vencido. / Si a poner el pie ha venido / sobre la
frente atrevida, / mal dirán, que fue vencida / la que alcanzó la victoria, /
dando al mundo tanta gloria, / y al mismo que le dio vida."

56 "san Juan, en su aparición / de hacerla de luz vestida / y en el cielo
aparecida, / do pecado no se asienta, / claro nos la representa / sin pecado
concebida."

57 "Como aurora esclarecida / que como alegre arrebol / manifiesta al
mundo el sol / sin queda del ofendida, / la Virgen con Dios unida / más
que ella resplandeció, / pues con la luz, que la dio, / al divino sol del
cielo, / para reparo del suelo, / quedando virgen parió."

58 "mas dos tiempos que pasaron / considerarse pudieron, / que si el segundo
entendieron, / que fue después que pecó, / a María excervó / la divina
omnipotencia, / si el primero de inocencia, / María de Adán nació."

59 "La Virgen en el que se muestra / con su pureza, nos dio / lo mismo que
el padre eterno / siendo ella menos que Dios."

60 "Pintose un cielo muy claro, y sereno, después de la tempestad, con el arco de
san Juan, y el sol que sale, y abajo en la tierra una paloma con un ramo de
olivo en la boca, y la letra dice. *Columba venit ad vesperam portans ramum olivae*

virentibus solis in ore suo. Genes. Cap. 6. 'Ana restauración del hombre ha sido, / pues cual paloma con ligero vuelo / nos trajo nuevas del sereno cielo.'"

3. *Pintor Divino*

1 "¿Pudiérese excusar la Pintura en el mundo?" (266).
2 "Si el mismo Dios apenas había criado el mundo, quando hizo en sí una pintura o imagen de hombre para hablar con nuestros primeros padres, y luego hizo una imagen del Serafín para que los echase del Paraíso" (268).
3 "Qué es todo esto sino imagines y pinturas de la mano y pincel de Dios, que nos habla en este lenguaje, que parece que se sigue desto, y nos dice que este Arte es necesario é inexcusable, y que no se excusan hombres que le imite, é imite a aquella universal Pintura de los Cielos, y sus luminarias ... ? [N]inguna Arte es de tanta importancia como esta, para la noticia de todas las cosas, y mayormente para la reverencia y alabanza de Dios, y de sus Santos, para los divinos y heroicos milagros, hechos para bien y edificación, para todas las historias divinas y humanas que hermosean y adornan las Repúblicas" (269–70).
4 As explained by Stuart Clark regarding Nicolas Sanders's *A treatise of the images of Christ, and of his saints* (1567), "God himself had created men and women in such a way that they could not learn, know, or understand any thing, without conceiving the same in some corporal image or likeness. Knowledge itself arose from the mind printing images and similitudes, indeed, graving them in the phantasie from information powered into it via common sense from the individual senses, chief of which were the eyes. To read of Christ on the cross was necessarily to form a mental image of him, with his hands stretched and nailed upon the wood, and to construct any outward version of this internal figure, must, in consequence, be equally allowable" (169).
   Nicolas Sanders was an English exile who participated in the final sessions at Trent as a theologian to the papal legate Cardinal Hosius. For a discussion of Sanders's importance and writings, see Clark 168–75.
5 Antonio Sánchez Jiménez and Adrián J. Sáez's recent edition, *Siete memoriales españoles en defensa del arte de la Pintura,* further documents the connection made between painting as a liberal art and theology in Spanish art treatises.
6 The at times violent debate in the early Church culminated with the decrees of the Council of Nicaea in 787, where images were first officially coded as a proper conduit for the veneration of the sacred: "The more frequently [holy figures] are seen in representational art, the more are those who see them drawn to remember and long for those who serve as models, and to pay these images the tribute of salutation and respectful veneration. Certainly, this is not the full adoration [latria] in accordance

with our faith, which is properly paid only to the divine nature, but it resembles that given to the figure of the honored and life-giving cross, and also to the holy books of the gospels and to other sacred cult objects. Indeed, the honor paid to an image traverses it, reaching the model, and he who venerates the image, venerates the person represented in that image" (http://www.ewtn.com/library/COUNCILS/nicaea2.htm).

7 See: http://www.ewtn.com/library/COUNCILS/nicaea2.htm. As defined by Catholic theologians, there are three distinct types of reverence or veneration (opposite to blasphemy or sacrilege): latria, which is reserved only for God; dulia, which is appropriate for saints and angels; and hyperdulia, set aside exclusively for the Virgin Mary. More detailed definitions can be found in Livingstone, *The Concise Oxford Dictionary of the Christian Church*.

8 The issue at hand was Christ's consubstantiality, defined as the sharing of substance (which can be variably expressed as spirit or as matter) with God *and* with humanity; in other words, Christ, an image that is God and is created by God, straddles the divine and the material, containing and revealing the mystery of the Incarnation.

9 English quotations are from the translation of Bonaventure's *On the Reduction of the Arts to Theology* by Zachary Hayes.

10 Tim Noone and R.E. Houser – referring to the Bonaventure's corpus more generally – explain how "[he] includes within theology both religious beliefs transformed by arguments from natural reason and natural reason changed by arguments based on religious revelation. If so, then theology must have the kinds of principles that make possible both kinds of arguments: the fundamental truths of faith drawn from the Bible and tradition, but also the fundamental truths of reason. What makes all such basic truths theological is their argumentative function. Theological arguments may draw from revelation by using revealed truths as premises, and they may draw from reason by using rational truths as premises. Both kinds of arguments are theological because of the use to which they are put" (http://plato.stanford.edu/archives/spr2013/entries/bonaventure/).

11 See Eco's *The Aesthetics of Thomas Aquinas*.

12 Clark adds: "Thus, in the semantic movement from signs to signified (from earthly *signum* to heavenly *res*, or in Augustine's terms, from visible sign to invisible grace – from what we see to what we believe), the outer and inner eyes performed very different but equally vital tasks, both of which could be described in the language of visual accuracy" (190).

13 For a detailed study of the Protestant position(s) on images, see Clark, especially the chapter titled "Images."

14 I am referring to Bourdieu's broad thesis in *The Field of Cultural Production*.

15 Art historian José Enrique García Melero has documented instances of this connection in his study of the treatise tradition in sixteenth- and seventeenth-century Spain, *Literatura Española Sobre Artes Plásticas*.

16 By revelation Marion means "a strictly phenomenological concept: an appearance that is purely of itself and starting from itself, that does not subject its possibility to any preliminary determination" (*The Visible* 47). Regarding the hermeneutical status of painting, Robyn Horner adds, "Saturated phenomena are excessive in that their intuitive content cannot be contained in a single concept, or even by a combination of concepts, but demands an endless hermeneutics" (123).

17 "El grupo de obras que se ocupa exclusivamente de la fundamentación del status de la pintura como arte liberal está particularmente bien representado en la España del siglo XVII. Estos textos se escriben sobre todo en el ambiente cortesano de Madrid, en el que los pintores mostraron una preocupación mayor que en otras ciudades por la revalorización social de su trabajo. Los textos eran consecuencia de acontecimientos en los que los artistas no se sentían tratados conforme a su status de personas que ejercían un arte liberal" (51).

18 Regarding these levies, Volk adds: "Archival material in Madrid indicates that there were intermittent levies after 1609, when the standing militia was re-established by Philip III, and until 1625. Then annual and occasionally biannual demands from the guilds were made without cease through the end of the century" (83).

19 For a comprehensive and illuminating analysis of the commercial structure of the art market in early modern Spain, see Muñoz González.

20 For the most recent translation of Alberti's *Della pittura*, see *Leon Battista Alberti: On Painting: A New Translation and Critical Edition*, edited and translated by Rocco Sinisgalli. Regarding the import of Alberti's treatise, Markowski notes: "[T]hat is precisely what Alberti says about represented things, which 'bring pleasure' to those able to see them. Here the concept of the autonomy of representation is born, together with another concept deriving from it, namely, the concept of aesthetic experience" (112).

21 Within the Renaissance *Studia humanitatis*, poetry, previously understood as secondary to grammar and rhetoric, had been elevated as the most eminent subject of study; Alberti's insistence on his understanding of the Horatian dictum follows what he hoped would be a reconsideration of painting as well. In the original Horace, the point was much more practical: that, like paintings, poems varied in quality and in the level of attention they demanded from the audience. A precedent for Horace was a saying attributed to the poet Simonides of Ceos, who was said to call painting silent poetry and poetry painting that speaks, thus providing the logic for the understanding of painting and poetry as sister arts.

22 Within our own context, Hans Georg Gadamer, through Hegel, reaches a parallel proposition: "The 'ideality' of the work of art does not consist in its imitating and reproducing an idea but ... in the 'appearing' of the idea itself" (Gadamer 138).

23 Moshe Barasch explains how "The image, at least the holy icon, reaches farther than the perception of the human eye in natural experience; it shows what lies beyond the real of visual experience ... the icon's main value ... is that it reveals to our eyes what otherwise cannot be seen" (*Icon* 219). Gadamer, when referring to religious symbols, follows a similar logic: "what is to be symbolized is undoubtedly in need of representation, in as much as it is itself non-sensible, infinite, and unrepresentable, but it is also capable of it. It is only because what is symbolized is present itself that it can be present in the symbol" (Gadamer 147).

24 As William Franke summarizes, "The irrepressible impulse to 'speak' essential silence is a constant ... of human experience confronted ever anew with what surpasses saying. While what is experienced remains inaccessible to speech, there is no limit to what can be said about ... this experience which, nevertheless, in itself cannot be described except as experience of ... what cannot be said" (2).

25 "On Sacred Scripture and Its Authors," in Harkins and van Liere, *Interpretation of Scripture* 215.

26 See Lubac 9.

27 Carducho includes here an indictment of what he believes is the debasement of art: "subjecting Art to humble concepts, as we see today, all these still lifes with lowly and vile ideas, and others with drunkards, of cheating card players, and similar things, without any wit, or topic, only the whim of the painter to draw four dirty rogues and two dishevelled women, demeaning Art, and with little reputation for Artifice" ["abatiendo el Arte a conceptos humildes, como se ven hoy, de tantos cuadros de bodegones con bajos y vilísimos pensamientos, y otros de borrachos, otros de fulleros tahúres, y cosas semejantes, sin más ingenio, ni más asunto, de habérsele antojado al pintor retratar cuatro pícaros descompuestos y dos mujercillas desaliñadas, en mengua del mismo Arte, y poco reputación del Artífice"] (253).

28 "[p]ara dar motivos a la imitación de aquellas virtudes de que fueron adornados" (250).

29 "se reputan por accidentales, respecto de los hechos y obras principales, y estas circunstancias se pueden en la pintura alterar, mayormente para mejor conseguir el fin que se pretende, que es ayudar a mover la devoción, reverencia, respeto, y piedad, y declarar más lo que se pretende" (255).

30 "Y no sólo no lo tengo por culpable, mas lo alabo por acto prudencial, el adornar y explicar lo sustancial de la historia con las circunstancias y accidentes más propios de decentes conocidos, y graves, porque de los pastos y misterios, y aquellas circunstancias y modos antiguos, ni son ahora practicados, ni causarán devoción, es necesario sustituirles otros, que aunque en lo material diferencien, vengan en el intento a ser los mismos, como en el lenguaje, las frases propias de una lengua traducida" (256).

31 "Predicadores y Escritores, adornando y vistiendo el suceso de la historia con palabras y frases elegantes, propias y conocidas, y con ejemplos graves" (258).

32 Connected to his description of this phenomenon, Bouza Álvarez recalls Foucault's epistemological scheme regarding the contiguous relationship of the sign to truth or reality: "In the early modern period, as Foucault has shown, it was thought that there existed a relationship between signs and the realities signified going beyond the merely expressive to the domain of the creative" (21).

33 "lo sustancial del misterio" (259).

34 "y así cuando se ofrece pintar un caso particular, en que hay alguna cosa incompatible a nuestra capacidad, y a nuestro entender, nos valemos deste género de pintura metafórica, para explicar y decir nuestro concepto" (263). Carducho bolsters his argument by tracing the way in which metaphorical images and symbols were employed by the Egyptians and the ancients, and cites Piero Valeriano's *Hieroglyphica sive de sacris Aegyptiorum litteris commentarii* (1556) as a source text.

35 Marion is a point of reference for this idea as well.

36 "milagroso medio ... que en un mismo instante nos muestra y hace capaces de lo que por lectura era fuerza gastar mucho tiempo, y ojear muchos libros, siendo ellos dicho con multitud de palabras, con mucha erudición y Teología para declararse, y muy posible después quedar menos entendidos" (Carducho 271).

37 Unfortunately, from our present standpoint, this revelatory capacity of the metaphoric image is especially needed, according to Carducho, for the sake of "women, and idiots that do not know, or cannot read" ["mujeres, y gente idiota que nos saben, o no pueden leer"] (271).

38 "Y si Seneca dice, que el Arte liberal tiene fuerza de hacer virtuosos, y buenos, quién más que la Pintura?" (272).

39 "no importa que la imagen en quien se hace la oración, o el sacrificio, está hecha con arte, o sin ella; porque no obra ni la forma ni la materia (sino lo que representa, y no más) y asno importa para esto que sea hecha con perfección, o sin ella" (280).

40 "Pues bien se supone de cuanta eficacia sea la buena pintura, que el mismo Dios se muestra a servile de que sus imágenes, y de su sacratísima Madre, y las de sus Santos sean hechas de suerte, que lo que representan, lo muestren con propiedad, y conveniencia ... que las tales causen mayor devoción, y que muevan los ánimos a los afectos a mayor fervor, amor y encendidos deseos de obrar en la virtud" (282–3).

41 "Aunque no causara tales efectos la pintura que no fuese bien formada, o la estampa de papel, que ya en esto se sentía bien desengañada esta Santa" (283).

42 "Basta que de lo dicho se infiere con cuánta diferencia mueve los afectos de la devoción y disposición la Pintura, con mayor perfección conducida, que no la inculta y toscamente fuere pintada" (284).

43 "Aunque ... se siente con semejantes pinturas" (285).

44 "[L]o que se debe a este Arte, pues tales mercedes y devociones se granjean por medio de las imágenes, que en hacerlas milagrosas, se muestra muchas veces Dios agradecido al devoto y religioso celo con que se obraron, no menos que a la cuidadosa y científica mano" (285).

45 "Y es muy cierto, que San Lucas fue Evangelista, y Pintor, en que vemos epilogado todo el encarecimiento, pues parece que Dios no quiso fiar este Arte a menos de a quien había fiado su santo Evangelio, y hizo retratos de nuestra Señora, y de nuestro Señor; y que traía consigo estos retratos, con que se convertía mucha gente, y hacía muchos milagros; y desto no hay que dudar: y así en toda la Iglesia se reconoce, y llama Pintor; y todas las Academias le tienen por abogado, honrando con tal Patrón de todo el Arte. Imitámosle en la vida, y en el modo de pintar devoto: en lo exterior, y interior, que es sin ninguna duda, que así como traía en su compañía aquellas Santas imagines pintadas, también tenía dentro del alma retratada toda la Santísima Trinidad contemplando sus soberanos atributos, a quien procuraba copiar; y a la purísima Reina de los Ángeles, procurando imitar sus Santísimas virtudes" (288).

46 "Yo venero, y reverencio la imagen: primero por lo que representa, y luego por la pluma que la pintó con tanta excelencia. Dios te guarde" (289).

47 See Sorensen.

48 For an account of Pacheco's sources, see Fernández López 53–8.

49 "Pacheco no fue un ortodoxo intransigente, su reacción vital ante su entorno social se manifiesta con los niveles de acatamiento de una realidad impuesta por un poder religioso y su elemento más representativo y represivo, la Inquisición" (Fernández López 58).

50 "la pintura es arte, pues tiene por ejemplar objetivo, y por regla de sus obras a la misma naturaleza, procurando siempre imitarla en la cantidad, relieve y color de las cosas, y esto hace valiéndose de la geometría, aritmética, perspectiva y filosofía natural, con infalible y cierta razón" (Pacheco 12).

51 "las cosas naturales ... son hechas de Dios con suma sabiduría" (11).

52 "se honraron ellos de profesalla, ejercitándola por sus manos y prefiriéndolas a otras artes liberals" (144).

53 "pintor católico y santo" (152).

54 "se preparaba con la confesión y comunión antes de pintarlas" (153).

55 "Pero la más aventajada grandeza de esta profesión es (a mi ver) que nuestro Felipo II y III (como es opinión de muchos) no carecieron de esta gloria y ejercicio del dibujo. Y de nuestro gran monarca, cuarto de este nombre

(siendo príncipe), tengo un San Juan Bautista mancebo en el desierto, abrazado con el cordero, de muy gallarda y diestra pluma, que envió a Sevilla un gran valido el Conde-Duque el año del 1619" (146–8).

56 "devoto artífice"; "Virgen, tenedme" (154–5).

57 "[A]penas la turbada lengua pronunció estas palabras, cuando la piadosa Señora sacó el brazo pintado de la pared y así el del pintor y le tuvo firme. El andamio con los vasos y colores vino a tierra con gran ruido, que todos los que allí se hallaron, creyendo que el techo de la capilla se venía abajo, levantaron los ojos y vieron a la Virgen, aún no pintada, con un brazo fuera de la pared, teniendo al venturoso hombre, y clamaron misericordia, alabando a la madre de ella: y puestas escaleras, habiendo bajado al suelo el pintor, la imagen volvió a encoger el brazo" (155).

58 "muchas cosas de los misterios sagrados" (160).

59 "[S]i bien pintó, como es cierto, las demás imágenes con el niño Jesús en sus brazos, no fue porque retratase a Cristo en aquella edad de la infancia, teniéndolo presente como tuvo a la Virgen; sino a semejanza de la Madre, y por información de ella o con particular favor y valiéndose del retrato primero hizo otras imagenes" (161).

60 "ilustrándola con tales y tan santos artífices" (162).

61 The *Pimander* was first translated by Marsilio Ficino in 1463, with many subsequent translations popular amongst humanist circles.

62 "Si lo que quieres investigar por los usos mortales, ya de la tierra, ya de la profundidad de las aguas, mira, o hijo, al hombre fabricado en el vientre, y escudriña exactamente la arte de esta fábrica; y aprende quien formó la hermosa y divina imagen suya. Quién pintó los ojos, quién abrió las narices y orejas, quién la boca, quién atendió los nervios y los ató" (163).

63 "vestido de nuestra carne la halló, para engrandecer la pintura, por mara-villosa y nueva manera" (163).

64 The version of the tale in which Ananais is a painter first appears in the Syriac work the *Doctrine of Addai* of around 400 AD. Pacheco is citing the German Laurentius Surius's *De probatis Sanctorum historiis ab Al. Lipomano olim conscriptis nunc primum a Laur. Surio emendatis et auctis*, which appears in Cologne in six volumes between 1570 and 1577. For more information on Surius, see Kirsch.

65 "se lavó el rostro en el lienzo, oh cosa admirable con que enjugaba el agua, y estampó su imagen, llevada al Rey, sucedieron grandes maravillas y milagros" (164).

66 "autorizó y honró la pintura de imágenes sagradas con los sucesos milagrosos que habemos contado" (166).

67 "mucho más ilustre y altamente puede hoy un pintor cristiano hacer obras que Apeles ni Protógenes" (172).

68 "no teniendo otra mira todas las sagradas imágenes ... que unir los hombres con Dios, que el fin de la caridad, manifiestamente se sigue que el ejercicio de formar imágenes se reducía a la misma caridad, y por esto será virtud dignísima y nobilísima" (173).

69 "[L]a pintura, como obra divina, entra por los ojos como por ventanas de nuestra alma mientras está encerrada en esta prisión, y representa en nosotros aquella luz por naturaleza inmortal. Y así penetra en la más secreta parte, que la hace dolerse, alegrarse, desear y temer, según la diversidad de las cosas que por los buenos pintores aparecen representadas en líneas y colores ..." (174).

70 "Resta, para conclusión de este discurso, la última causa que se atribuye al origen de la pintura, la cual nace de virtud: porque sucede muchas veces que los hombres, por beneficios recibidos o por estima grande hacen de otros, sientan dentro de sí una ardiente voluntad de dar a conocer estos nobles y justos pensamientos, y no entendiéndose de hacer esto en palabras solas, procuran juntar otras demostraciones más durables y gloriosas. De aquí comenzaron muchos motivos de grandes respetos (a su parecer dignos de memoria) a formar las imágenes y estatuas en honor de otros: manifestando lo que tenían concebido en el ánimo ... [C]omo fue honrar por este medio al soberano Señor en su celestial jerarquía, e ilustrar su Iglesia santa. Mas esto pertenece a las sacras imágenes de que nos viene a cuento tratar" (178).

71 "criado para cosas santas, no se contenta en sus operaciones con mirar tan bajamente, atendiendo sólo al premio de los hombres y comodidad temporal, antes levantando los ojos al cielo, se propone otro fin mucho mayor y más excelente, librado en cosas eternas" (184).

72 "fin supremo" (185).

73 "la filosofía de la pintura" (45).

74 The manuscript did not see publication until 1866.

75 "entendimiento y especulación" (270–1).

76 "Esto lo causa el relevado ingenio con que obran y meditan, y es tanta la bizarría de su discurso, que lo hacen todo fácil, mostrando en sus obras que parece lo hacen todo de un golpe, y sin pena alguna" (Martínez 81).

77 "Esta viene por gracia divina, y por eso se dijo viendo las obras de los grandes sujetos: este es pintor con filosofía divina" (45).

78 "Bien contrario juicio hiciera Séneca si viera lo que se ha pintado y se pinta debajo la religión católica, y no solo tuviera por arte liberal la pintura, sino por muy divina ... dijera, muy al contrario, viendo que induce a toda virtud y veneración en las sagradas imágenes por donde el Altísimo Señor ha obrado y obra maravillosos milagros" (46).

4. *Visiones Imaginarias*

1 "Los que tales pinturas hizieron, fue, que levantaron con la contemplación el vuelo más alto, y con cierta Filosofía consideraron, que aquello que pintaban no era caso sujeto al sentido de la vista corporal, mas visiones imaginarias, o apariciones intelectuales, representadas a nuestro entendimiento o imaginativa" (Francisco Pacheco, *Arte de la pintura* 227).

2 In commemoration of the 150th anniversary of the dogma in 2005, the *Conferencia Episcopal* of Spain organized an exposition at the Santa María la Real de la Almudena Cathedral; the accompanying four-hundred-page catalogue, titled simply *Inmaculada*, includes a selection of over 350 images, most of them dating to the late sixteenth and seventeenth centuries. Most recently, José Casar Pinazo and Pablo González Tornel published a fifty-three-painting catalogue for the "Intacta María" exhibition at the Museo de Bellas Artes of Valencia, with a specific focus on examples that demonstrate the political use of the image.

3 For a detailed historical and theological account of the four senses, see Lubac.

4 Two pivotal studies on the topic of early modern theories of sight and vision are John Shannon Hendrix and Charles H. Carman's edited volume, *Renaissance Theories of Vision*, and Clark's *Vanities of the Eye*.

5 "Los cuerpos cuyas imágenes representa la pintura son de tres géneros: naturales, artificiales o formados con el pensamiento y consideración del alma ... Los cuerpos del pensamiento son los que la imaginación forma: sueños, devaneos, de grotescos y de fantasías de pintores. Y son asimismo los que figura el entendimiento con sabia consideración. Ángeles, virtudes, potencias, empresas, jeroglíficos, emblemas ... visiones imaginarias o intelectuales que percibieron y revelaron los Profetas y suelen los pintores representarlas en su arte" (10).

6 Malinowski's "The Problem of Meaning in Primitive Languages" appears as an addendum in *The Meaning of Meaning*, edited by C.K. Ogden and I.A. Richards.

7 See my discussion on religious art as saturated phenomena, as defined by Marion, in chapter 3. See also Marion's *In Excess*.

8 "La pintura, en una época teocéntrica como la Edad Moderna, alcanzaba su justificación última por su condición de instrumento que facilitaba el culto y la comunicación entre el fiel y la divinidad ... Por ello resulta muy significativo que sea una relación con pinturas o esculturas religiosas donde mejor se puede estudiar las características de lo inefable; lo que nos sirve para entender hasta qué punto el asunto ... incide en un aspecto fundamental de la concepción artística de la época" (167).

9 In this regard, Stoichita recalls that "There is a crucial point in the evolutionary history of the iconography of the Immaculate Conception: it is when the object of worship becomes an actual representation of a vision, or more precisely, what John had on Patmos and which he described in chapter 12 of the Apocalypse" (109).

10 As best systematized by San Juan de la Cruz in his three poems, *Noche oscura del alma, Cántico espiritual*, and *Llama de amor*, the *vía mística* is achieved through the passage of three stages – *purgativa, iluminativa*, and *unitiva* – that require the faithful to relinquish the memory of carnal pleasures and empty the mind of the logic of human reason in order to become, so to speak, a blank canvas upon which the presence of God can be made manifest. See Juan de la Cruz, *Obra completa*.

11 In contrast to Juan de Jáuregui's 1614 *The Apocalyptic Woman*, an illustration for Luis de Alcázar's preterist *Vestigatio arcani sensus in Apocalypsi* showcases the narrative plot of Revelations 12:1–4, including the birth of the child in the sky and the appearance of the seven-headed dragon.

12 "El Dragón, enemigo común, se nos había olvidado a quien la Virgen quebró la cabeza triunfando del pecado original. Presenos había de olvidar. La verdad es que nunca lo pinto de buena gana, y lo excusaré cuando pudiere, por no embarazar mi cuadro con él" (483–4).

13 "Pero en todo lo dicho tienen libertad los pintores de mejorarse" (484).

14 For a detailed account of all of Pacheco's known works, see Valme Muñoz Rubio.

15 For example, the 1624 *Inmaculada* placed in the altarpiece of the Immaculate Conception chapel at the Church of San Lorenzo in Seville, and the 1630 *Inmaculada Concepción* found in the Colección Granados.

16 Juan Ochoa de Basterra commissioned the painting for the cathedral in Seville, where it is still housed today.

17 See González Polvillo, whose article places all three donors represented in the Pacheco paintings as members of the "Congregación de la Granada," a secret society which came out of the *alumbrado* movement in the previous century and which by the early seventeenth had taken to reform the Church by proving Mary's absolute purity. Although his claims are highly controversial – Bonaventura Bassegoda i Hugas states, for example, "they have no iconographic or historical support" ["que no tienen soporte iconográfico ni histórico alguno"] (47) – it is a potentially fascinating connection to a group whose religious imaginary lent itself to "millenarian presuppositions, visions, and prophesies" ["presupuestos milenaristas, visiones y profecías"] (González Polvillo 48). For further documentation on the relationship between the members of the "Congregación de la Granada" and Sevillian painters, see Vicente Lléo Cañal.

18 See Stoichita 30–44.

19 See Valdivieso 299.

20 See Stratton, *The Immaculate Conception in Spanish Art* 82. For a detailed account of all of Velázquez's known works, see López-Rey and Delenda's *Velázquez*.

21 See López-Rey and Delenda, *Velázquez* 20.

22 See also Stoichita 114–15.

23 Alfonso E. Pérez Sánchez states: "From the compositional point of view, both canvases are entirely conservative and are related to the style of Pacheco's drawings and paintings, but the rounded volumes, the intense chiaroscuro, the range of color, of warm, extremely personal tones with thickly daubed notes of gray-whites, and the vivid individualism of the faces place these paintings in the absolute vanguard of the naturalist style" ("Velázquez and His Art" 29).

24 This imaginary mechanism is facilitated, no doubt, by Velázquez's use of paid models. See Bray 94.

25 See Stratton, *The Immaculate Conception in Spanish Art*, chapter 3, where the critic offers a political reading of the Immaculate Conception iconography.

26 This number does not include drawings and other paintings of Mary that, even if not assigned the title of *Immaculate Conception*, explicitly borrow some or all of the iconography.

27 For a discussion of compositional and conceptual precedents for these paintings, see the previous section in this chapter on Pacheco's donor paintings.

28 For a detailed account of all of Zurbarán's known works, see Delenda's *Zurbarán: Catálogo razonado y crítico*. See also Delenda's *Zurbarán: Una nueva mirada*.

29 "Su pintura clara, monumental y perfectamente legible, así como su naturalismo sencillo puesto al servicio de un discurso didáctico, puede explicar sin duda alguna su extraordinario éxito en la Sevilla del Segundo cuarto del siglo XVII" (Delenda, *Francisco de Zurbarán* 59).

30 Pérez Sánchez explains: "But the language of the intimate and the domestic, the invasion of the supernatural into the everyday, and the marvelous transformation of the divine into the familiar that permeate Zurbaran's compositions were not the invention of the artist; rather, they culminate in his work. The general development of all Spanish painting prior to Zurbaran, especially in Seville, had in fact led in this direction" ("The Artistic Milieu in Seville during the First Third of the Seventeenth Century" 38).

31 See Stoichita 48.

32 See Baticle 62. See also Delenda, *Francisco de Zurbarán*, 125.

33 Louis Réau offers the following list of the attributes for hope: "Anchor, hive, a crown presented by an angel, the cross of the Resurrection, cornucopia,

and a sphere. On the head a ship with its sails filled by the wind" ["Ancla, colmena, corona presentada por un ángel, cruz de Resurrección, cuerno de abundancia, esfera. En la cabeza un navío las velas infladas por el viento"] (226).

34 Felipe de Silva's 1712 *El rey Felipe V de España, la reina María Luisa Gabriela de Saboya y el príncipe Luis niño matando al dragón de la herejía delante del monasterio de El Escorial* (Palacio Real de Aranjuez) provides a clear example of the visual codification for Faith. Réau offers the following list of attributes for faith: "Chalice, a heart in flames, a lighted candle, the cross, manna, and the Tables of the Law. On the head a church or a tiara. Stepping on Heresy" ["Cáliz, corazón en llamas, cirio encendido, cruz, maná, Tablas de la Ley. En la cabeza una iglesia o una tiara. Pisotea a la Herejía"] (226).

35 As noted by Réau, "The representation of the virtues was renewed for the last time with the *Iconology* of Cesare Ripa, whose first illustrated edition appeared in 1603 and whose successive reeditions inspired in the seventeenth and eighteenth centuries the art of the Counter-Reformation, not only in Italy, but in all of Europe" ["La representación de las virtudes se renovó por última vez con la *Iconología* de Cesare Ripa, cuya primera edición ilustrada apareció en 1603 y cuyas sucesivas reediciones inspiraron en los siglos XVII y XVIII el arte de la Contrarreforma, no solo en Italia, sino en toda Europa"] (225).

36 Some of the better-known examples are Giorgio Vasari's 1541 *Allegory of the Immaculate Conception* (Uffizi Gallery, Florence), Peter Paul Rubens's 1631–2 *Franciscan Allegory of the Immaculate Conception* (Philadelphia Museum of Art), and Juan de Roelas 1615 *Allegory of the Immaculate Conception* (National Museum of Sculpture, Valladolid).

37 See also James Hall, Réau, and Carmona Muela.

38 As discussed above, see the 1632 *Immaculate Conception* (National Museum of Art of Catalonia), where the Virgin is contemplated by two young noblemen, and the 1639–40 *Immaculate Conception with Saint Anne and Saint Joachim* (National Gallery of Scotland, Edinburgh).

39 For a detailed account of all of Murillo's known works, see Valdivieso.

40 "una vision celestial movida y dinámica" (211).

41 As explained by Valdivieso, "Painters were continuously called upon by the clientele to interpret this theme, which occupied a prominent place in all the homes [of Seville] and, above all, presided in the main stairwell of all the houses of medium importance" ["[L]os pintores fueron continua-mente requeridos por la clientela para interpretar este tema que figura en todos los domicilio [de Sevilla] y, sobre todo, presidía la escalera principal de todas las casas de mediana importancia"] (210).

5. *Concepción Maravillosa*

1 "redes de pensamiento que respaldan la noción, nada unívoca, de cultura femenina" (72).

2 "El monacato femenino fue un marco de vida liberador aunque dentro del orden establecido. Esto quiere decir que estuvo sujeto a limitaciones, pues no permitió a las mujeres proponer significados culturales del todo nuevos ... [C]abe relativizar el alcance de esta limitación, porque no toma en consideración la subjetividad femenina y su capacidad para resignificar símbolos y valores de la cultura común y experiencias propias. Cuando esta práctica de significación, ilimitada en sus horizontes, la crean y perpetúan relaciones de mujeres, generadoras de contextos de sentido, podemos reconocer en ella formas de cultura femenina" (78).

3 For a history of the development of Scholastic theology, see Leinsle.

4 Interestingly, as we shall see later in this chapter, Isabel de Villena cites Clairvaux's works in the *Vita Christi*.

5 See Howe, "Let Your Women Keep Silence," and *Women and Gender in the Early Modern World*.

6 See Howe, "Let Your Women Keep Silence" 124.

7 Holmes asks a similar set of questions. See page 6 of her text. Related interrogations have been addressed by a number of critics in Spanish early modern studies, Jessica Boon, Myriam Criado, Jesús Gómez López, Beatriz Ferrús Antón, Lola Luna, María Carmen Marín Pina, Isabelle Poutrin, Ángela Muñoz Fernández, and Ronald Surtz, among others.

8 Twomey and Curbet have excellent studies of Isabel de Villena's life and text.

9 "al considerar [en la *Vitae Christi*] la incorporación de la experiencia femenina, la creación de nuevos modelos de mujer, y la importancia de las mujeres en la redención humana" (Criado 77).

10 "la qual concebra de vos una fillia de tanta excelencia e dignitat" (1:11). All English translations of Villena are from *Portraits of Holy Women*, translated by Robert D. Hughes; here page 51.

11 "la imperial, que no es entesa ni compresa en nenguna ley comuna" (1:12; Hughes 51). As noted in chapter 1, there is a strain of Conceptionism that advocates for Mary having been implanted fully formed into Saint Anne's womb without the need for Saint Joachim's semen.

12 "no temau, temple meu, que ab tot vos Adam, no sereu compresa en la ley per lo seu peccat constituyda, ans sobre aquella privilegiada per gracia mia en singular grau. Quia ego elegi te" (12). A few lines below, Villena reiterates this point and cites Ecclesiasticus 1:9, "*Ipse creavit eam in spiritu suo, vidit et dinumeravit et mensuravit*," or "Our Lord God has

created this excellent lady according to his pleasure and will, as well as to the contentment of his spirit" (1:52; Hughes 52).

13 "E de contient que la gloriosa anima sua sia creada e unida al cors, la vol vesir e arrear de la sua gracia en singular grau" (1:13; Hughes 52).

14 "que seruixquen e acompanyen sa senyoria dins lo ventre de sa mara e en tot lo temps de la sua vida" (1:14; Hughes 52–3).

15 "en nostre senyor Deu vol que concebau huna Filla tan singular, que peccat original, venial ni mortal en ella james sera trobat. Pura de tota culpa la concebreu, e pura la criareu. E en puritat e nedea sera tota la sua vida, car de aquesta Senyora ha dit nostre senyor Deu, por boca de Salamo: Pulchra es amica mea, et macula non est in te" (1:18; Hughes 56).

16 "e, lauors, de aquelles singulars e virtuoses filles vos sereu molt alegre e gojosa quant conexereu esser per mi tam amades y estimades, per les grams obres sues, que als homens passaran en fortalea de amor. E perço los he donat per capitana e Senyora la mia Mare, perque les guart e les defena de aquells que delles mal volran parlar" (3:37; Hughes 141).

17 "car es estada començ de la nostra salut" (1:20; Hughes 58).

18 "per donar exemple als seruents seus que seguissen la via sua, si pervenir volran al repos seu" (1:25; Hughes 63).

19 "Perche podem dir que nostre senyor Deu la ha feta naxer en lo mon per esser advocada de natura humana e refuge en totes les necessitats sues" (1:27; Hughes 65).

20 See also Boon's "The Glory of the Virgin" and her Introduction to *Mother Juana de la Cruz, 1481–1534.*

21 "dont le trait dominant état l'affirmation d'un contact direct avec le monde celeste ... [E]t enfin par l'ecriture de textes inspirés, voire dictés par des médiateurs célestes" (81).

22 Certainly, this is one of the aspects in which Juana de la Cruz serves as a precedent for Ágreda.

23 "como la conoscían y sabían quien hera, a quien avia serydo, e que les pareció no aber necesidad" (Gómez López 15). All citations of Juana de la Cruz's sermon on the Immaculate Conception are found in Gómez López's article.

24 Curiously, Mary's immaculacy is obvious and evident, whereas Christ's status as God incarnate seems to not be, and thus needed to be described and explained by the apostles.

25 "Porque de la carne de dios tomo carne, mucha razón hera que fuesse linpíssima y purísima e castísima y escogida entre todas las criaturas" (15).

26 "santa humanidad" (15).

27 "que es más pura e aventajada que todas las criaturas, assi en su concebimiento e nascimiento como en todas las otras cosas de su vida e niñez" (16).

28 "para fazer una rosca ceñada e blanca y espejada e sin ningún agros ni corrompimiento de levadura" (16).

29 "E que lo mesmo fizo la santisima Trinidad; la qual puede ser figurada por la muger que masa una masa: que quando quiso masar la massa del hombre e aun antes que la cerniese, conviene a saber, quando quiso criar al hombre e aun antes que la criase, supo e conoscio como avia de ser corruto por el pecado original ... E que como el supiese que avia menester pa si una muger escogida e pura e cenceña de toda levadura e corrución de pecado ... e lo dice el espiritu santo, fablando de parte suya: dende antes de los siglos, dende ab inicio soi criada, e facta el siglo que es por venir, no sere acabada" (16–17).

30 "la crio e la escogió e la saco en su voluntad y entendimiento e sabiduría antes que criase el primer hombre" (17).

31 "Porque nuestra señora era tan limpia que dios se avia enamorado tanto della, que avia de tomar su carne e ayuntarse con ella, e fazerse hombre sin simiente de hombre, mas por obra maravillosa del espíritu santo el qual lo obró de esta manera: Que tuviese nuestro señor Jesu Cristo madre en la tierra e padre en el cielo" (17).

32 "e dentro del mesmo primer hombre quedo encerrada la muger, e después la pario adan, porque del mesmo saco la muger el señor" (17).

33 "E que así como Eva fue nacida de varón sin muger, assi por semejante nuestro redentor Jesu Cristo nacido de muger sin varón" (17).

34 "limpias y virginales entrañas" (22).

35 "negra soi, que no lo dixo porque ella tuviese ninguna negrura de pecado original ni atual ni venial ni mortal ... [P]equña soi e no soi dina que dios se acuerde de mi, mas soi fermosa por quanto el mesmo dio e señor acató la humildad de su sierva e fizo aun grandes cosas el que es poderoso. E por tanto me ensalzo e me fizo la mas grande e fermosa e limpia de todo pecado, e adornada de tantas virtudes y eselencias, que jamás hubo ni abra" (20).

36 "mirad señor mio e nieto mio muy amado como vengo preñada e traygo aqui la estrella de la mar e la gloria del cielo" (21).

37 "E por tanto no se deve angustiar ningun hombre ni muger por feo e disforme que sea. Que si buenas obras fazen e merecen yr al cielo, alla estaran fermosas e blancos e adornados, e ella no terná ninguna tacha ni fealdad ni negrura" (21).

38 "E tales personas traen en esta vida sus espíritus desasosegados, mas allá en la otra resciviran algunos señalados pena por ello" (22).

39 "por lo cual estava fecha muy fermosa donzella" (23).

40 "angustias e tribulaciones e penas" (27).

41 "tan ayrado contra el mundo" (27).

42 "E que por sola ella faze más mercedes que todas las criaturas celestiales e terrenales. Por quanto ella fue la que le fizo venir del cielo hasta la tierra" (27).

43 As Philip Schaff explains, "Justin Martyr, Irenaeus, and Tertullian, are the first who present Mary as the counterpart of Eve, as a 'mother of all living' in the higher, spiritual sense, and teach that she became through her obedience the mediate or instrumental cause of the blessings of redemption to the human race, as Eve by her disobedience was the fountain of sin and death" (414). See note 5 attached to this citation, which traces in detail the fundamental theological texts where this idea is reproduced and elaborated upon, including Saint Jerome and Saint Augustine.

44 "escritora agustina de prosa intelectual" (91).

45 "madre de la Madre" (Prólogo).

46 "substancia perfectísima y no hay inconveniente ni dissonancia" (124 A).

47 "la puso y depositó en la parte más principal del cuerpo de Adam" (125 A).

48 "Así pues aquesta divina substancia de que habemos dicho, por el testimonio de tantos y tan graves doctores, tan conservada por tantas edades de siglos, y llevada por tantos Patriarcas de la milagrosa mano de Dios; había llegado, y estaba ya en depósito, en el santo Patriarca Joaquín" (125 B).

49 John F. Wippel discusses this concept in the writings of several medieval scholastic philosophers in his "Godfrey of Fontaines (B. CA. 1250; D. 1306/09), Peter of Auvergne (D. 1303), and John Baconthorpe (D. 1345/48)." See especially the discussion of Godfrey on pages 225–6.

50 "que en tan dichosos y felicísimos casados, quedase aqueste celestial tesoro y sustancia, de que había de ser formado el cuerpo de la Reyna de los Ángeles, en el vientre santísimo de Ana ... y pariese Ana el mejor parto, que el cielo ni la tierra de pura criatura, a reconocido ni conoce ... y naciese en el mundo la gloriosa Virgen María, y que se había otorgado la dispensación, para casarse la naturaleza divina con la humana, y aunque humana había de ser con singular privilegio concebida" (126 A/B).

51 "la hizo única" (128).

52 "idiotas" and "gentil bobería" (131).

53 "[D]igo pues cuanto los padres de la gloriosa Virgen María: ellos de su parte procedieron, aunque con más casta y limpia intención, pero como los demás hombres ... porque había de ser esta sangre y carne, con razón aventajada, con singular privilegio, para que no pudiese haber mácula de pecado en ella" (131 A/B).

54 "y su limpieza soberana agradece a Dios, y no tuviese la naturaleza divina asco de la humana" (131 B).

55 "aquí la madre de Dios recibe de su hijo, y de sus padres, sola la naturaleza humana, mas como era su verdadero padre y criador el que había de ser su hijo y su esposo, levantándola de punto, cercola del Sol, no tuvo tierra en medio, todo era cielo, no pudo eclipsarse su luz or ser impecable: que no se apartó Dios de ella, desde el punto y hora de su concepción" (132 A).

56 "supremo artifice y pintor divino" (147 B).

57 "pintó a su madre con aquella esencia divina, tal cual convenía para madre suya" (147 B).

58 "que al infundir al alma en aquel cuerpo, iba la culpa a vestirle aquella cota pesada: salió el Verbo divino defendiéndola, tomado aquel golpe sobre sí, remitiéndolo a la Cruz, rescatola al tiempo que iba a ser captiva, y así no lo fue" (134 B).

59 "escribiendo contra Pelagio dice [Agustín], que Cristo no tuvo pecado venial ni actual ni mortal, porque no tuvo la original culpa" (152).

60 "la Virgen no tuvo pecado venial ni mortal, luego bien se prueba que no tuvo el pecado original" (152).

61 "siendo probado, como lo vereis por el concilio Tridentino, que no solo en ella no cupo pecado mortal, pero ni aun venial" (137 B).

62 "concepto de Theología" (141 A).

63 "siendo ella como fue la causadora de nuestro daño" (149 B).

64 "De esta suerte la hidalguía y privilegio de la Virgen María, y el ser preservada de culpa, con esto se prueba, y que le está muy bien a todos los estados: Al cielo, y a la tierra, a Dios, y a los hombres; y así parece que estamos obligados a juzgar, que convino para todos. Al padre Eterno, para ser su esposa, y al Verbo divino, para ser su madre, y al Espíritu Santo, para ser sagrario suyo, y a los Ángeles, para ser su reina; y a los justos, para ser su guiadora, su luz, y su lumbrera; y a los pecadores, para ser abogada y medianera nuestra. Últimamente a todo el orbe criado, le está bien reconocerle ventaja que es honra y gloria de la tierra, gozo y alegría del cielo, donde todos pretendemos entrar por medio de su intercesión, por la que nos conceda misericordia" (152 B).

65 The travails of the manuscript are well known: Ágreda's confessor requires she burn her copy in expectation of the 1650 Inquisitorial interview; and yet, despite the apparently extreme nature of this request, Philip IV, who had a close relationship with the nun for twenty-two years, clandestinely preserved a second, secret copy. See Risse for a discussion of the context around this second manuscript copy and narrative strategies of the *Mística ciudad de Dios*, and my article, "Friends in High Places," for an examination of the friendship held by Ágreda and Philip IV.

66 "y así la vieron antes que los buenos se determinasen al bien y los malos al pecado; y fue como señal de cuan admirable había de ser Dios en la fábrica de la humana naturaleza ... en pura criatura y en la más perfecta y santa que, después de Cristo nuestro Señor, había de criar" (95; 1.8.95, 36). Translations of *Mística ciudad de Dios* are my own but were informed by the 1914 translation by Reverend George J. Blatter.

67 "[S]e les puso otro tercero precepto, de que habían de tener juntamente por superior a una mujer, en cuyas entrañas tomaría carne humana este Unigénito del Padre; y esta mujer había de ser su Reina y de todas las criaturas

y que se había de señalar y aventajar a todas, angélicas y humanas, en los dones de gracias y gloria ... Lucifer y sus confederados, con este precepto y misterio, se levantaron a mayor soberbia y desvanecimiento ... Y en cuanto al ser inferior a la Madre del Verbo humanado y Señora nuestra, lo resistió con horrendas blasfemias, convirtiéndose en desbocada indignación contra el Autor de tan grandes maravillas" (1.7.90, 34–5).

68 "[T]uvo María purísima cierta igualdad de proporción con su Hijo Santísimo ... de manera que ella como Madre y Cristo como Hijo tuvieron igual proporción de dignidad, de gracia y dones y de todos los merecimientos, y ninguna gracia criada hubo en Cristo que no estuviese con proporción en su Madre purísima" (227; 1.18.278, 87–8).

69 "que por esta poderosa Señora y Abogada alcanzasen la vida eterna" (239; 1.19.295, 92).

70 Ágreda capitalizes both Madre and Verbo.

71 "Advierte que todas las cosas las hago nuevas" and "Mirad al tabernáculo de Dios con los hombres y habitará en ellos. Y ellos serán su pueblo y el mismo Dios estará con ellos y será su Dios" (1.17.245, 76).

72 "nueva tierra y nuevo Cielo" (1.17.247, 77).

73 "Porque todos estos sacramentos comenzaban de María Santísima y se fundaban en ella, dice el Evangelista que la vio en forma de la Ciudad Santa de Jerusalén, etc., que de la Reina habló con esta metáfora ... Por los misterios que Dios obró en la Ciudad Santa de Jerusalén, era más a propósito para símbolo de la que era su Madre y el centro y mapa de todas las maravillas del Omnipotente. Y por esta misma razón lo es también de las Iglesias Militante y Triunfante, y a todas se extendió la vista del águila generosa Juan, por la correspondencia y analogía que entre sí tienen estas Ciudades de Jerusalén místicas. Pero señaladamente miró de hito a la Jerusalén suprema María Santísima, donde están cifradas y recopiladas todas las gracias, dones, maravillas y excelencias de las Iglesias Militante y Triunfante; y todo lo que se obró en la Jerusalén de Palestina, y lo que significa ella y sus moradores, todo está reducido a María Purísima, Ciudad Santa de Dios, con mayor admiración y excelencia que en lo restante del cielo y tierra y de todos sus moradores. Por esto la llama *Jerusalén nueva*, porque todos sus dones, grandeza y virtudes son nuevas y causan nueva maravilla a los Santos; y nueva, porque fue después de todos los Padres Antiguos, Patriarcas y Profetas y en ella se cumplieron y renovaron sus clamores, oráculos y promesas; y nueva, porque viene sin el contagio de la culpa y desciende de la gracia por nuevo orden suyo y lejos de la común ley del pecado; y nueva, porque entra en el mundo triunfando del demonio y del primer engaño, que es la cosa más nueva que en él se había visto desde su principio" (1.17.248–9, 77).

74 "Madre del Verbo eterno" (1.17.251, 78).

75 "dones de la divinidad" (1.17.252, 79).

76 "habiendo enviado al mundo a María santísima sin culpa original, ya da por hecho todo lo que pertenece al misterio de la encarnación, pues estando María purísima en la tierra no parece que se podía quedar el Verbo eterno solo en el cielo sin bajar a tomar carne humana en sus entrañas" (1.17.259, 81–2).

77 "por medio de esta obra de Cristo y María" (1.17.259, 81–2).

78 "Aquí declara que la Ciudad Santa de Jerusalén que le mostró es la mujer esposa del Cordero, entendiendo debajo de esta metáfora – como ya he dicho – a María santísima, a quien miraba San Juan madre o mujer y esposa del Cordero, que es Cristo. Porque entrambos oficios tuvo y ejercitó la Reina divinamente. Fue esposa de la Divinidad, única y singular, por la particular fe y amor con que se hizo y acabó este desposorio; y fue mujer y madre del mismo Señor humanado, dándole su misma sustancia y carne mortal y criándole y sustentándole en la forma de hombre que le había dado" (1.18.266, 84).

79 "fabricada y formada, no en la tierra, donde era como peregrina y extraña, mas en el cielo, donde no se pudo fabricar con materiales de tierra pura y común; porque se de ella se tomo la naturaleza, pero fue levantándola al cielo para fabricar esta ciudad mística al modo celestial y angélico, y aun divino y semejante a la divinidad" (1.18.266, 84).

80 "Y por eso añade, que tenía la claridad de Dios; porque el alma de María Santísima tuvo una participación de la Divinidad y de sus atributos y perfecciones, que si fuera posible verla en su mismo ser, pareciera iluminada con la claridad eterna del mismo Dios. Grandes cosas y gloriosas están dichas en la Iglesia católica de esta ciudad de Dios (Sal., 86, 3) y de la claridad que recibió del mismo Señor, pero todo es poco, y todos los términos humanos le vienen cortos; y vencido el entendimiento criado, viene a decir que tuvo María Santísima un no sé qué de Divinidad, confesando en esto la verdad en sustancia y la ignorancia para explicar lo que se confiesa por verdadero. Sí fue fabricada en el Cielo, el Artífice sólo que a ella la fabricó conocerá su grandeza y el parentesco y afinidad que contrajo con María Santísima, asimilando las perfecciones que le dio con las mismas que encierra su infinita Divinidad y grandeza" (1.18.267, 84).

81 "Advierte que esta gran Princesa honra a los que la honran, enriquece a los que la buscan, ilustra a los que la ilustran y defiende a los que en ella esperan; y para hacer contigo estos oficios de madre singular y usar de nuevas misericordias, te aseguro que espera y desea que la obligues y solicites su maternal amor" (1.19.305, 95).

82 For a more detailed discussion of the relationship between Ágreda and Philip IV, see my article, "Friends in High Places."

83 "Pero también advierte que Dios de nadie necesita, y es poderoso para hacer de piedras hijos de Abraham y si de tanto bien te haces indigno,

puede reservar esta gloria para quien el fuere servido, y menos lo des-
mereciere ... porque no ignores el servicio, con que hoy se dará por
obligada esta Reina, y Señora de todos, entre muchos, que te enseñará
tu devoción y piedad, atiende al estado, que tiene el Misterio de su inmaculada concepción en toda la Iglesia, y lo que falta para asegurar con
firmeza los fundamentos de esta ciudad de Dios" (1.19.306, 95).

84 "Y nadie juzgue esta advertencia, como de mujer flaca, e ignorante, o
nacida de particular devoción, y amor a mi estado, y profesión debajo de
este nombre, y religión de María sin pecado original; pues a mí me basta
mi creencia, y luz, que en esta Historia he recibido ... Obedezco en ella [en
mi exhortación] al Señor que da lengua a los mudos, hace presta las de los
niños infantes" (1.19.305–6, 95).

85 Villena offers, as far as I have found, the first account of Mary's infancy as
related to the Immaculate Conception and her existence *ab initio*. Pérez de
Valdivia, who postdates Villena and whose treatise I examined in chapter 2,
offers the following description of the same period in the Virgin's life: "that
from the time of her conception our most blessed Virgin had the gift of
reason, so that from then on she began to exercise all the virtues and gifts
that God had given her in the womb of her mother: the blessed daughter
had a very high and lively knowledge of God, she displayed profound acts
of faith and held the ample certainty of hope; she was consumed by love,
made prudent use of her time, and honoured our Lord with magnificent
reverence; she offered herself for suffering, humiliated herself profoundly,
and with saintly purpose determined she would exercise all types of mortification" ["que desde el punto de su concepción tuvo la benditísima Virgen
uso de razón, de tal manera que desde aquel punto comenzó a ejercitar
todas las virtudes y dones que le había dado Dios dentro de las entrañas
de su madre: la benditísima hija tenía un altísimo y vivísimo conocimiento
de Dios, tenía unos actos de fe agudísimos y firmísimos y una esperanza
amplísima y certísima; abrasábase en amor, disponía el tiempo prudentísi-
mamente, honraba con maravillosa reverencia la divina Majestad; ofrecíase
a padecer, humillábase profundísimamente y con santos propósitos deter-
minaba de ejercitar toda mortificación" (46)]. It is possible that Ágreda was
familiar with this text as well as Villena's and used it as an inspiration for
her own development of Mary's biography.

86 Nancarrow, Bergmann, and Villaseñor Black have focused on what
these paintings and narratives tell us about the ideologies that framed
the education of girls, specifically in early modern Spain. Additionally,
Nancarrow and Villaseñor Black make note of the iconography that
links these paintings to the doctrine of the Immaculate Conception –
the red dress, the blue mantle, the flowers. Villaseñor Black, moreover,

cites Ágreda's account of Mary as a child to support her own positive assessment of these paintings as an early modern model for the education of girls.

87 Pope Pius XII: "Munificentissimus Deus – Defining the Dogma of the Assumption," par. 44. Vatican, 1 November 1950. Following this logic, Em McAvan – taking on Deleuze's dictum "difference is monstrous" – offers a reading of Mary as a monstrous figure: "Recently, Slavoj Žižek and John Milbank have re-drawn our attention to that wonderful phrase of Hegel's, 'the monstrosity of Christ.' For Hegel, Christ is a monster because he is a meeting point of two otherwise radically impossible positions – God and man. Mary, too, is an equally monstrous figure in drawing together two impossible positions – girl (defined in the Christian tradition as virgin) and mother" (http://rhizomes.net/issue22/mcavan/index.html).

88 "O, Senyora! Y quant es lo mon obligat a beneyr y lohar lo pare vostre e mare quius han engenrat, la memoria dels quals immortal restara en totes les generacions presents e esdeuenidores" (1:28; Hughes 66).

89 "car certs dies de la semana no mamava sino una vegada, sabent que la penitencia e dejuni eren vida de la anima" (1:25; Hughes 63).

90 "aquella cruel dolor e malaltia enfectionada, devallant de Adam e comprenent tots los fills seus" (1:26; Hughes 64).

91 "suplicant la clemencia divina doans si en aquest exil de Adam e dels fills seus, els reduhis a la gracia e amor sua" (1:27; Hughes 64).

92 "E, pensat que aquell loch de tant sobiran delit era tancat e clos per lo peccat de Adam, habundava en infinides lagrimes" (1:27; Hughes 64).

93 "Veniu, seynor Joachim, e hoyreu les rahonetes de la vostra amada Filia, e viura la vostra anima ab la consolacio inestimable que pendreu hoyint la paraula sua" (1: 27–8; Hughes 65).

94 "salas de vostre palau" (1:26).

95 "nal presencia qui glorifica e alegra tots los mirants e contemplants en Vos" (1:27; Hughes 64).

96 "qui sou font de sauvitat e dolçor, que no reporte delit singular en el anima sua, segons yo ara sent en hoyruos e veureus e teniruos en los meus braços?" (1:28; Hughes 65).

97 "era juntamente el tesoro mayor de Cielo, y Tierra en pura criatura, sólo a Dios inferior, y superior a todo lo criado" (1.12.171, 56).

98 "en alma y cuerpo" (1.19.331, 103).

99 "Pidiole acelerasse el remedio del linaje humano, que por tantos siglos le aguardaba, multiplicándose los pecados, y pérdidas de las almas. Oyó el Altíssimo esta petición ... y prometió a su madre ... que luego desempeñaría sus promesas, y bajaría al mundo tomando carne humana para redemirle" (1.19.334, 104).

100 "adornada entonces, como esposa que descendía del cielo con todo
    género de hábitos infusos, [pero] no fue necesario que luego los ejercitase
    todos, mas de sólo aquellos que podía y convenían al estado que tenía en
    el vientre de su Madre" (1.16.226, 71).

101 "adornan y perfeccionan la parte racional de la criatura" and "ciencia
    infusa y hábitos de todas ellas y de las artes naturales, con que conoció y
    supo todo lo natural y sobrenatural que convino a la grandeza de Dios"
    (1.16.227, 71).

102 "desde el primer instante en el vientre de su Madre, fue más sabia, más
    prudente, más ilustrada y capaz de Dios y de sus obras, que todas las
    criaturas, fuera de su Hijo santísimo, han sido ni serán eternamente"
    (1.16.227, 71).

103 "no estaba unida sustancialmente a la divinidad y así no comenzó a obrar
    como comprensora, porque que entraba en la vida a ser peregrina. Mas
    en este orden, como quien era la más inmediata a la union hipostática,
    tuvo otra visión proporcionada y la más inmediata a la visión beatífica"
    (1.16.236, 73).

104 "un cuerpecito animado de la cantidad de una abejita" (1.15.222, 70).

105 "comenzando desde aquel punto con fervoroso afecto a bendecirle,
    amarle y reverenciarle" (1.16.231, 72).

106 "siendo aquel cuerpecito, en el primer instante que recibió el alma
    santísima, tan pequeño que apenas se pudieran percibir sus potencias
    exteriores ... con el conocimiento y dolor de la caída del hombre llorase
    y derramase lágrimas en el vientre de su madre, conociendo la gravedad
    del pecado contra el sumo bien" (1.16.232, 72).

107 "pidió luego, en el instante de su ser, por el remedio de los hombres y
    comenzó el oficio de medianera, abogada y reparadora" (1.16.233, 72–3).

108 "los dones que recibía, aunque con profunda humildad y postraciones
    corporales que luego hizo en el vientre de su Madre y con aquel cuer-
    pecito tan pequeño" (1.16.228, 71).

109 "la violencia del amor" (1.24.380, 117).

110 "En estos coloquios y otros muchos, que no alcanza toda nuestra capaci-
    dad, pasaba la niñez María Santísima con sus Ángeles, y con el Altísimo,
    en quien estaba transformada. Y como era consiguiente crecer en el
    fervor y ansias de ver al Sumo Bien, que sobre todo pensamiento amaba,
    muchas veces, por voluntad del Señor, y por manos de sus Ángeles era
    llevada corporalmente al Cielo Empíreo, donde gozaba de la presencia de
    la Divinidad" (1.24.383, 117–18).

111 "ocultando debidamente la ciencia y la gracia, y excusando la admiración
    de ver hablar a una recién nacida" (1.17.252, 79).

112 "Y como no fui esclava de la culpa, no obraba las virtudes como sujeta
    a ella, sino como Señora sin contradicción, y con imperio; no como

semejante a los hijos de Adán, sino como semejante al Hijo de Dios, que también era Hijo mío" (1.21.341, 106).

113 "muy dificultoso es para la criatura racional, no exceder en las palabras" (1.25.394, 120).

114 "Niña grande" (1.25.395, 120).

115 "pero jamás le dio a entender [a Santa Ana] el Sacramento, que tenía en su pecho, de que ella era la escogida para Madre de el Mesías" (1.25.399, 121).

116 "retirábase algunas veces en tiempos oportunos, para gozar a solas con más libertad de la vista, y coloquios Divinos de sus Ángeles Santos, y manifestarles con señales exteriores el amor ardiente de su Amado" (1.25.403, 122).

117 "en comenzando a usar de las fuerzas corporales en aquella edad, las estrenó con la penitencia y mortificación, para ser en todo madre de misericordia y medianera de la gracia, sin perder punto, ni tiempo, ni operación, por donde pudiese granjearla para sí y nosotros" (1.25.403, 122).

118 "comenzó a señalarle mucho en el afecto y caridad con los pobres ... daba al pobre limosna, no como quien le hacía beneficio de gracia, sino como quien pagaba de justicia la deuda" (1.26.404, 122).

119 "enseñándola a leer y otras cosas; y todo lo admitía y desprendía la que estaba llena de ciencia infusa de todas las materias criadas, y callaba y oía a todos; con admiración de los ángeles, que en una niña miraban tan peregrina prudencia" (1.25.405, 122–3).

120 Galerie Canesso webpage catalogue entry, "The Virgin Mary as a Child, Asleep." See also Delenda's "La Virgen niña dormida."

121 There are three additional Virgin child paintings held in private collections attributed to Zurbarán and his workshop that are very close in composition and style to these better-known examples.

Works Cited

Agamben, Giorgio. *The Kingdom and the Glory: For a Theological Genealogy of Economy and Government/(homo Sacer Ii, 2)*. Translated by Lorenzo Chiesa and Matteo Mandarini, Stanford University Press, 2011.

Ágreda, María de Jesús. "Primera Parte." *Mística ciudad de Dios*. Viuda de Gerónimo Verdussen, 1696.

Alberti, Leon Battista. *Leon Battista Alberti: On Painting: A New Translation and Critical Edition*. Edited and translated by Rocco Sinisgalli, Cambridge University Press, 2011.

Alcántara, Pedro de. "La redención preservativa y el débito remoto." *Salmanticensis*, vol. 1, 1954, pp. 301–42.

Althaus-Reid, Marcella. *Indecent Theology*. Routledge, 2001.

Althusser, Louis. "Ideology and Ideological State Apparatuses." *Mapping Ideology*, edited by Slavoj Žižek, Verso, 2012, pp. 100–40.

Alva y Astorga, Pedro de. *Militia Immaculatae Conceptionis*. Louvain, 1663.

Apollonio, Alessandro M. "The Decisive Contribution of Bl. John Duns Scotus to the Dogma of the Immaculate Conception. Objections Old and New." *Blessed John Duns Scotus and His Mariology*, Academy of the Immaculate, 2009, pp. 43–70.

Ara Gil, Clementina, Francisco de la Plaza Santiago, and María Meléndez Alonso. *Inmaculada*. Santa Iglesia Catedral de Santa María la Real de la Almudena, 2005.

Augustine of Hippo. *City of God*. Translated by Henry Bettenson, Penguin Classics, 2003.

Avis, Paul D.L. *God and the Creative Imagination: Metaphor, Symbol, and Myth in Religion and Theology*. Routledge, 1999.

Azevedo, Ángela de. "Dicha y desdicha del juego y devoción de la Virgen." *Women's Acts: Plays by Women Dramatists of Spain's Golden Age*, edited by Teresa S. Soufas, University Press of Kentucky, 1997, pp. 4–44.

Bandera, Cesáreo. *The Sacred Game*. Penn State UP, 1994.

Baranda, Nieves. "Beyond Political Boundaries: Religion as Nation in Early Modern Spain." *Women Telling Nations,* edited by Amelia Sanz Cabrerizo, Francesca Scott, and Susan Van Dijk, Rodopi, 2014, pp. 63–83.

– *Cortejo a lo prohibido: Lectoras y escritoras en la España moderna.* Arco Libros, S.L. 2005.

– "Reflexiones en torno a una metodología para el estudio de las mujeres escritoras en justas del Siglo de Oro." *Memoria de la palabra: Actas del VI Congreso de la Asociación Internacional Siglo de Oro,* Burgos–La Rioja 15–19 July 2002, coordinated by Francisco Domínguez Matito and María Luisa Lobato López, vol. 1, 2004, pp. 307–16.

Barasch, Moshe. *Icon: Studies in the History of an Era.* New York University Press, 1992.

Barbieri, Costanza. "To Be in Heaven: St. Philip Neri between Aesthetic Emotion and Mystical Ecstasy." *The Sensuous in the Counter-Reformation Church,* edited by Marcia B. Hall and Tracy Elizabeth Cooper, Cambridge University Press, 2013, pp. 206–29.

Bassegoda i Hugas, Bonaventura. "El dibujo como fundamento del pensamiento de Francisco Pacheco: Procesos y Principios." *Pacheco: Teórico, artista, maestro (1564–1644),* Museo de Bellas Artes de Sevilla, 2016, pp. 37–48.

Baticle, Jeannine. "Francisco de Zurbarán: A Chronological Review." *Zurbarán,* edited by Baticle and translated by Jean-Marie Clarke, Metropolitan Museum of Art, 1987, pp. 53–68.

Belting, Hans. *Likeness and Presence: A History of the Image before the Era of Art.* Translated by Edmund Jephcott, University of Chicago Press, 1994.

Bergmann, Emilie. "Learning at Her Mother's Knee? Saint Anne, the Virgin Mary, and the Iconography of Women's Literacy." *Women's Literacy in Early Modern Spain and the New World,* edited by Anne J. Cruz and Rosilie Hernández, Ashgate, 2011, pp. 243–61.

Blatter, Rev. George J., translator. *Mystical City of God,* by María de Ágreda, The Theopolitan, 1914.

Bonaventure, Saint. *On the Reduction of the Arts to Theology.* Translated by Zachary Hayes, Bookmasters, 1996.

– *The Works of Bonaventure: Cardinal, Seraphic Doctor, and Saint.* Edited and translated by José De Vinck, St Anthony Guild Press, 1960.

Boon, Jessica A. "The Glory of the Virgin: The Mariology of the Incarnation in Two Early Modern Castilian Mystical Sermons." *La corónica,* vol. 4, no. 1, 2012, pp. 35–60.

– Introduction. *Mother Juana de la Cruz, 1481–1534: Visionary Sermons.* Edited by Ronald E. Surtz, Iter Academic Press, 2016, pp. 1–33.

– "Mother Juana de la Cruz: Marian Visions and Female Preaching." *A New Companion to Hispanic Mysticism,* edited by Hilaire Kallendorf, Brill, 2010, pp. 127–48.

Boss, Sarah Jane. "The Development of the Doctrine of Mary's Immaculate. Conception." *Mary: The Complete Resource*, by Boss, Continuum, 2007, pp. 207–37.

– "Francisco Suárez and Modern Mariology." *Mary: The Complete Resource*, by Boss, Continuum, 2007, pp. 256–83.

Bourdieu, Pierre. *The Field of Cultural Production: Essays on Art and Literature*. Edited and introduced by Randal Johnson, Columbia University Press, 1993.

Bouza Álvarez, Fernando J. *Communication, Knowledge, and Memory in Early Modern Spain*. University of Pennsylvania Press, 2004.

Bray, Xavier, editor. *The Sacred Made Real: Spanish Painting and Sculpture 1600–1700*. National Gallery Company, 2009.

Broggio, Peter. "The Religious Orders and the Expulsion of the Moriscos: Doctrinal Controversies and Hispano-Papal Relations." *The Expulsion of the Moriscos from Spain: A Mediterranean Diaspora*, edited by Mercedes García-Arenal Rodriquez and Gerard A. Wiegers, Brill, 2014, pp. 156–78.

Brown, Sylvia Monica. Introduction. *Women, Gender and Radical Religion in Early Modern Europe*, by Brown, Brill, 2014.

Calderón de la Barca, Pedro. *La Hidalga Del Valle: A María, El Corazón; Dos Autos Sacramentales Marianos*. Aguilar, 1963.

Cantavella, Rosanna, and Lluïsa Parra. *Protagonistes Femenines a la "Vita Christi."* LaSal, 1987.

Cañedo-Argüelles, Cristina. *Arte y teoría: La Contrarreforma y España*. Arte Musicología, Universidad de Oviedo, 1982.

Carducho, Vicente. *Diálogos de la pintura*. Edited by D.G. Cruzada Villaamil, Manuel Galiano, 1865.

Carmona Muela, Juan. *Iconografía cristiana*. Ediciones Akal, 2003.

Carrillo, Martín. *Elogios de mujeres insignes del viejo testamento*. Pedro Bluson, Universidad de Huesca, 1627.

Casar Pinazo, José Ignacio, and Pablo González Tornel. *Intacta María. Política i Religiositat en L'Espanya Barroca*. Generalitat Valenciana, 2017.

Cascardi, Anthony. *Ideologies of History in Golden Age Spain*. Pennsylvania State University Press, 1997.

Cervantes, Miguel de. *Don Quijote de la Mancha*. Edited by Francisco Rico, Punto de Lectura, 2012.

– *Don Quixote*. Signet Classics. Translated by Tom Lathrop, Penguin Books, 2011.

Christian, William A., Jr. "Images as Beings in Early Modern Spain." *Sacred Spain: Art and Belief in the Spanish World*, edited by Ronda Kasl, Yale University Press, 2009, pp. 75–100.

Clark, Stuart. *Vanities of the Eye: Vision in Early Modern European Culture*. Oxford University Press, 2007.

Cocking, J.M. *Imagination: A Study in the History of Ideas*. Introduction and notes by Penelope Murray. Routledge, 1991.

Colomer, José Luis. "Luoghi e attori della 'pietas hispanica' a Roma all'epoca di Borromini." *Francesco Borromini. Atti del convegno internazionale. Roma. 13–15 gennaio 2000*, edited by Christoph Luitpold Frommel and Elisabeth Sladek, Electa, 2001, pp. 346–57.

Coolidge, Grace E. Introduction. *The Formation of the Child in Early Modern Spain*, by Coolidge, Ashgate, 2014, pp. 1–15.

Coreth, Anna. *Pietas Austriaca: Austrian Religious Practices in the Baroque Era*. Translated by William D. Bowman and Anna Maria Leitgeb, Purdue University Press, 2004.

Council of Nicaea in 787. In *Decrees of the Ecumenical Councils*, edited by Norman P. Tanner, www.ewtn.com/library/COUNCILS/nicaea2.htm.

Covarrubias, Sebastián de. *Emblemas Morales*. Luis Sánchez, 1610.

Criado, Miryam. "La *Vita Christi* de Sor Isabel de Villena y la teología feminista contemporánea." *Lemir*, vol. 17, 2013, pp. 75–86.

Cruz, Anne J., and Mary E. Perry. *Culture and Control in Counter-Reformation Spain*. University of Minnesota Press, 1992.

Curbet, Joan. Introduction. *Portraits of Holy Women: Selections from the Vita Christi*, by Isabel de Villena, translated by Robert Hughes, Barcino, 2013, pp. 9–36.

Curran, Angela. *Routledge Philosophy Guidebook to Aristotle and the Poetics*. Routledge, 2016.

Damascus, John of. "Apologia against Those Who Decry Holy Images." *From St. John Damascene. On Holy Images*, translated by Mary H. Allies, Thomas Baker, 1898, www.fordham.edu/halsall/basis/johndamascus-images.asp#PART%20I.

Dandelet, Thomas James. *Spanish Rome, 1500–1700*. Yale University Press, 2001.

Delenda, Odile. *Francisco de Zurbarán*. Arco/Libros, 2007.

– "La Virgen niña dormida." *Miriam*, vol. 351, 2007, pp. 103–4.

– "The Virgin Mary as a Child, Asleep." Catalogue Entry. Galerie Canesso, www.canesso.art/The-Virgin-Mary-Child-Asleep-DesktopDefault.aspx?tabid=6&tabindex=5&objectid=587325&lg=it.

– *Zurbarán: Catálogo razonado y crítico. Vol. I y Vol. II*. Fundación Arte Hispánico, 2009.

– *Zurbarán: Una nueva mirada*. Museo Thyssen-Bornemisza, 2015.

Desmond, William. *God and the Between*. Blackwell Publishing, 2008.

Domínguez Ortiz, Antonio, Alfonso E. Sánchez, and Julián Gallego. *Velázquez*. Metropolitan Museum of Art, 1989.

Dreyer, Elizabeth A. *Accidental Theologians: Four Women Who Shaped Christianity*. Franciscan Media, 2014.

Duerloo, Luc. *Dynasty and Piety: Archduke Albert (1598–1621) and Habsburg Political Culture in an Age of Religious Wars*. Ashgate, 2012.

Eco, Umberto. *The Aesthetics of Thomas Aquinas*. Translated by Hugh Bredin, Harvard University Press, 1988.

– *Art and Beauty in the Middle Ages*. Translated by Hugh Bredin, Yale University Press, 2002.

Edwards, Kathryn. "Popular Religion." *Reformation and Early Modern Europe: A Guide to Research*, edited by David M. Whitford, Truman State University Press, 2008, pp. 331–54.

Enos, Theresa, editor. *Encyclopedia of Rhetoric and Composition: Communication from Ancient Times to the Information Age*. Routledge, 1996.

Evangelisti, Silvia. *Nuns: A History of Convent Life 1450–1700*. Oxford University Press, 2007.

Fernández Dueñas, Ángel. "Órdenes militares de la Inmaculada Concepción. La Real y Distinguida Orden de Carlos III." *Boletín de la Real Academia de Córdoba de Ciencias, Bellas Artes y Nobles Artes*, vol. 134, 1998, pp. 71–3.

Fernández García, Ricardo. *La Inmaculada Concepción en Navarra*. Universidad de Navarra, 2004.

Fernández López, José. *Programas iconográficos de la pintura barroca sevillana del siglo XVII*. Universidad de Sevilla, 2002.

Fernández de Mesa, Blas. *La fundadora de la santa concepción*. Edited by Nancy K. Mayberry, Peter Lang, 1996.

Ferrús Antón, Beatriz. "Mayor gloria de Dios es que lo sea una mujer: Sor María de Jesús de Ágreda y Sor Francisca Josefa de la Concepción del Castillo (Sobre escritura conventual en los siglos XVI y XVII)." *Revista de Literatura*, vol. 70, no. 139, 2008, pp. 31–46.

Foucault, Michel. *A History of Sexuality Vol. 1: An Introduction*. Translated by Robert Hurley, Random House, 1990.

– *The Order of Things: An Archeology of the Human Sciences*. Routledge, 2002.

Franke, William, editor. *On What Cannot Be Said: Apophatic Discourses in Philosophy, Religion, Literature, and the Arts*. University of Notre Dame, 2007.

Gadamer, Hans-Georg. *Truth and Method*. Edited and translated by Joel Weinsheimer and Donald G. Marshall, Bloomsbury, 2004.

García Melero, José Enrique. *Literatura Española Sobre Artes Plásticas*. Ediciones Encuentro, 2010.

Gillespie, Michael Allen. *The Theological Origins of Modernity*. University of Chicago Press, 2008.

Godzieba, Anthony J. "The Catholic Sacramental Imagination and the Access/Excess of Grace." *New Theology Review*, vol. 2, 2008, pp. 14–26.

Gómez López, Jesus. "El 'Conorte' de Sor Juana de Jesús y su sermón sobre la Inmaculada Concepción de María." *Hispania Sacra*, vol. 74, 1984, pp. 601–27.

González García, Juan Luis. *Imágenes sagradas y predicación visual en el siglo de oro*. Alkal, 2015.

González Polvillo, Antonio. "La Congregación de la Granada, el Inmaculismo sevillano y los retratos realizados por Francisco Pacheco de tres de sus principales protagonistas: Miguel del Cid, Bernardo de Toro y Mateo Vázquez de Leca." *Atrio*, vol. 15–16, 2009–10, pp. 47–72.

González Tornel, Pablo. "La iglesia de los santos Idelfonso y Tomás de Villanueva en Roma: un monumento barroco a la *pietas hispánica*." *Archivo Español de Arte*, vol. 88, no. 349, 2015, pp. 69–84.

Goodwin, Robert. *Spain: The Centre of the World 1519–1682*. Bloomsbury, 2015.

Gorringe, Timothy. *Earthly Visions: Theology and the Challenges of Art*. Yale University Press, 2011.

Granada y Mendoza, Leandro. *Luz de las maravillas*. Herederos de Diego Fernández de Córdova, 1607.

Greene, Ronald, and Stephen Cushman, editors. *The Princeton Encyclopedia of Poetry and Poetics*. 4th ed., Princeton University Press, 2012.

Hall, James. *Dictionary of Subjects and Symbols in Art*. 2nd ed., Westview Press, 2008.

Hall, Linda B. *Mary, Mother and Warrior: The Virgin in Spain and the Americas*. University of Texas Press, 2004.

Hall, Marcia B. Introduction. *The Sensuous in the Counter Reformation Church*, edited by Hall and Tracy Elizabeth Cooper, Cambridge University Press, 2013, pp. 1–27.

– *The Sacred Image in the Age of Art*. Yale University Press, 2011.

Halliwell, Stephen. *Aesthetics of Mimesis*. Princeton University Press, 2002.

Hamburger, Jeffrey F., and Anne-Marie Bouché. *The Mind's Eye: Art and Theological Argument in the Middle Ages*. Department of Art and Archaeology, Princeton University, in association with Princeton University Press, 2006.

Harkins, Franklin T., and Frans van Liere, editors. *Interpretation of Scripture: Theory: A Selection of Works of Hugh, Andrew, Richard, and Godfrey of St. Victor, and of Robert of Melun*. New City Press, 2013.

Hellwig, Karin. *La literatura artística española del siglo XVII*. Translated by Jesús Espino Nuño, Visor, 1999.

Hendrix, John Shannon, and Charles H. Carman, editors. *Renaissance Theories of Vision*. Ashgate, 2010.

Hernández, Rosilie. "Friends in High Places: The Correspondence of Felipe IV and Sor María de Ágreda." *Perspectives on Early Modern Women in Iberia and the Americas: Studies in Law, Society, Art and Literature in Honor of Anne J. Cruz*, edited by María Cristina Quintero and Adrienne Martín, Arte Poética, 2015, pp. 422–42.

– Book review: *The Comedia of Virginity: Mary and the Politics of Seventeenth-Century Spanish Theater*, by Mirzam C. Pérez. *Theater Research International*, vol. 39, no. 2, 2014, pp. 158–9.

– "The Politics of Exemplarity: Biblical Women and the Education of the Spanish Lady in Martín Carrillo, Sebastian de Herrera Barnuevo, and María de Guevara." *Women's Literacy in Early Modern Spain and the New World*, edited by Anne J. Cruz and Hernández, Ashgate, 2011, pp. 225–42.

– "Reproductive Genesis: Mothers and Children in Martín Carrillo's *Elogios de mujeres insignes del viejo testamento.*" *The Formation of the Child in Early Modern Spain*, edited by Grace E. Coolidge, Ashgate, 2014, pp. 19–40.

Holmes, Emily A. "Introduction: Mending a Broken Lineage." *Women, Writing, Theology: Transforming a Tradition of Exclusion*, by Holmes, Wendy Farley, and Michelle Voss Roberts, Baylor University Press, 2011.

Horner, Robyn. *Jean-Luc Marion: A Theo-logical Introduction*. Ashgate, 2013.

Howe, Teresa. "'Let Your Women Keep Silence': The Pauline Dictum and Women's Education." *Women and Gender in the Early Modern World: Women's Literacy in Early Modern Spain and the New World*, edited by Anne J. Cruz and Rosilie Hernández, Ashgate, 2011.

– *Women and Gender in the Early Modern World: Education and Women in the Early Modern Hispanic World*. Ashgate, 2008.

Hugh of St Victor. "On Sacred Scripture and Its Authors." *Interpretation of Scripture: Theory – Volume 3. The Victorine Texts in Translation*, edited by Franklin T. Harkins and Frans van Liere, translated by Frans van Liere, Brepols, 2012.

Jervis, John. *Sympathetic Sentiments: Affect, Emotion and Spectacle in the Modern World*. Bloomsbury, 2015.

Johnson, Christopher D. *Hyperboles: The Rhetoric of Excess in Baroque Literature and Thought*. Harvard University Press, 2010.

Johnson, Trevor. "Mary in Early Modern Europe." *Mary: The Complete Resource*, edited by Sarah Jane Boss, Continuum, 2007, pp. 363–84.

Juan de la Cruz. *Obra Completa*. Edited by Luce López Baralt and Eulogio Pacho, Alianza Editorial, 2003.

Juana de la Cruz. "De la Inmaculada Concepción de Nuestra Señora." *El "Conorte" de Sor Juana de Jesús y su sermón sobre la Inmaculada Concepción de María*, edited by Jesús Gómez López, *Hispania Sacra*, vol. 74, 1984, pp. 601–27.

Justa Poética en Defensa de la Pureza de la Inmaculada Concepción de la Virgen Santísima. Coordinated by Sancho Zapata, Diego la Torre, 1619.

Justiniano, Vicente. *Tratado de la Inmaculada Concepción de la Virgen Santísima Nuestra Señora*. Luis Sánchez, 1615.

Kappes, Christiaan W. *The Immaculate Conception*. Academy of the Immaculate, 2014.

Kearney, Richard. *The Wake of Imagination: Ideas of Creativity in Western Culture*. Hutchinson, 1998.

Kempis, Thomas à. "The Imitation of Christ." *A New Reading of the 1441 Latin Autograph Manuscript*, translated by William C. Creasy, Mercer University Press, 2007.

Kirsch, Johann Peter. "Laurentius Surius." *The Catholic Encyclopedia, Vol 14*. Robert Appleton Company, 1912. www.newadvent.org/cathen/14343c.htm.

Kreitzer, Beth. *Reforming Mary: Changing Images of the Virgin Mary in Lutheran Sermons of the Sixteenth Century*. Oxford University Press, 2004.

Kristeva, Julia. *This Incredible Need to Believe*. Columbia University Press, 2009.

Lasance, Francis Xavier. *My Prayer Book*. Benziger Brothers Press, 1908.

Laven, Mary. Introduction. *The Ashgate Research Companion to the Counter-Reformation*, edited by Alexandra Bamji, Geert H. Janssen, and Laven, Routledge, 2013, pp. 1–14.

– "Legacies of the Counter-Reformation and the Origins of Modern Catholicism." *The Ashgate Research Companion to the Counter-Reformation*, edited by Alexandra Bamji, Geert H. Janssen, and Laven, Routledge, 2013, pp. 451–70.

Leinsle, Ulrich G. *Introduction to Scholastic Theology*. Translated by Michael J. Miller, Catholic University of America Press, 2010.

Levenson, Jay. A. *1492: Art in the Age of Exploration*. National Gallery of Art, Washington, and Yale University Press, 1991.

Levi, D'Ancona M. *The Iconography of the Immaculate Conception in the Middle Ages and Early Renaissance*. College Art Association of America in conjunction with the *Art Bulletin*, 1957.

Livingstone, E.A., editor. *The Concise Oxford Dictionary of the Christian Church*. Oxford University Press, 2013.

Lléo Cañal, Vicente. "La Congregación de la Granada y los artistas sevillanos del Barroco." *Temas y formas hispánicas: Arte, cultura, y sociedad*, edited by Carlos Mata Induráin y Anna Morózova, BIADIG, 2015, pp. 201–17.

Lope de Vega. *El milagro por los celos y D. Álvaro de Luna*. Imprenta de Carlos Sapera, 1770.

– *La Limpieza No Manchada: Comedia de la Concepción Inmaculada de la Beatísima Virgen María*. Librería Cervantes, 1972.

López-Rey, José, and Odile Delenda. *Velázquez: Complete Works*. Wildenstein Institute, Paris, and Taschen, 2014.

Loyola, Ignatius. *The Spiritual Exercises and Selected Works*. Edited by George E. Ganss, Paulist Press, 1991.

Lubac, Henri de. *Medieval Exegesis: The Four Senses of Scripture*. Vol. 2. Translated by E.M. Macierowski, W.B. Eerdmans, 1998.

Luna, Lola. "Sor Valentina Pinelo, intérprete de las Escrituras." *Cuadernos Hispanoamericanos*, vol. 464, 1989, pp. 91–104.

Malinowski, Bronisław. "Supplement I: The Problem of Meaning in Primitive Languages." Addendum to *The Meaning of Meaning*, edited by C.K. Ogden and I.A. Richards, Routledge and Kegan Paul, 1923, pp. 296–336.

Manrique, Rodrigo. *Sermón de la Limpia Concepción de la Virgen María nuestra Señora*. Francisco Lira, 1615.

Marín Pina, María Carmen. "'Cuantas fueren las cabeças tantos han de ser los pareceres': censura al 'Libro de Santa Ana' de Valentina Pinelo." *Voz y Letra*, vol. 17, 2006, pp. 33–50.

– "Los certámenes poéticos aragoneses del siglo XVII como espacio literario de sociabilidad femenina." *Bulletin hispanique*, vol. 115, no. 1, 2013, pp. 145–64.

Marion, Jean-Luc. *In Excess: Studies of Saturated Phenomena*. Translated by Robyn Horner and Vincent Berraud, Fordham University Press, 2002.

– *The Visible and the Revealed*. Translated by Christina M. Gschwandtner, Fordham University Press, 2008.

Markowski, Michał Paweł. *Pragnienie obecności. Filozofie reprezentacji od Platona do Kartezjusza*. słowo/obraz terytoria, 1999.

Martínez, Jusepe. *Discursos practicables del nobilísimo arte de la pintura, sus rudimentos, medios y fines que enseña la experiencia, con los ejemplares de obras insignes de artífices ilustres*. Edited by Valentín Carderera y Solano, Real Academia de Bellas Artes de San Fernando, 1866.

Martínez Peñas, Leandro. *El confesor del rey en el antiguo régimen*. Editorial Complutense, S.A., 2007.

Marx, Anthony W. *Faith in Nation*. Oxford University Press, 2005.

McAvan, Em. "The Becoming-Girl of the Virgin Mary." *Rhizomes: Cultural Studies in Emerging Knowledge*, no. 22, 2011. http://rhizomes.net/issue22/mcavan/index.html.

McDonald, Lee Martin. *The Biblical Canon: Its Origin, Transmission, and Authority*. Baker Academic, 2007.

McGinn, Bernard. "On Mysticism and Art." *Daedalus*, vol. 132, no. 2, 2003, pp. 131–4.

Mir y Noguera, Juan. *La Inmaculada Concepción*. Sáenz de Jubera Hermanos, 1905.

Mitchell, W.J.T. *Picture Theory: Essays on Verbal and Visual Representation*. University of Chicago Press, 1994.

Molina, Tirso de. *Doña Beatriz de Silva*. Linkgua Ediciones, 2008.

Monsalve, Pedro de. *Canciones a la Inmaculada Concepción de la Virgen*. Alonso Rodríguez Gamarra, 1615.

Morán Turina, Miguel, and Javier Portús Pérez. *El arte de mirar: La Pintura y su público en la España de Velázquez*. Istmo, 1997.

Mujica, Bárbara. "Beyond Image: The Apophatic-Kataphatic Dialectic in Teresa de Ávila." *Hispania*, vol. 84, no. 4, 2001, pp. 741–8.

Mulcahy, Rosemarie. *Spanish Paintings in the National Gallery of Ireland*. National Gallery of Ireland, 1988, pp. 89–91.

Muñoz Fernández, Ángela. "El monacato como espacio de cultura femenina. A propósito de la Inmaculada Concepción de María y la representación de la sexuación femenina." *Pautas históricas de sociabilidad femenina rituals y modelos de representación: Actas del V Coloquio Internacional de la Asociación Española de Investigación Histórica de las Mujeres*, coordinated by M. Gloria Espigado Tocino, Mary Nash, and María José de la Pascua Sánchez, Asociación Española de Investigación de Historia de las Mujeres (AEIHM), Universidad de Cádiz, 1999, pp. 71–89.

Muñoz González, María Jesús. *El mercado español de pinturas en el siglo XVII*. Fundación Arte Hispánico and Fundación Caja Madrid, 2008.

Nancarrow, Mindy. "Francisco Suárez's *Bienaventurada Virgen* and the Iconography of the Immaculate Conception." *Imagery, Spirituality and Ideology in Baroque Spain and Latin America*, edited by Jeremy Roe and Marta Bustillo, Cambridge Scholars Publishing, 2010, pp. 3–14.

– "Murillo's *St. Anne Teaching the Virgin to Read* and the Question of Female Literacy and Learning in Golden Age Spain." *Konsthistorisk tidskrift/Journal of Art History*, vol. 68, 1999, pp. 31–46.

– "Theology and Devotion in Zurbarán's Images of the Infant Virgin in the Temple." *South Atlantic Review*, vol. 72, no. 1, 2007, pp. 76–92.

Noell, Brian, et al. "On Visual Exegesis." *Speculum Theologiae*. http://brbl-archive.library.yale.edu/exhibitions/speculum/v-exegesis.html.

Noone, Tim, and R.E. Houser. "Bonaventure." *The Stanford Encyclopedia of Philosophy*, edited by Edward N. Zalta, 2013. https://plato.stanford.edu/entries/bonaventure.

Núñez Bosch, Pedro. *Relación Verdadera de la Imagen de la Inmaculada Concepción de la Virgen María, que se halló en la Raíz o Cebollita de una Azucena de los Valles del Monte del Carrascal de la Villa de Alcoy, en el Reino de Valencia*. Benito Mase, 1665.

O'Malley, John W. *Trent and All That: Renaming Catholicism in the Early Modern Era*. Harvard University Press, 2000.

– "Trent, Sacred Images, and the Catholics' Sense of the Sensuous." *The Sensuous in the Counter-Reformation Church*, edited by Marcia B. Hall and Tracy E. Cooper, Cambridge University Press, 2013, pp. 28–48.

Osuna Rodríguez, Inmaculada. "Literary Academies and Poetic Tournaments." *The Routledge Research Companion to Early Modern Spanish Women Writers*, edited by Nieves Baranda and Anne J. Cruz, Routledge, 2018, pp. 153–68.

Pacheco, Francisco. *Arte de la pintura*. 2nd ed. Edited by D.G. Cruzada Villaamil, Manuel Galiano, 1866.

Paleotti, Gabrielle. *Discourse on Sacred and Profane Images*. Translated by William McCuaig, Getty Publications, 2012.

Palmén, Ritva. *Richard of St. Victor's Theory of Imagination*. Brill, 2014.

Peinado Guzmán, José Antonio. "La monarquía española y el dogma de la Inmaculada Concepción: Fervor, Diplomacia, y Gestiones a favor de su proclamación en la edad moderna." *Chronica Nova*, vol. 40, 2014, pp. 247–76.

Peña Sueiro, Nieves. "Estado de la cuestión en el estudio de las Relaciones de sucesos." *Pliegos bibliofilia*, vol. 13, 2001, pp. 43–66.

Pérez, Mirzam C. *The Comedia of Virginity: Mary and the Politics of Seventeenth-Century Spanish Theater*. Baylor University Press, 2012.

Pérez Sánchez, Alfonso E. "The Artistic Milieu in Seville during the First Third of the Seventeenth Century." *Zurbarán*. Metropolitan Museum of Art, 1987.

– "Velázquez and His Art." *Velázquez*, edited by Antonio Domínguez Ortiz, Alfonso E. Sánchez, and Julián Gallego, Metropolitan Museum of Art, 1989.

Pérez de Valdivia, Diego. *Tratado de la singular y purísima concepción de la Madre de Dios, 1582*. Edited by Juan Cruz Cruz, Universidad de Navarra, 2004.

Pinelo, Valentina. *Libro de las alabanzas y excelencias de la gloriosa Santa Ana*. Clemente Hidalgo, 1601.

Pius XII. "Munificentissimus Deus – Defining the Dogma of the Assumption," par. 44. Vatican, 1950.

Planes, Gerónimo. *Tratado del examen de las revelaciones verdaderas y falsas y de los raptos*. Viuda de Juan Chrysóstomo Garriz, 1633.

Poska, Allyson M. *Regulating the People: The Catholic Reformation in Seventeenth-Century Spain*. Brill, 1998.

Poutrin, Isabelle. *Le Voile et la Plume: Autobiographie et Sainteté Féminine dans L'Espagne Moderne*. Casa De Velázquez, 1995.

Prodi, Paolo. Introduction. *Discourse on Sacred and Profane Images*, by Gabrielle Paleotti, translated by William McCuaig, Getty Publications, 2012, pp. 1–42.

Réau, Louis. *Iconografía del arte cristiano: Introducción general*. El Serbal, 2006.

Reynolds, Brian K. *Gateway to Heaven. Vol. 1*. New York City Press, 2012.

Reza, Alma Linda. "Devoción inmaculista en Barcelona. Una imagen triunfal de la monarquía española." *Pedralbes*, vol. 2, 2008, pp. 761–78.

Ribadeneyra Pedro de. *Flos Sanctorum*. Luis Sánchez, 1616.

Ricœur, Paul. *Figuring the Sacred: Religion, Narrative, and Imagination*. Translated by David Pellauer and edited by Mark I. Wallace, Fortress Press, 1995.

Ripa, Cesare. *Iconologia*. Lorenzo Salviati, 1603.

Risse, Katherine. "Revising a Matrimonial Life: An Alternative to the Conduct Book in María de Ágreda's *Mística ciudad de Dios*." *Modern Language Notes*, vol. 123, 2008, pp. 230–51.

Roberts, Edward A. *A Comprehensive Etymological Dictionary of the Spanish Language with Families of Words Based on Indo-European Roots: Vol. II*. Xlibris Corporation, 2014.

Rodríguez G. de Ceballos, Alfonso. "The Art of Devotion: Seventeenth-Century Spanish Painting and Sculpture in Its Religious Context." *The Sacred Made Real: Spanish Painting and Sculpture 1600–1700*, edited by Xavier Bray, National Gallery Company, 2009, pp. 45–58.

Ruiz, Miguel. *Sermón de la Inmaculada Concepción de la Virgen María*. Gabriel Ramos Vejarano, 1617.

Sánchez, Magdalena S. *The Empress, the Queen, and the Nun: Women and Power at the Court of Philip III of Spain*. Johns Hopkins University Press, 1998.

Sánchez Jiménez, Antonio, and Adrián J. Sáez, editors. *Siete memoriales españoles en defensa del arte de la pintura*. Iberoamericana Vervuet, 2018.

Sánchez Luzero, Gonzalo. *Dos discursos teológicos en defensa de la Inmaculada Concepción de la Virgen*. Luis Sánchez, 1614.

Schaff, Philip. *History of the Christian Church. Vol III: Nicene and Post-Nicene Christianity 311–600*. 6th ed. Charles Scribner's Sons, 1908.

Schroeder, Rev. H.J., translator and editor. *The Canons and Decrees of the Council of Trent*. TAN Books, 2011.

Sebastián, Santiago..*Contrarreforma y Barroco: Lecturas Iconográficas e Iconológicas*. Alianza, 1981.

Solá, Francisco de P. "Doctrina del doctor eximio y piadoso Francisco Suárez sobre la Concepción Inmaculada de María." *Estudios eclesiásticos*, 28, vol. 110–11, 1954, pp. 501–32.

Sorensen, Lee. "Pacheco, Francisco." *Dictionary of Art Historians*. http://www.arthistorians.info/pachecof.

Stoichita, Victor I. *Visionary Experience in the Golden Age of Spanish Art*. Reaktion Books, 1995.

Stratton, Suzanne L. *The Immaculate Conception in Spanish Art*. Cambridge University Press, 1994.

– "Murillo in America." *Bartolomé Esteban Murillo (1617–1682): Paintings from American Collections*, edited by Suzanne Stratton and Harry N. Abrams, in association with the Kimbell Art Museum, 2002, pp. 91–109.

Suárez, Francisco. *Misterios de la vida de Cristo*. Translated by Romualdo Galdós, La Editorial Católica, 1948–50.

Suárez de Castilla, Pedro. *Diálogo entre Maestro y Discípulo en que se trata la purísima Concepción de nuestra Señora la Virgen María, concebida sin mancha de pecado original, con la declaración de lo tocante al misterio*. Viuda de Juan Gracián, 1615.

Surtz, Ronald E. *The Guitar of God: Gender, Power, and Authority in the Visionary World of Mother Juana de la Cruz (1481–1534)*. University of Pennsylvania Press, 1990.

Taylor, Dianna, editor. *Michel Foucault: Key Concepts*. Routledge, 2014.

Thomas Aquinas. *Commentary on the Letters of Saint Paul to the Corinthians*. Translated by Fabian R. Larcher, Aquinas Institute for the Study of Sacred Doctrine, 2012.

– *Summa Theologica*. Translated by the Fathers of the English Dominican Province, Benziger Brothers, 1947–8.

Tiffany, Tanya J. *Diego Velázquez's Early Paintings and the Culture of Seventeenth-Century Seville*. Pennsylvania State University Press, 2012.

Tirso de Molina. *Doña Beatriz de Silva*. Red ediciones S.L., 2012.

Torres, Francisco de. *Consuelo de los devotos de la Inmaculada Concepción de la Virgen Santísima*. Pedro Cabarte, 1620.

Twomey, Lesley K. *The Fabric of Marian Devotion in Isabel de Villena's Vita Christi*. Tamesis, 2013.

– *The Serpent and the Rose: The Immaculate Conception and Hispanic Poetry in the Late Medieval Period*. Brill, 2008.

Urban VIII. *Relación de la institución en Roma, de la Orden Militar, de la Inmaculada Concepción de la Virgen María Nuestra Señora. Por la Santidad del Papa nuestro*

Señor Urbano VIII: copia de dos cartas, escritas en Roma, a dos señores Prebendados de la Santa Iglesia mayor desta Ciudad de Sevilla. Antonio Álvarez, 1624.

Valdivieso, Enrique. *Murillo: Catálogo razonado de pinturas*. El Viso, 2010.

Valme Muñoz Rubio, María del. *Pacheco: Teórico, artista, maestro*. Museo de Bellas Artes de Sevilla, 2016.

Villaseñor Black, Charlene. *Creating the Cult of St. Joseph: Art and Gender in the Spanish Empire*. Princeton University Press, 2005.

– "Paintings of the Education of the Virgin Mary and the Lives of Girls in Early Modern Spain." *The Formation of the Child in Early Modern Spain*, edited by Grace E. Coolidge, Ashgate, 2014, pp. 93–122.

Villena, Isabel de. *Portraits of Holy Women: Selections from the Vita Christi*. Edited by Joan Curbet, translated by Robert Hughes, Barcino, 2013.

– *Vita Christi*. Vol. 1. Edited by R. Miquel y Planas, Biblioteca Catalana, 1916.

– *Vita Christi*. Vol. 3. Edited by R. Miquel y Planas, Biblioteca Catalana, 1916.

Volk, Mary Crawford. *Vicencio Carducho and Seventeenth Century Castilian Painting*. Garland Publications, 1977.

Weaver, Andrew H. *Sacred Music as Public Image for Holy Roman Emperor Ferdinand III: Representing the Counter-Reformation Monarch at the End of the Thirty Years' War*. Ashgate, 2012.

Webb, Stephen H. *Blessed Excess: Religion and the Hyperbolic Imagination*. State University of New York Press, 1993.

Westfall, Carroll William. "Painting and the Liberal Arts: Alberti's View." *Journal of the History of Ideas*, vol. 30, 1969, pp. 487–506.

Wippel, John F. "Godfrey of Fontaines (B. CA. 1250; D. 1306/09), Peter of Auvergne (D. 1303), and John Baconthorpe (D. 1345/48)." *Individuation in Scholasticism: The Later Middle Ages and the Counter-Reformation, 1150–1650*, edited by Jorge J.E. Gracia, State University of New York Press, 1994, pp. 221–56.

Index

Toronto Iberic

CO-EDITORS: Robert Davidson (Toronto) and Frederick A. de Armas (Chicago)

EDITORIAL BOARD: Josiah Blackmore (Harvard); Marina Brownlee (Princeton); Anthony J. Cascardi (Berkeley); Justin Crumbaugh (Mt Holyoke); Emily Francomano (Georgetown); Jordana Mendelson (NYU); Joan Ramon Resina (Stanford); Enrique García Santo-Tomás (U Michigan); Kathleen Vernon (SUNY Stony Brook)